Rebel

REBEL

The Short Life of Esmond Romilly

———

Kevin Ingram

Weidenfeld and Nicolson
London

ISBN 0 297 78707 1

Printed in Great Britain at The Bath Press, Avon

To my parents

Contents

Illustrations

Acknowledgements

First and foremost my profound thanks are to Jessica Mitford for allowing me access to Esmond Romilly's letters and papers, and for answering my numerous questions.

I am also indebted to Peter Nevile for sharing his memories of Esmond Romilly, and for making available his correspondence with Esmond and Jessica from the couple's elopement in 1937.

My thanks also to John Peet for a colourful and evocative essay on the birth of the magazine, 'Out of Bounds', and for his insights into the character of the juvenile Romilly; and to Selden Rodman for allowing me to quote from his Esmond Romilly correspondence, and to transcribe, from his journal, several vivid accounts of Esmond Romilly in the United States.

Thanks are also due to the late Philip Toynbee, whom, sadly, I met only once before his death in 1981.

I also wish to express my gratitude to: Mary Marshall, Simona Pakenham, Lucinda Romilly, The Lady Soames, Lady Wakeman for providing me with information on Esmond's childhood; to John Gardner, Rupert Horsley, Anthony Robinson, Trevor Russell-Cobb, Cecil de Sausmarez, Leslie Sayers, Major Bowes Stoney, Henry Swanzy for their accounts of Esmond's schooldays; and to Phillip Gillan and the late Arthur Ovenden, Esmond's comrades in the Thaelmann Battalion of the International Brigades, for their impressions of Romilly in Spain.

For other accounts of Esmond Romilly, on both sides of the Atlantic, my thanks are to: John Boulting, Alister and Puggy Cameron, Maurice Carstairs, Robert Dewhirst, Virginia Durr, Gavin Ewart, David Gascoyne, Katherine Graham, Bernard Gutteridge, J.N.Hall, Donald Harborow, Alexander Lourie, Arthur Calder-Marshall, Sir Stephen Spender, Michael Straight, H.W.Stubbs, Harry Watts, Basil Wright.

I should also like to thank the administrators of the G.S.B.Romilly estate for making available the Esmond Romilly papers in their possession.

Mark Baker, the Wellington College archivist until 1982, and his successor, Dr Heather Tomlinson, kindly provided background information to Romilly's schooldays; my thanks to them, and to the headmasters of Wellington College and Newlands for allowing me to visit their schools.

My editors, William Abrahams at Dutton, and John Curtis and Linden Lawson at Weidenfeld, have made many useful suggestions for which I am grateful.

Kevin Ingram, Tysoe, April 1985

The author and publishers are grateful for permission to quote from the following:

'Song for the New Year' and 'Spain 1937', reprinted from *The English Auden: Poems, Essays and Dramatic Writings 1927–1939*, edited by Edward Mendelson, by permission of Faber and Faber Ltd and Random House, Inc. (copyright © 1940, renewed 1968 by W.H.Auden and Random House, Inc.); 'London Rain', reprinted by permission of Faber and Faber Ltd from *The Collected Poems of Louis MacNeice; Hons and Rebels,* copyright 1960 by Jessica Mitford, by permission of Victor Gollancz Ltd and Curtis Brown Ltd, New York; *Boadilla,* by Esmond Romilly, © 1935; *Out of Bounds,* by Esmond Romilly and Giles Romilly, first published in 1935, by permission of Hamish Hamilton Ltd; *Clementine Churchill: The Biography of a Marriage*, by Mary Soames, copyright © 1979 by Thompson Newspapers Ltd, by permission of Cassell Ltd and Houghton Mifflin Company; and *Friends Apart,* by Philip Toynbee, published in 1980, by permission of Sidgwick and Jackson Ltd.

1
The Red and the Blue

Both Esmond and I would have scouted the idea that anything in our conduct was remotely attributable either to heredity or to upbringing, for, like most people, we regarded ourselves as 'self-made', free agents in every respect, the products of our own actions and decisions. Yet our style of behaviour during much of our life together, the strong streak of delinquency which I found so attractive in Esmond and which struck such a responsive chord in me, his carefree intransigence, even his supreme self-confidence – a feeling of being able to walk unscathed through any flame – are not hard to trace to an English upper-class ancestry and upbringing.

JESSICA MITFORD, *Hons and Rebels*

In 1878 Esmond Romilly's maternal grandmother, the wayward Lady Henrietta Blanche Ogilvy, married, against her parents' wishes, the recent divorcee, Sir Henry Hozier. The marriage lasted twelve years and, as Blanche's father, the seventh Earl of Airlie, had foreseen, it was not a happy match. Long before the separation in 1891 Henry's and Blanche's paths had diverged, Henry's leading him outside the realm of this story, Blanche's leading her into a series of love affairs from which emerged her four children: Kitty, Clementine, and the twins Nellie and Bill. Kitty and Clementine, the two eldest daughters, were, according to Blanche, fathered by that society figure and horseman, Bay Middleton; the twins ... it is not known for certain by whom, although Hozier, for one, was convinced they were not his. There was, of course, speculation. Wilfrid Scawen Blunt, the poet and orientalist, perhaps? Or the pleasure-loving politician, Ellis Ashmead Bartlett? There were several strong contenders.

Soon after the Hozier separation, Blanche and her heterogeneous brood moved across the Channel to Dieppe. The move was made with a mind toward both economy and safety. Blanche was not well off and it was far cheaper to live in France than in England. It was also a safe distance away from her husband, whom she suspected of planning to kidnap the two eldest children. Yet the emigration, made with all the best intentions, proved an ironic, tragic decision.

On a visit to her mother's house in Dieppe in 1924, an unhappy Clementine Hozier, now Mrs Winston Churchill, wrote to her husband:

> This is a sad old place and to me it is extraordinary that Mother should make it her home. To me it is haunted and decayed and melancholy. My sister Kitty died here of typhoid fever, and Bill is buried here in the cemetery at the top of the hill.... It is extraordinary to reflect that if Mother had not on that first occasion come to Dieppe both Kitty and Bill might be alive today. I say Bill as well as Kitty, because it is here that Mother first began her regular gambling habit and it is here that Bill saw gambling from his early childhood and used to come after he was grown up when on leave from his ship on weekend gambling expeditions.*

As she got older Lady Blanche's interests were transferred from the society salons of London to the gambling tables of the Dieppe casino. Gambling became an all-consuming passion, and longer and longer periods were spent in the French port, where the addiction was indulged. Eventually Blanche stopped returning to England altogether; there was no need. She bought two cottages, St Antoine and Petit St Antoine, situated on a hill overlooking the casino, and took her place, a commanding one, in the British 'colony' which had begun to take root in that small dent of Normandy coastline.

Blanche gambled right up until her death in 1925, at the time of which she was living in a hotel room on the sea-front, the St Antoines having been rented out to supplement her gambling money. The hotel was, of course, carefully chosen for its proximity to the casino.

Esmond's mother Nellie was also bitten by the gambling bug. 'I went with Nellie to the casino the other night,' wrote a horrified Clementine, 'and I was astounded at the reckless manner in which both Mother and Nellie gambled.... It made me feel quite ill and ashamed to watch them and I went home to bed ... Bill's grim lonely end has not made the slightest difference....'

'Both my grandmother and Aunt Nellie were terrific gamblers,' says Lady Soames (*née* Mary Churchill), 'I think there must have been a

---

* Kitty died in Dieppe on 5 March 1900, aged sixteen. Bill committed suicide in a Paris hotel room on 14 April 1921, aged thirty; it is thought over a gambling debt.

gambling gene.' Esmond's wife, Jessica Mitford, believes her husband would gamble on anything, although he had a particular penchant for dog racing: 'We often made the trek down to the White City dog track on a Friday night, where he would systematically go through both his wages and mine. Everything gone. Not even the bus fare home.'

Nellie Romilly had been in the same situation many times. On opening her writing table, after her death in 1955, Giles, the eldest son, was confronted by a chaos of counterfoils: redundant receipts for items pawned and never reclaimed.

Nellie had inherited her mother's temperament or, at least, the core of it; for in form it was quite different; less exact, at times almost amorphous. 'The bud herself [Nellie] is a curious study', wrote Prime Minister Asquith in 1915 'I like her (not vehemently) and she is really much cleverer and more original than Clemmie. But her pose of a sort of simple fatuity is apt to take one in and sometimes one is not quite sure whether it is a pose or the real person.'

Nellie was, in fact, two people. She was the intelligent and sophisticated younger member of the much talked of 'Hozier girls'. She was also the sentimentalist; the excitable, ingenuous, wide-eyed romantic, the girl who, in August 1914, left her home and followed the martial drum to war.

Nellie had joined her friend Angela Manners' private nursing unit, Clementine wrote to Winston, and had gone off to Belgium as the unit's secretary and interpreter. Of course, it was 'all cheap emotion. Nellie is not trained, she will be one more useless mouth to feed in that poor little country which in a few days will be the scene of horrible grim happenings.'

Nellie's unit arrived in Belgium in mid-August, and was immediately captured by an insurgent German Army. Thereafter, it worked behind the German lines, ministering to both British and German wounded, until December, when the German war office allowed it to return to England.

Strangely enough, Nellie's war experiences appear to have made no impression on her sentimental armour – at least no lasting impression. Eighteen years after her return from Belgium, and at a time when her two sons were beginning to question such jingoistic sentiments as *dulce et decorum est pro patria mori*, Nellie published her life story. The book – an autobiographical novel – was titled *Misdeal*, and was dedicated to: 'The men of the tattered battalion which fights till it dies.'

Not everyone took to Nellie's duality of character. Most, however, found it disarming and attractive. On leave from France in 1915 Colonel

Bertram Romilly was not only attracted to this mercurial young woman, he was bowled over, totally infatuated, and ready and willing to propose marriage, and after just one meeting. Nellie remained unmoved. The dapper Colonel may have been known as Romeo to his regiment, but he was no Don Juan to sweep a girl off her feet in twenty-four hours. Besides, did men really fall in love so quickly? 'What nonsense it all was.' The Colonel's proposal was rejected, and that as far as Nellie Hozier was concerned was the end of the matter.

Then in May 1915, only weeks after his English leave and stillborn proposal to Nellie Hozier, Colonel Romilly suffered a serious head wound. At first he was not expected to live, but with the help of a distinguished surgeon he pulled through and in the summer returned to England to recuperate. It was now that Bertram began his real campaign to capture the beautiful and volatile Nellie. This was no lightning attack – that was not the young officer's way – but it was a very effective war of attrition. Battered by the constant bombardment, Nellie eventually surrendered and married the victorious Colonel. The ceremony was performed at the Guards Chapel on 4 December 1915; symbolically, the ill-matched newlyweds walked through an arch of swords formed by members of Colonel Romilly's regiment.

Long years spent in isolation from the fair sex, manning the outposts of Empire, may not have enhanced Colonel Romilly's seduction technique, but they had taught him the value of perseverance, and it was this quality that had finally won the day. Indeed, the word 'persevere' had a special significance for Bertram Romilly, it was his family motto – an imperative summoned by his great-grandfather, Sir Samuel, as a mark of respect for those earlier Romillys who had worked relentlessly to establish themselves within their new country.

In 1709 Stephen Romilly of Montpelier, France, landed in England. He was on the run, fleeing, like so many other Huguenots, from the religious persecution which followed the 1685 Revocation of the Edict of Nantes. Like most of his persuasion, Stephen was an artisan, so too was his son Peter, a Soho watchsmith, who rose to become jeweller to King George III. Peter Romilly was proud of his success, and he was adamant that his sons should be successful too; but not successful craftsmen. The next generation of Romillys would be professionals.

Sir Samuel Romilly, Peter's youngest son, was perseverance personified, or so it appeared, labouring long and hard in his legal profession to make not one but two fortunes. The first of these was for his parents, the second for himself and the future Lady Romilly, a Miss Anne Garbett, whose hand in marriage he denied himself until his Olympian task was completed.

This same determination was exhibited by Sir Samuel in public life also, where, as Secretary General and MP for Queensborough, he applied his great energy and ability unremittingly to the much neglected area of social reform. There was, however, a limit to Sir Samuel's perseverance, and this was reached in 1818, on the death of Lady Romilly. 'My head is burning,' Sir Samuel repeated constantly during the Sunday of 1 November 1818, 'My head is burning.' It was just three days since the death of his beloved wife following a long and painful illness and the statesman's grief, which had grown daily during the previous months, now consumed him totally. His family tried to maintain a constant vigil but it proved an impossible task. Left alone for several minutes on the Sunday afternoon, Sir Samuel rose from his bed, slashed his wrists and, in the words of his memoirist, 'what was once the ornament of the senate and the bar became a lifeless corpse.'

Although Sir Samuel Romilly's youngest son, Frederick (Esmond's great-grandfather), did not achieve his father's eminence, he did acquit himself well in his chosen career, becoming Lt-Colonel in the Scots Guards and thereby setting a precedent which lasted three generations. Frederick's place in this story is however pre-empted somewhat by his elder brother Henry, who, having worked to establish himself on the West Country estate of Huntington Park, left everything to Frederick's son, Samuel Henry, thus placing Esmond's branch of the family within the ranks of the landed gentry.

Esmond's grandfather, the very fortunate Samuel Henry, was not required to persevere at anything. Having been called to the Bar (1874) he retired early to his Huntington estate where, in the course of a long life, he became JP for both Herefordshire and Glamorgan, and lorded over his domain in true squirearchical fashion. It was in the main an untaxing existence (which may explain its longevity; he died aged ninety-one) and left him time for other pursuits, among them literature, an interest he shared with his wife Lady Arabella Carnegie, who wrote poetry and articles for gentlemen's magazines and entertained in her London salon such literary giants as Henry James and Oscar Wilde. She also entertained one Blanche Ogilvy. Indeed, Blanche referred to Arabella as one of her greatest friends.

The Samuel Romillys had five children; three girls and two boys. Of the two sons, it was the younger, Eric, who followed his father into the law, the elder, Bertram, entering the Scots Guards as both his uncle and grandfather before him.*

A model had emerged within the Romilly family; a model founded on the bedrock of the landed gentry, and supported by those twin pillars of order, the Army and the law. It was a structure both simple and compact and contained neither nook nor niche for the accommodation of Bertram's and Nellie's younger son, the many-sided Esmond.

In essence, Esmond would have little in common with the Romillys (unless there is such a thing as an atavistic running-away gene). Even the family motto 'persevere', a command apparently forged to the young Romilly's soul, is not the pertinent axiom it may seem. 'In everything he was as persistent as a hound', wrote Philip Toynbee of Esmond, capturing his friend's indefatigable nature. But 'persevere' has a heavier, almost burdensome quality; a stoical toiling against the odds. And there was certainly this aspect to the Romilly character; Samuel Henry's black-dog moods, Bertram's periods of melancholic reclusion, Esmond's brother Giles's almost Sisyphean struggle with depression.

Nellie was under no delusion as to Bertram's character; his sober-mindedness was, in fact, what most appealed to her; the broken war-hero image of her romantic illusions. But what of her other feelings? Was she in love with him? The ever-perturbed Clementine was in no doubt as to the answer. She wrote to Winston on 12 November 1915:

> I don't think she loves him at all but is simply marrying him out of pity.... She vacillated (for the last week) between breaking off entirely, postponement, and immediate marriage with every hour of the day, but now she has hardened into a sort of mule-like obstinacy and says with a drawn wretched face that she loves him, is divinely happy and will marry on the 4th. She is now furious with me for my former support of her postponing intentions, and says that if I say one word against her marriage on December 4th she will leave the house and never come near me when she is married.

The marriage, the most reckless gamble Nellie was ever likely to take, went ahead.

'What's this?' asked the prefect Anthony Robinson, picking up a new grey-bound book, the only one on Esmond's Wellington bookshelf (the year was 1932). '*Misdeal* by Anna Gerstein?'†

---

* Bertram Romilly entered the Scots Guards in 1899. In 1902, at the age of twenty-four, he was awarded the DSO for acts of bravery while serving in South Africa. He later served in Egypt where from 1911 to 1914 he commanded the Egyptian Camel Corps.
† *Misdeal* was written by Nellie Romilly under the pseudonym Anna Gerstein.

'That's my family history,' Esmond replied, and smiled. . . .

When the heroine Nancy Rivers marries the broken war-hero, Colonel Gerald Durane, she is not absolutely sure of her feelings towards him. She is 'haunted by the thought that his chance of a real renewal of life did indeed depend on her', she is also, at the age of twenty-five, 'agonizingly shy of becoming an old maid', but is she in love with him or has she merely succumbed to his passionate persistence?

Nancy soon finds out that she and her husband are not at all compatible, that they are like 'two wild animals penned in a cage'. 'Soon she found he actually did not like her affectionate ways. He was frantic when she pulled his matchbox out of his pocket without warning. He tried, of course, to hide his consternation, but it was a dismal failure and she felt like a cat walking on hot bricks.'

The situation is exacerbated by Gerald's long absence from his regiment. Months pass before he is considered fit to return to France, and then only to be invalided out of the war again that same year. After this Gerald gives up all hope of pursuing his career and withdraws from society, placing an even greater strain on the relationship '. . . he irritated her at times beyond bearing. His face was fine but it was the face of a man broken in the wars, and the eyes which were generally downcast reflected from their blue irises the agony of a disappointed career.'

Then, unexpectedly, Colonel Gerald Durane is offered another post in his old stomping ground, India, and is given a new lease of life. Meanwhile, however, Nancy has fallen in love with the dashing Cyril Landon and is placed in a dilemma. She explains to Cyril: 'I love Gerald like a cause – something you believe in . . . something you die for sometimes. . . . But I love you like a human being. I want to live for you, Cyril – with you, that's what it is. I understand it now. Oh, help me to bear it all.'

But Nancy realizes there can be no divorce. 'She was committed to one of those marriages which it is almost impossible to dissolve in this country' and there is in any case 'too little money to make a separation possible, for the affairs of her lover were in such a state of chaos that a complete break from Gerald with Cyril as her future husband could only make confusion worse confounded.' There is moreover a third, overriding reason why the marriage chains cannot be broken – 'There were two children to forge the iron links.'

2
Childhood

Tommy, the eldest, was her heart's delight and astonishingly good looking. Sylvia, her daughter, was more difficult, aloof, impertinent and obstinate.

Misdeal

The Romillys' first son, Giles Samuel Bertram, was born on 19 September 1916. Esmond Marcus David followed two years later, on 10 June 1918. Both children were, according to the *Daily Mail* (2 February 1934), 'war babies', that is children 'born during the late war years when their mothers were suffering acute anxiety'; an anxiety creating in their offspring 'a rebelliousness and not always quite normal mind as we speak of the normal mind of the schoolboy'. Esmond, on whom this attack was centred, felt bound to concur. 'Speculation about the last war,' he wrote in *Out of Bounds** has of necessity led many to a Socialist standpoint.'

Esmond was born at No. 15 Pimlico Road, sw1, a house rented by the Romillys soon after their marriage and remaining with the family up until Giles's death in 1967. No. 15 stands a few yards aloof from the busy Buckingham Palace Road, a brisk walk from Victoria Station. It is narrow, erect and Victorian, and of a type encountered throughout middle-class London – three storeys and a basement, a piece of ground, the garden, at the back.

In the Romillys' day the house was divided into a first-storey drawing room and dining room, a second-storey master bedroom and a third-storey nursery and boys' bedroom. The basement was the province of Mrs Perriman, the Romillys' cook-cum-housekeeper, on whom Nellie bestowed the dubious title of 'best chip maker in London'. It was a small house, but neat and tastefully decorated. Like that other much

---

* *Out of Bounds: The Education of Giles Romilly and Esmond Romilly*. All references to the book will be in italics; all references to 'Out of Bounds', the magazine, will be in roman type and inverted commas.

harried mother, Saki's Francisca Bassington, Nellie took pride (and solace) in a home which reflected the conventional and organized elements in her life while belying the impending chaos. The chaos in Nellie's case lying under the drawing-room bureau (in a jumble of pawn tickets) and in a large decrepit bag which never left her side. 'With this bag I could leave for Peru tomorrow', she was fond of telling sister Clemmie, revealing in that statement the other side of the story.

Pimlico Road accounted for both the largest and the most uneventful part of Esmond's childhood. It was a dull centre of a universe which contained such bright satellites as Chartwell and Dieppe. And it was the satellites not the centre that exercised their magnetic force on childhood emotions. Esmond, a hyper-active child, was attracted most by the freedom of movement which both the Churchills' Kent estate and the Normandy resort provided. At Chartwell this was created by the country atmosphere and the continual coming and going of the various characters and personalities. As for Dieppe, there freedom was a small, intimate and totally accessible community; a place without bounds. It is hardly surprising that it gained Esmond's unqualified approbation : 'My summer holidays at Dieppe I remember as a time I really enjoyed, and to which I can look back with pleasure. I took part with zest in all the activities that there were, and was never bored or unhappy in the slightest degree.'

The Romillys descended upon Dieppe every year, at first as the guests of Nellie's mother, Lady Blanche and later, after the old lady's death in 1925, as the owners of the much renowned Grande St Antoine. A large wedge of a house set into the ascending rue des Fontaines, Grande St Antoine peers out across the rooftops of the small nucleated town below. In Esmond's day this vista was much the same as that which had greeted his grandmother some three decades previously. The town had changed however, imperceptible though this change was to the summer visitor. Dieppe had lowered its tone – that was the opinion of the English colonists at least. The old place was going downhill.

Back in the 1890s Dieppe had been at the height of fashion ; a centre for dandy and impressionist alike. Here Max Beerbohm drew his caricatures of the English denizens, Sickert captured ephemeral moments in perpetual afternoon, and Wilde and his cronies discussed the same. That had all gone. What remained was a small indigenous community of fishermen and shopkeepers with its incongruous upper echelon of Little Englanders. This group – made up for the most part of crusty colonels and their families – regarded the French town as yet another outpost of Empire and themselves as the burdened white man. And their burden had increased with the entry of the lower French orders who began to view Dieppe as a summer seaside resort. The old boundaries were becoming as blurred as a Sickert canvas. But what was to be done? Move? Impossible. Where else could one live so well, so cheaply? They were none of them well off.

Esmond was oblivious to Dieppe's declining fortune. To him the town represented the height of civilization and emancipation. His days were a blithe frenzy of bicycling, swimming and tennis and any other sport or activity which the English colony chose to organize, and all performed – such are the halcyon days of childhood summers – to a continual musical accompaniment. Morning, afternoon and evening, music cascaded across the casino roof and floated out into the town, and not merely background music, but a great variety of themes and styles. In the morning there was Monsieur Gladenewsky and his Cossack Band, dressed in full Russian regalia and playing as if their lives depended upon it. Their position was always the same, outside Charlie's bar, underneath the casino arches. Here a crowd would often gather and the more extroverted join the hand clapping and foot stomping. After lunch the musical venue changed from the informality of the arches to the glass-domed elegance of the casino's small concert hall, where the resident orchestra played selections from the German and French greats, while their audience reposed in the comfortable *fauteuils*. The evening opera brought the day's music to a close, the casino playing host to the best of the Paris performers. Dieppe may have been sinking but the band played on.

Like Seaford, its Sussex coast counterpart, Dieppe generally experiences a pleasantly warm summer climate. Yet, like its opposite number, it can also fall victim to the sudden onslaught of brittle sea air, ravaging the most balmy day, sending sunbathers scurrying crab-like across pebble beach in pursuit of newspaper, sunhat and plastic (bakelite) cup. It was in such unpredictable conditions as these that the young Romilly evolved his own, equally unpredictable, game of tennis.

Every day during his Dieppe vacation, the weather appearing tolerable, Esmond made for the 'two windy and stony courts' which formed his tennis club (not to be confused with 'the expensive, fashionable casino club' up the road) and there played against anyone willing to tolerate him for a couple of sets. He was an enthusiastic player, but no stylist. Many years later (or what seems like many years), when Esmond was living in the States, the Bryn Mawr Professor Alister Cameron observed his tennis from the opposite side of the court: 'He was' says Cameron 'one of the most unconventional players I have ever faced. He held his racket like a weapon, and charged around the

10

court, scrabbling for every ball, almost willing it over the net.... He was a difficult player to beat. He took every game seriously.'

Tennis was one of Esmond's childhood passions. The Dieppe fair was another. Every year this noisy, colourful colossus settled on the beach, providing, for the younger members of the community at least, a welcome distraction from those events taking place at the casino. Esmond's attention was arrested by one side-show in particular, 'where one had to knock off the heads of moving effigies of celebrities with a pop gun'. Every afternoon for a fortnight Esmond and an equally enthusiastic Giles made for the fair, where they spent 'at least ninety francs' at the pop gun side-show in a bid to win a large rococo clock for their parents. Unfortunately, on the day the brothers' score tipped the required number of points Giles was ill in bed. Alone, Esmond collected the coveted reward to bear it home. The inevitable happened: the clock slipped and shattered into a mess of coil and shell. It was yet another incident in Esmond's continuing estrangement from the practical universe. His friend Peter Nevile often observed that Esmond was incapable of opening or closing a door because his mind couldn't fathom the workings of a doorknob. This was no exaggeration. Practical considerations of any kind were the constant bane of his life, the simplest task transforming an otherwise extrovert character into a hesitant jelly of procrastination. And yet, this congenital incompetence was never prohibitory. The doorknob may have been an irksome fact of life, but it was never a barrier. If it was necessary for Romilly to enter a room he would do so – somehow. Unlike those people intimate with the mechanics of doorknobs, Esmond was never confounded by the words 'NO ENTRY'.

Still, an impious disregard for practical considerations can have its drawbacks, as Esmond often found. Over the clock he was inconsolable, and spilled red-hot angry tears against insidious fate. The thought that he was not in total control of his own destiny was never one he bore easily: 'I sobbed for hours and refused to be comforted by being told that a clock of better value could be bought in the town for thirty francs.'

The Dieppe fair was responsible for yet another emotional outburst. It was agreed by the local *cognoscenti* that the fair was louder, brighter and better after 11 p.m. Naturally, Esmond wanted to be allowed to go at night. He was told he was too young. He persisted with his plea and, 'after many stormy scenes', was taken. 'I usually succeeded in getting what I wanted,' he matter-of-factly observed.

In the account of Esmond's childhood it is tempting to write of the young rebel's 'passionate nature' and 'autonomous spirit', but the facts would remain to undermine these euphemisms. In truth, Esmond was not an easy child to cope with. Even the much-adoring Nellie admitted he was 'difficult'. To the Dieppe colonists he was more than 'difficult', he was a spoilt brat. They said as much. They also said why.

There was that time, for example, when Esmond went missing. Nellie, distraught, phoned round the colony for help. No, she had no idea where he was. He had just vanished, probably kidnapped. In next to no time a search party was organized, Esmond's erstwhile detractors rallying to the cause. Meanwhile, the object of all this concern was cycling towards Rouen. Old Colonel Price bumped into him several hours later. What was he doing? Running away. Why? He wouldn't say. Of course, it was Nellie's fault. No discipline.

And then there were the casino bar escapades. Simona Pakenham, another of Dieppe's summer visitors, recalls the uproar Esmond caused when he made one of his frequent sorties on the town's centre of culture:

Our parents particularly deplored their (Giles' and Esmond's) habit of descending on the bar at the casino and making raids on all the tables. If anyone's eye was averted for a moment both Giles and Esmond – but Esmond was considered the ring-leader – would seize any cocktail glass they could get at and drain it. This made them extremely unpopular, and fairly sloshed. . . . The boys were considered to be very badly brought up – Nellie's fault, we were told, not their father's, but I never saw Bertram Romilly make any attempt at controlling them.

The other young inhabitants of the colony were constantly being warned against associating with the Romilly boys. They were scruffy and troublesome. Simona Pakenham believes very few children needed the warning. 'We were terrified of them.' Already, Esmond's roller-coaster tendencies were starting to repel the more pedestrian spirits of his generation. And this was not the only offensive aspect of the young Romilly. Simona Pakenham again:

One morning I called at St Antoine with my nurse and found Denise, the Romilly cook-general, remaking Esmond's bed. There was a large damp patch in the mattress. 'Il a une faiblesse', said Denise to Nanny. I gathered that he was an habitual bedwetter and I was shocked and horrified – nasty little snob that I was. I fancy that this put him permanently out of count as far as I was concerned. He must have been at least seven and I could see no excuse.

A highly-strung child, Esmond's behaviour was both unpredictable and excessive, and, unfortunately, all too often exacerbated by his mother. 'Over the bedwetting my mother behaved ridiculously', Giles told his wife many years later. 'She made a great business out of stripping the bed and washing the sheets. This upset Esmond a great deal.'

Sometime in the middle of August, having spent a month or more on French soil, the Romillys crossed the Channel, refurbished their wardrobe and made for the English West Country where, three miles from the Hereford town of Kingston, Esmond's grandfather resided on his Huntington Park estate.

Huntington Park no longer exists. The accumulation of taxes accrued through the deaths of Samuel Henry Romilly on 14 March 1940 und his eldest son Bertram just two months later rapidly drained the life-blood out of the family home. And yet, the Huntington of Esmond's childhood was a healthy and thriving thousand acres of rugged Welsh borderland. This was (and is) sheep country, the land yielding reluctantly to cultivation. The exception to this general recalcitrance was provided by the Huntington grounds themselves which, landscaped and prodigiously colourful, also contrasted favourably with the house: a uniformly dull, brick monolith standing to attention at their centre.

With neither hot running water nor electric light, Huntington House remained, like the country over which it ruled, firmly and intractably set in its ways. Not that this perturbed its occupier, the stalwart octogenarian Samuel Henry, nor for that matter his less robust son Bertram, who made a point of visiting his childhood home at least twice a year. On Esmond and Giles its effect was less congenial. On the subject of his Huntington vacations Esmond was tersely dismissive, writing – 'Half our summer holidays used to be spent at Dieppe, and half at our Grandfather's country house in Herefordshire. We both preferred the former. The latter meant being tucked away in the country and a succession of long walks.'

Huntington did have its perks, of course; the food, for instance – four large, delicious meals a day – and the relatives, a whole clan of them, to provide a suitable distraction from all that nature. Among the Huntington summer sojourners were cousins Lucinda Romilly and Pamela Hunter-Little (now Lady Wakeman). Both retain vivid memories of a boisterous Esmond. Lucinda Romilly:

He was always scruffy, always in need of a good bath. I suppose Nellie could never pin him down long enough to clean him. He was a tremendously active character, constantly rushing around, constantly coming up to one to make some terribly urgent speech on absolutely nothing; reckless, at times extremely funny. I remember one Easter vacation at Huntington when he held an auction in the attic, selling all his toys including two beautiful working models of traction engines, one of which may have belonged to Giles. Esmond was a great one for 'borrowing' things.

'Esmond was tough', Lady Wakeman recalls, although she also discerned a warmer, more generous side to her tearaway cousin. She was first introduced to this 'other person' at Pimlico Road, when Esmond emptied his pockets and gave all his money to a pavement artist. There were times too at Huntington when his gentler nature surfaced. Esmond had a soft spot for the simple-minded Tom Bevan, a gardener's son, and 'went out of his way to be a special companion'. He was also very fond of Miss Scott – a superannuated Huntington governess who had become part of the family – and on one occasion in particular was of great comfort to the old lady. 'We were sitting in the conservatory after breakfast one morning,' says Lady Wakeman, 'when Miss Scott received a telegram to say an old friend had died. Seeing she was upset, Esmond, only a small boy of nine or ten, asked if she would like to go for a stroll around the grounds. Miss Scott accepted. They went off together, Esmond chatting away like an old friend.'

Esmond was an extrovert, both cousins agreed; Giles was different, quieter, more contemplative. 'He was also on the lazy side,' added Lucinda, 'just like the Romillys.' The two brothers differed quite considerably in looks too. Giles, dark and slightly built, again resembled the Romillys. Esmond, with his brown hair and fair complexion, took after his mother's side of the family. Even his smile with its broad display of top gum was inherited from Nellie. Physically, Esmond was a tubby child, and remained so until leaving school. Of the two children Giles was considered the prettier. He was also 'Nellie's favourite'. 'You knew that, of course?' Lucinda Romilly asked. 'Oh quite clearly the favourite', Lady Wakeman agreed.

Just two miles from the Kent town of Westerham, and only an hour's drive from the capital, lies Chartwell, the Churchills' country home. Neither isolated nor antiquated, Chartwell was, during Esmond's childhood, the setting for regular family gatherings, including the much-celebrated Churchill Christmas party. Lady Soames:

... year after year the same party gathered at Chartwell: Jack and Goonie Churchill with their three children, Johnny, Peregrine and Clarissa. Clementine's sister, Nellie, with her husband, Bertram Romilly, and their two sons, Giles and Esmond (curiously known as 'The Lambs'). ... The crowd of young cousins were close in age, and provided the necessary raw material for the jollity, special friendships, and in-fighting inseparable, and indeed, indispensable on such occasions.

The Chartwell Christmas, a spectacle as rich and flamboyant as a Churchill speech, began on Christmas Eve, when 'the double doors between the drawing room and the library were flung open to reveal the Christmas tree, glowing with light, and radiating warmth – too much warmth on one occasion when 'the tree caught fire, and only Randolph's presence of mind, and speed in fetching an extinguisher, saved us from catastrophe'. This, at any rate, is Lady Soames's story. Esmond, in a diary entry, Christmas 1932, told another:

The Christmas tree caught fire in the afternoon, which I thought rather exciting. Aunt Clemmie and Mummy lost control of themselves (the former just screamed out: 'Shout fire!', while the latter rushed about the room, alternately shouting and doing silly things like opening windows. I must say I expected her to be more useful in that sort of situation.) Cousin Moppet was absolutely in her element. She, of course, got the fire extinguisher and put out the fire. I think she slightly enjoyed the comparison between her and Mummy, Randolph (who did nothing) and Aunt Clemmie. But I think she also slightly despised them. I thought I myself was rather clever. I stood there at first, thinking what a marvellous blaze it was, slightly lost my head, and thought of getting out of the front door. However, I then saw Cousin Moppet rush in with a fire extinguisher, followed by Mary who was sobbing hysterically, with a large basin of water. This I seized from her in a masterly fashion and poured it over the blaze, which was now completely under the control of Cousin Moppet. My action just failed to look as noble as it should have done, but I at least impressed Mummy. Questioned by her this morning as to the part I played, I replied that I had rushed out to get water, and what's more I think I believed it when I said it.

For the young, Christmas at Chartwell was a very exciting event, and in *Clementine*, her biography of her mother, Lady Spencer Churchill, Lady Soames records the activities with evident relish. She even describes the great Christmas snow of 1927 when 'the bigger children built a wonderful igloo; there was skating on the lakes, and the lane below the house was so deep in snow that a tunnel had to be dug to allow traffic to pass'. She does not, however, evoke a memory of a more sombre occasion several years later when both she and Esmond were interned in an upstairs bedroom while somewhere below Christmas continued without them. Lady Soames:

I think we both had chicken pox, anyway we had to be isolated. We were forced into each other's company and so Esmond had to tolerate me although I was four years younger.... I remember he tried to teach me to play cards which was a dismal failure, so we reverted to conversation. He sat back on the bed, lit a cigarette – I thought this very dashing and daring – and started a discourse on various subjects. Eventually we got round to religion.

'I don't believe in God,' he said. 'It's absolute tosh.'

'Well, I do,' I said.

'I don't believe you believe what you're talking about,' he continued. 'I bet I could make you deny Jesus Christ in sixty seconds flat.'

I said, 'You most certainly could not.' So he drew a basin of cold water, frog-marched me to it, and held my head under. When I came up he said, 'Now do you believe in Jesus Christ?' Of course, after the second time I jacked the whole thing in.

This was not the only occasion on which Lady Soames fell foul of her cousin: it was indeed rare that an encounter did not end aggressively:

I must have been about eight and still unable to ride a bike. Esmond thought it about time I learned, so one morning in the Easter holidays he took me down to the tennis court to teach me. He had little patience and his method consisted mainly of hefty shoves and 'pedal you idiot, pedal'. It was quite an ordeal, but I did learn to ride the bike. I can never remember a kind word, but I adored him. I think I was even a bit in love with him.

Christmas 1933 was Esmond's last Chartwell Christmas. He was fifteen and at the height of adolescent intolerance and pomposity. For some time now he had been making sweeping gestures against authority, several of which were made sartorially – a favourite adolescent form of protest. He had, for example, taken to wearing a large black Homburg – a symbol no doubt of his anarchism. At Chartwell this gesturing was taken one step further when he refused to dress for dinner. 'Almost everyone was seated', Lady Soames remembers, 'by the time Esmond ambled in minus black tie. How brave, I thought. Whatever would Papa say?' Much to Esmond's chagrin, Papa didn't even notice.

Although somewhat amused by his nephew's political precocity, there is no evidence to suggest that Churchill was any more inclined towards Esmond than towards any of the other young relatives who hovered around Chartwell. Esmond, on the other hand, had a special affection for his uncle, and this remained constant despite the ever-widening gulf which separated them politically. In *Out of Bounds* Esmond wrote:

It is easy enough for me to say that I think he represents all the worst elements of Tory reaction. But there is just this disadvantage. I have not known him primarily as a politician. When I have heard him talk, my capacity has not been that of a journalist – either professional or amateur. And I think it would be hardly appropriate to usurp that function now. With certainty, however, I can say that he is one of the most charming people I have ever met, and I can think of few people who would not find it a privilege to enjoy his company.

It was not, however, Esmond's affection for his uncle, but his resemblance to him, in build, posture and temperament, that led both friends and family to speculate as to the 'real' familial connection.

The rumour that Esmond was Churchill's son was ever slightly afloat [says Jessica Mitford], but I don't remember Esmond paying too much attention to it. The only time I got what seemed like some sort of solid information was from Nancy [Mitford] in the 1960s. Giles had gone mad (or fairly mad), and I was in Paris seeing Nancy. I said oh dear I do hope it's not hereditary (thinking of Dinky [Esmond's daughter]). Nancy said that anyway the madness would have been inherited from Colonel Romilly who was not Esmond's father: 'Everyone knows he's Winston's son', she said. I pressed for details and she told me about a Mediterranean cruise on which the Romillys and the Churchills went some months before Esmond's birth and during which Churchill had an affair with his sister-in-law. It didn't occur to me that, had this cruise existed, it would have taken place in the middle of the war! Nevertheless, I don't think I took the story too seriously. Nancy had a wonderfully active imagination.

It is certainly a plausible supposition, one which may even have intrigued Esmond himself, but it has no substance: Churchill was not Esmond's father. Indeed, what indication there is that Esmond was illegitimate – this contained within Nellie Romilly's *Misdeal* – soundly refutes any such claim. As for Esmond's attraction towards his uncle, that may be attributed to nothing more than a simple case of hero worship, although there is also the following to be considered. Lady Soames:

Esmond's father, Bertram Romilly, was a very ineffectual parent (this my mother told me much later on). Uncle Bertram was severely wounded in the First World War and although he made a good recovery and was certainly perfectly all right mentally, he was, I seem to remember, particularly sensitive to noise or stress. Consequently, I believe he never played a truly paternal role with his rumbustious sons and Aunt Nellie was always at great pains to protect him from childish uproars, etc. In these circumstances, it was doubly unfortunate for Giles and Esmond that their Mother should have been so suffocatingly over-maternal, which she undoubtedly was. Do you not think that given the above circumstances Esmond may have found emotionally in his Uncle a father-figure?

In these circumstances it was doubly unfortunate for Giles and Esmond that their Mother should have been so suffocatingly over-maternal.... Esmond was spoilt, that's the verdict of his childhood contemporaries. And it was Nellie's fault. It could hardly have been otherwise. Bertram was never on the scene. This was partly due to the exigencies of an army career; it was predominantly the result of personal preference. The family was too raucous for Bertram's quiet taste. His club was much more satisfactory, his father's tranquil country estate better still. To Huntington he would escape for a month at a time to shoot and fish, and forget his family problems. He was not missed – that is, not missed in any physical sense. Psychologically, his sons missed him a great deal.

'Nellie indulged both boys,' says Lady Soames. 'She adored them and told everyone they were brilliant. She fed their precocity.' Simona Pakenham goes further. 'One of the things we always thought about the boys was that they couldn't expect to grow up tolerable with a mother who was always saying, in their hearing – "Isn't he beautiful? Have you ever seen such lovely boys?" Perhaps that, more than anything, put the average child (in Dieppe) off them.'

'Both Esmond and Giles had complexes about their mother', Stephen Spender has observed of the teenage Romillys, 'but Giles' complex seemed all-consuming. He hated Nellie, or so it appeared, but he wouldn't or couldn't leave home and free himself of her influence.'

'Giles as a schoolboy didn't know whether to hate his protective mother or to love her', wrote T.C.Worsley. 'Esmond was undivided in his hate – the lack of any such division in his character was his great strength.'

It would seem likely that of the two Romilly children the highly excitable Esmond would have been most affected by Nellie Romilly's overpowering personality, yet it was the irresolute elder brother, the much adored Giles, who succumbed most to Nellie's over-indulgence. Not that there was any discernible sign of stress in either one in childhood. The effect came later, in adolescence, when the strain of living under Nellie's stifling canopy began to tell on both children, and on Giles in particular:

> And Maxwell, hovering round like a kite
> Said, 'Read this poem I wrote last night.
>   It's good.'
> While by himself the elder Romilly
> Delivered an introspective homily
>   on motherhood.*

* Poem by Gavin Ewart appearing in the *Wellingtonian*, November 1933.

3
School

In the second of Nellie Romilly's large decayed family scrapbooks there is a telegram dated 9 November 1929 : 'Congratulations on scholarship Giles – Gibbs.' This terse message plus a school sports programme contained in the same tome are the only indication that the Romillys' formal education began not at Newlands Prep. School ('Seacliffe' of *Out of Bounds*) but at Gibbs Day School, 134 Sloane Street, SW1. Neither Esmond nor Giles mention Gibbs in the account of their education, no doubt discounting it as irrelevant to their purpose. Esmond even goes as far as to alter his age of entry into Newlands to make the existence of a previous school less likely. 'I had first gone to Seacliffe at the age of seven and a half', he wrote in *Out of Bounds*. In reality he had entered the school in May 1927 aged eight years and ten months. Esmond was never troubled by what Virginia Woolf termed 'those miserable impediments called facts'.

Newlands is situated in the Sussex coastal town of Seaford, its home since 1905. Today the school houses one hundred and seventy boys, thirteen masters and four matrons. In Esmond's day there were forty-one boys, four masters and 'Matron', a woman of gigantic proportions, 'whose "Good morning" was a thunderclap that not even the heaviest sleeper could ignore'.

In 1927 Newlands was just one big happy family. That according to Esmond was the whole problem ; the school, under the leadership of the archaic Mr Doberell,* had receded to just a handful of boys. Forty years previously Doberell had represented 'all that was absolutely modern' in education, but he had now, plainly, 'outlived his generation', and there was a movement abroad, among the parents, to oust the well-meaning but ineffectual old-timer. Even Colonel Romilly joined the affray. Esmond :

* All the Seaford masters' names are pseudonyms.

About a year before Giles left my father wrote, intimating that there was a strong possibility of his removing his sons from the school, and at the same time tactfully inquiring as to whether there was any chance of Doberell's retirement in the near future, as this would considerably influence his decision. The old man replied, saying that he was delighted to assure Colonel Romilly that there was no chance of his retiring for at least ten years, and that therefore he need have no fears for his sons' education.

Writing some four or five years after they had left Newlands, Esmond and Giles took the opportunity to send-up the old school. Their accounts, though irreverent, are not malicious, however, and the humour conceals, for the most part, a fond regard for the quaintness of education before public school Newlands, Esmond and Giles style, is more fact than fiction, but on the whole it is a place not to be taken too seriously.

In *Out of Bounds* the task of introducing the reader to Newlands – and later to Wellington – falls to Giles; Esmond, the generator of all the publicity, confining himself to a straightforward account of his inchoate rebellion. The partnership works well, Esmond's loose anecdotal approach riding on the surface of his brother's earlier pensive analyses.

Giles begins his section by describing his first day at school:

I can remember no day so vividly as that on which I first went to Seacliffe School, Seaford, unless perhaps the first day at Wellington College, Berkshire. I can remember what kind of day it was – warm, and stuffy, like the inside of a taxi cab – and what time I got up in the morning, and what I had for lunch. I remember the discomfort of my new flannel suit, with its short trousers, its waistcoat, and its Eton collar. I remember the slight sensation of nausea, contingent on clean clothes and trunks in the hall, and incessant running up and down stairs. I remember the napkin tucked into my collar at lunch to prevent me from slopping food over my new coat. I remember my mother checking up lists of clothes and writing out labels. I remember marking my own handkerchieves in ink. Above all, I remember the hallucinated sense of unreality which prevented me from being absolutely depressed. As though I were having an operation, and things were being done to me which I had no power or will to resist.

The above reads like a summary of how Giles existed; not quite in a state of depression – not always anyway – but in suspended animation, waiting for events to overtake him and relieve him of the burden

21

of living them. The rest of the account is more motivated, however, and reveals a humorous edge to Giles's character.

Stephen Spender, who met him several years later, recalls: 'Giles could be very amusing. He was always sending up the Communists, and their meetings. He had a strong verbal sense, very interesting with words. The word "spontaneous" as used by the CP amused him a lot. "Let us now send a 'spontaneous' telegram to Harry Pollitt", he would announce in his droll manner.' Giles had a caricaturist's ability for picking out the salient features of a person or situation and satirizing them. On his first day at school this landed him in some trouble:

On the very day I arrived I managed to put my foot in it. I passed in the corridor a boy with a pronouncedly hooked nose. 'Look!' I rashly cried, 'there's a boy with a nose like a beak.' He was a senior boy and he had little sense of humour, and he was very angry. I became from that moment on 'a cheeky little brat' and liable to be hunted down and cuffed by him and friends larger than himself.

In *Out of Bounds* Giles's eagle eye falls not upon Newlands pupils but upon the staff. There was Matron, for example, whose 'face had a comical shapelessness' and whose 'figure was like a sack in which everything has been shaken down to the bottom'. And Mr Boil, the science master, whose ability to impale the currants from the school pudding on his thick bristly moustache was greeted with genuine interest and astonishment, while his science experiments only elicited a burlesque mockery of enthusiasm.

Equally outrageous, according to Giles, were Mr Doberell's scripture lessons – where pandemonium reigned between intermittent pleas of 'I say, you fellows, can't you attend to what I'm saying' – and his early morning exercises, during which time 'We performed "twirligigs" at the double and other complex movements of that kind ... while Mr Doberell hovered uncertainly on the fringe ready with his "Come, come you fellows, that won't do," when the movement became too chaotically out of hand.' It would appear in fact that the eccentric headmaster had the fatal facility of attracting anarchy to whatever activity he supervised, academic, moral or cultural:

Once a week we had a dancing lesson. The floor of the gym was cleared and polished, and all the boys went up to their cubicles to change into Eton suits. Then, after roll call, we sauntered along to the gym and surprised Mr Doberell treading in the floor polish with his pumps. We would then slide ecstatically up and down with whoops and shouts until the eagerly awaited 'I say, you fellows, stop that, stop that', restored us to merely momentary order. Suddenly the door would open and in would come a very genteel lady in a black frock escorted by a no less genteel, though less substantial accomplice with a music case. 'Good afternoon Miss Sutton', would rise the well-bred chorus, and, 'Good afternoon, boys', the genteel reply. Then, after Mr Doberell, with much old-world ceremony and flourish, had helped Miss Sutton off with her coat and established her accomplice at the piano, we would pair off for the foxtrot or the waltz: and then perhaps after a hard hour of orthodox foxtrotting and waltzing, we would be allowed to attempt a country dance or perhaps even a Charleston. And Mr Doberell was, as usual, the readiest pupil of us all

For obvious reasons Mr Doberell was a favourite with the boys. Another favourite was Mr Browne, the history master, who was an authority on naval matters and bore 'more than a touch of the "quarter deck manner"'.

While we sat [in class] waiting, the door would fling open, Mr Browne charge right across the room with a pile of books up to his chin, and crash them down on his desk. Then 'Dates!' he would say, and look fiercely at us; and almost before we could open our notebooks he would begin to run through a list of principal dates of English history....

It was generally agreed that Mr Browne's history classes were the most entertaining, although Giles enjoyed English with Mr Hurst, too. Here he could escape into the world of *Lorna Doone*, *Ivanhoe* and *The Cloister and the Hearth* and lose himself in the machinations of his own essays, concerning which he recalls, with some irony, the pedagogical reproach 'not to let my pen run away with me'.

'After the first shock of "going to school"', Giles admits, 'I began to find that I did not altogether dislike Seacliffe.' Exceptions to this general equanimity were his mother's occasional visits – such occasions tending to highlight the iniquities of his educational servitude – and the mirthless Newlands Sunday, filled with depressing thoughts and the opprobrious school walk.

There were two basic routes for the school walk: either along the sea-front or over the Downs. If the school trudged the sea-front in the morning it would plod the Downs in the afternoon – 'over Beachy Head perhaps to Hove Gap where we would throw stones at a piece of seaweed, and watch other people paddling among the rocks'. Once or twice a term Newlands made the trek 'over a very smelly beach' to Newhaven to cheer the departure of a Channel boat. This was regarded as a treat, although Giles for one 'was never particularly thrilled on these occasions, perhaps because the Channel boats were already old friends (and old enemies) of mine'.

The Sunday walk understandably came in for a good deal of criticism. And this was both overt and vociferous when, during the summer term ('I shrink to remember'), a third walk was as often as not announced after tea.

This final trudging of the same stretch of Downs was effected with the utmost weariness of spirit. As soon as it was announced a chorus of protest would arise, and be tyrannically silenced. Cowed and exhausted, we would return home (a euphemism) for prayers; and after prayers a talk on cleanliness or the scout spirit; and after that bed, with its well-known Sunday night blues, which very few people could resist, and had a good deal to do with the menacing return of Monday.

'This time one day where shall I be?' began the old refrain,

> Not in this academy
> No more beetles in my tea
> Making googly eyes at me,
> No more Latin, no more Greek
> No more beatings to make me shriek.

The Michaelmas term of 1929 was Giles's last at Newlands. At the beginning of November he travelled up to Wellington College to sit the scholarship exam. One of the questions was, 'make a list of the surnames you have heard which you consider odd'. One of the names Giles wrote was 'Malim' (the Wellington headmaster's). Later, he regretted this 'piece of impertinence', and for two weeks lived in trepidation of the result. It was a pass. The elder Romilly – who, it should be added, was the most intelligent boy at Newlands – had won a £50 scholarship to Wellington. The school was given a half-day holiday in celebration. 'It was an emotional moment.'

But why Wellington? It was 'my own mad choice', Giles admits:

Both Esmond and I had been entered for Eton at an early age. But one day in a taxi the thought of Eton collars and 'bum-freezers' became too much for us, and we cried: 'Oh, please need we go to

24

Eton? Please can't we go to Wellington instead?' Wellington was associated with soldiers, and naturally we were both very military. It was our father's hope that we should both end up in the Brigade of Guards.

In January 1930 Giles entered his chosen seat of learning. Esmond, two years his junior, remained at Newlands to witness a few changes in the old order.

At the end of the 1929–30 academic year Mr Doberell retired and a new, progressive era began at Newlands, instigated by his successor, the vigorous Mr Lancaster. New rules were drawn up and placed at strategic points throughout the school, and the 'green card' system introduced with its pluses and minuses for good or bad behaviour. 'Discipline improved enormously as a result of the change', wrote Esmond, although his approval did not extend to Mr Lancaster's brainchild, the 'green card'; that 'was about the stupidest [system] that could ever have been evolved'.

The plus and minus system had been devised by Mr Lancaster to control the boys' behaviour and stimulate a greater interest in work. Minuses were awarded for misdemeanours like 'spilling a glass of water or walking naked in the passage'; pluses for 'reading a good book or opening the door for a master'. All those boys amassing a certain number of pluses in a term were allowed to go on the school outing, the others had to remain at school to mourn their fate or ponder upon their lack of application. This was the theory at any rate. In practice the system was open to abuse. Esmond:

... the situation became perfectly ludicrous. For wherever a master went, he would be followed by a swarm of boys all intent on opening some door for him. If a boy made a sufficient nuisance of himself, the master would award him a plus to get rid of him. If he continued to make a nuisance of himself, then the probability was that he would be given a minus for performing the same action.

And there were worse, or better, abuses, depending upon one's perspective:

Only boys below the third class had to have their plusses and minuses signed: hence, among the rest, anyone who was doing badly could add to his score by a few strokes of the pen. From time to time there was an outcry when it was patent that somebody had cheated too

25

obviously. We all of us joined in the outcry, while we all of us cheated just the same. I myself used to increase my figure regularly each week.

The younger Romilly was troubled by few moral scruples and freely admits to having 'both enjoyed and abused my power' in the final year at Newlands. For this was the year Esmond found himself at the pinnacle of the Newlands hierarchy : a little 'big noise' in the land.

Esmond entertained only one thought on entering his last year at prep. school : 'to rise to a place of authority'. This ambition was realized on the first night of the autumn term when he was made head boy ; it was consolidated some weeks later when he became senior patrol leader. Esmond was as surprised as the next by his meteoric rise. It was a tradition at Newlands to place bets of one's sweet ration upon the contenders for the titles. While being head of the school in marks, Esmond's overall behaviour was so bad that 'it was impossible to get even money on my chances'.

Had the authorities placed the difficult Romilly in a position of responsibility to curb his boisterousness? If so, they must have been disappointed with the result. 'My appointment', writes Esmond, 'was not followed by any greater sense of responsibility or improved behaviour.' Nor was it followed by a greater effort to control his temper.

At the beginning of Esmond's final year a new master entered Newlands – a 'hearty "Public School" type', called Mr Barnaby. 'You think you're a big noise here don't you?' Mr Barnaby had challenged the twelve-year-old Romilly soon after his arrival, 'Well, I'll soon show you you're not.' Several weeks later, while Mr Barnaby was supervising the preparation period, Esmond began talking and giggling with some other older boys. 'Romilly, take minus ten, will you?' came the voice of authority. Esmond was horrified. No boy had ever been given more than 'minus five' for the gravest of offences, and now the head of the school, in front of about twenty-five boys, was given 'minus ten'. The shame was too much. 'I picked up a Latin Grammar, and threw it at him.'

The matter was not reported to the headmaster, which Esmond appreciated, instead Mr Barnaby reduced him to tears in private. The feud continued. It was one of several maintained by Esmond during that last year, the most bitter being the Hoskins affair.

The Hoskins feud had begun during the first days of term, when Hoskins and another boy named Bennett (they were rumoured to be blood brothers) had been Esmond's deadly rivals for the coveted positions of head boy and senior patrol leader. Later, the battle over, Esmond and Bennett had resolved their differences and become friends, but Esmond's relations with the envious Hoskins had continued to decline. By mid-term the enemies' open antagonism towards each other was such as to demand only one solution.

One afternoon, when we were out for one of our many walks over The Downs, Hoskins and I lagged behind the rest of the school until we were alone. Then we took off our coats and began to hit each other hard in the face. It was an extremely painful affair, and has made me dislike boxing ever since. [The following year Esmond won the school boxing trophy.] Suddenly, after a good many blows had been exchanged, my opponent collapsed onto the ground, lay there groaning for a few seconds, then relapsed into complete silence, I was absolutely terrified. In vain I shook him. It was a genuine 'knock out'.

Esmond ran to fetch the master – the irascible Mr Barnaby. Hoskins was revived and the two pugilists were marched back to school to collect their reward. Fortunately for Esmond he was just recovering from an allergy. His punishment was to go to bed and stay there. ('Personally, I had never felt more in need of a good rest!') Hoskins was not so lucky. He was told to go to Mr Lancaster's room and await his punishment. 'Mr Lancaster's room', writes Esmond, 'was at the bottom of the corridor. From my bed I could hear poor Hoskins's squeals of pain and, for once, my conscience was troubled.'

The precocious Marquis was yet another of Esmond's enemies, possibly the deadliest. This character, Esmond reluctantly admits, was more conceited than himself, more impertinent, and had even less self control. Worse, although Esmond's junior, he was his intellectual equal and constantly vied with him for first position in the period marks. And if this wasn't enough, Marquis was also the recipient of a Lancing scholarship – an award gained only weeks after Esmond had failed in a similar bid at Wellington.

Esmond does not disguise the fact that as a result of his intellectual jousting with Marquis his normally footsure ego had taken a tumble. His spirits revived, however, when in the spring term a fourth patrol was formed with Marquis as its leader.

I felt sure and hoped that he [Marquis] would be unable to justify his appointment, as he was very unpopular. He was nicknamed 'Froggie', partly on account of his French origin, and partly on account of his resemblance to a frog. During physical training, his orders,

27

issued in a high-pitched, squeaky voice were greeted to my undis guised delight, with croaks and derisive cries of 'Froggie!' After a few weeks he was deposed. I felt I had scored decisively.

Patrol leader Romilly's laugh was loud but not loud enough to drown the echoes which reverberated around his own crystal fortress – as later events showed.

Counting the newly formed Foxes there were four patrols at Newlands. The other three were the Wolves, the Otters and the Peewits. Giles describes them thus: The Wolves, 'rather shabby and intellectual', the Otters, 'rather tough and crude', and the Peewits, 'rather feeble'. 'I', writes Giles proudly, 'was an ornament of the Wolves.' Esmond had been a Wolf until September 1930, when he was transferred as patrol leader to the 'tough and crude' Otters. This was a position he had coveted since entering Newlands and he was naturally delighted. But his excitement was tempered by his fear of exposing an execrable lack of practical ability.

Only days after Marquis' downfall, and while the memory of that event was still vivid, the moment Esmond most dreaded arrived: Newlands annual scout camp was announced. All those boys able to attend the camp were to give their names to Mr Browne. Those not able to attend were to come up with some very good excuse. 'I am sure I could have made many excuses,' wrote Esmond, 'for I hardly saw myself at home in a scout camp. But my courage failed me, and I made none. How I dreaded that camp, which I suppose I ought to have looked forward to with eagerness. There was bound to be something, I felt, which would expose too blatantly my hopeless incompetence.' As it turned out, his fear was unfounded. 'Actually, I quite enjoyed the camp – it lasted five days and cost my parents the modest sum of £1. It poured with rain most days, and we seemed to spend nearly all our time cooking meals and washing up and cooking the next meal.'

His major ordeal over, Esmond managed to survive the next few months without incident. This he did by keeping a low profile and delegating, whenever possible, responsibility to other members of the troop. Thus, when the Otters scooped up the much-prized Crispen Cup for best patrol of the year their commander was forced to admit that this was not in the least due to his leadership. Mr Browne thought likewise. According to him, Esmond was the worst senior patrol leader the school had had for years.

Esmond left Newlands in July 1931, in what he himself described as 'a crescendo of triumph' which was 'quite undeserved'. In a scrapbook kept by Mr Browne, and still housed within the school, Esmond's final triumphs are recorded. They form an impressive list – Patrol Leader (Otters), Cricket XI, Rugger XV Captain, Head Boy, Tennis Cup 1931, Boxing Cup 1931, Crispen Cup 1930–31, fourth place in Townsend Warner History Exam 1931. The Romilly page of the scrapbook also contains a photograph of a nine-year-old Esmond smirking through one and a half adult teeth. This, unfortunately, is Mr Browne's only interpretation of his subject, although sometime later in a letter to another ex-Newlander at Wellington he was slightly more forthcoming: 'I have been reading of the exploits of the brothers Romilly', he wrote, 'what fools they are! Esmond always had some bee in his bonnet.'

'Mr Browne', wrote Giles, 'was undoubtedly the pleasantest and most intelligent master there.'

4
Memento Mori

The peculiar character of this College is that it is a
Commemoration. Like all other Colleges it is for the
living; unlike them, it is a remembrance of the dead....
Like all others, its daily voice is 'Learn how to Live';
but unlike others, from it arises in every pause of that
living hum, as the tolling of some funeral bell when
the mighty pass away, the solemn utterance, 'Memento
mori'.

BISHOP SAMUEL WILBERFORCE
speaking at Wellington College, 16 July 1863

Esmond entered his new school on 18 September 1931 – at the beginning
of that chilling period of contemporary history known provocatively
as 'The Slump' or the 'Great Depression'.

The economic decline had in fact begun its ineluctable progress two
years previously in the wake of the Wall Street Crash, but it was not
until the summer of 1931, with over two million people unemployed
and the 1929 export figure halved, that the country became impressed
by the situation's gravity. In August 1931 the May Commission, established by the Labour Government to report on National Expenditure,
prognosticated a £96 million Budget deficit (a forecast which, incidentally, worsened the situation by causing a run on gold) and recommended hefty cut-backs in public-sector spending. Divided over the
nature and severity of the cuts the Labour Government resigned and
on 24 August the tripartite National Government, headed by ex-Labour
leader, Ramsay MacDonald, took office.

Unassailed by its predecessor's doubts, the National Government
immediately took hold of the situation, rushing through a series of
austerity measures by Emergency Act and Orders-in-Council, expe-
diency processes rarely seen outside times of war. One of the most
severe of the late summer measures was a one shilling a day across-the-
board reduction in the Royal Navy's pay-packet: a figure which represented for the able seaman a 25 per cent reduction in his four shillings

30

a day wage. On Tuesday 15 September 1931, the day the Navy, anchored at Cromarty Firth, was ordered to put to sea, the seamen went on strike, demanding a more equitable wage cut. The strike, referred to by the foreign press as a 'mutiny', lasted just forty-eight hours. Smelling that thirties chimera, Red-revolution, the Government capitulated and amended the anomaly.

It was time for a democratic mandate. With the Labour Party in tatters and the Liberals becalmed in the political back-waters the result was, of course, a foregone conclusion : a victory for the Tory-dominated National Government. The 26 October National landslide was, never-theless, a very poor indication of the country's mood, as the thirteen-year-old Romilly noted in a letter to his mother, 25 October 1931 :

It must be very exciting during the elections in London ... I saw a few days ago in the *Daily Sketch* that Uncle Winston got mobbed at a meeting. I have been reading lots of articles in the *Morning Post, Daily Mail, Daily Sketch, Daily Mirror*, and it struck me that lots of the Conservative meetings are being broken up....

This studied observation was made from the confines of the school sanatorium, where Esmond had spent ten days recovering from some schoolboy ailment. The period of reclusion had left him plenty of time for reading, he told his mother, and he had read Lytton Strachey's *Queen Victoria*, Uncle Winston's *My Early Life* ('I especially like "The Battle of Omdurman" and his escape from the Boers') and a 'very funny' book by P.G.Wodehouse called *If I Were You*. He had also read all the newspapers and had followed closely the election run-in. But Esmond's interest in politics was not fervent, and even his uncle's de-clining fortunes failed to incite comment – 'I see in the paper [letter, 8 November] that the cabinet has been formed, and that Uncle Winston hasn't got a post'.

At the beginning of his first term at Wellington College, Esmond Romilly was preoccupied by thoughts quite different to those oppressing the outside world.

It was left to Giles to situate Esmond at his new school. Not wanting him in his own dormitory – The Blucher – as he was sure they would quarrel, Giles plumped for The Murray. It was here – or, rather, in the dormitory's annex shared with three other boys – that Esmond met his fellow entrant X – 'a pretty conceited pseudo tough' – who immediately became a more than willing participant in another Esmond feud.

31

'The story of Esmond's first term', writes Giles, 'is the story of his rise to equality with and triumph over X. This is what I listened to after every meal.' There was another drama too, as Giles well knew from experience – it was called The Importance of Being Conformist and began on the newcomer's very first day with the tolling of the school bell.

An early Wellington headmaster, Bertram Pollock, had often boasted that he knew exactly what each one of his pupils was doing at any point during the day. The headmaster during Esmond's period at the school, F.B.Malim, was not one to boast, nor was he one to be interested in the technical day-to-day workings of his school. Nevertheless he could be certain that his charges were always gainfully employed. Such was the Wellington timetable. Giles:

I can remember little of my first term as distinct from other terms, except that I had a terror of being late for things, and was constantly on the run. And though I said I was depressed almost from my first day, that cannot be strictly true; for during my first term at Wellington there was no time for such lazy self-indulgence. I hurried from work to call-over, from call-over to games, from games to work again, inky, harassed and perplexed, and had never a moment of the day to myself.

In similar terms, Giles analysed his brother's initial reaction to life at Wellington: 'Esmond was not unhappy his first term; there was too much that was new and bewildering for that. But like me, he registered instinctively that it was hateful despite its sometimes thrilling newness. What first drew us together, in fact, was a common hatred of Wellington.'

The Romillys' hatred of Wellington was inspired chiefly by the school's doctrine of suppression, a doctrine expressed to some extent through the tight timetabling but propounded more fully in the restrictions of the dormitory system.

The dormitory system had originally been adopted by public schools as a simple and practical method of dividing up students into manageable units for administrative purposes and, as such, it worked well. Not so commendable was its insistence upon creating petty group loyalties which were zealously upheld, not for any rational purpose, but because, by an arbitrary stroke of an administrator's pen, a boy happened to find himself amongst one group rather than another. At Wellington in the thirties the dormitory spirit was taken to ridiculous extremes. Not only were students discouraged from speaking to members of other dormitories, they were also advised against forming friendships with people other than contemporaries within their own dormitory; and 'contemporaries' did not mean those people who arrived the same year, but those several students, rarely more than four, who arrived in the same term.

In *Out of Bounds* Esmond recalls one particularly irksome ordeal created by the narrowness of the system:

I used to hate the meals at Wellington; one saw the same faces opposite one every day, breakfast, lunch or tea, term after term, year after year, always there was the same monotonous conversation. As a boy became older, he moved up the table and was able to swear and curse at the people below him; the number of terms one had been at school counted for everything. The boy who came a term before you, was (for the first year or so at least) an infinitely superior being. Similarly, you would never dream of so demeaning yourself as to make friends with a boy who came after you.

In an earlier section of the book Giles outlined an equally valid objection to the dormitory ethos:

Almost as soon as a boy arrived he became tarred with the dormitory brush, contaminated. There began to emanate from him, physically and mentally, an aura of Orange, Beresford, Lynedoch, whatever it was. Thus, for instance, in the Orange, everyone, except an occasional scholar, was 'spotty, dissipated and mad on jazz'. A boy of thirteen imprisoned in a society which has developed these tendencies is almost certain to be too weak to resist them. Usually he does not want to resist, but is only too willing to conform, and to deride 'intellectuals' who wear black homburgs and are 'always trying to be different.'

Of course, it is evident from the above that Giles's and Esmond's criticisms are as much a comment upon themselves as upon Wellington College. Both precocious, both spoilt, they were neither of them happy in an environment which refused to humour them or accommodate their idiosyncrasies. The Romillys were not, however, the school's only detractors. Wellington College 1930–40 was a school under fire, as we shall see. But first some history.

33

When, in 1852, the Duke of Wellington died, there arose the problem of commemorating one of England's great national heroes. Obviously a monument was required, but what form was this monument to take? The most acceptable idea came from the Palace. A college to give free education to the orphans of army officers, suggested the Prince Consort. Lord Derby, the Prime Minister, approved. A monument fund was therefore established and with subscriptions resting at £100,000 the building went ahead.

The architect chosen to design this school-monument was a Mr Shaw, among whose previous work was the much-praised Royal Naval College at Newcross. In the autumn of 1856, Mr Shaw's design approved, building began on Bagshot Heath, at that time a grim piece of scrub-land uninhabited except for the small village of Sandhurst and, appropriately enough, the Royal Military College, both located some two miles to the south-east.

With construction underway the school governors began formulating the school curriculum, adopting as their model the practical art and science programme of the Prussian gymnasium, as opposed to the classics-biased syllabus of the English public school. The object of this new school, it was agreed, was to furnish the underprivileged child with a basic education and no more; an education enabling him to support himself as soon as possible in, for example, an office job, although naturally it was hoped that many boys would avail themselves of the Services.

On 20 January 1859, nine days before Wellington College's official opening, the first seventy-six recruits filed through Great Gate (or the gap where Great Gate would eventually be inserted) and into the school. They were wearing green plaid uniforms and peaked caps and looked a little like station porters, which may explain why visiting dignitaries arriving at the local station were in the habit of slipping an idling pupil a penny and sending him ahead with the bags.

In the seventy-two years which elapsed between the arrival of the first students in 1859 and Esmond Romilly's entry in 1931, Wellington had been transformed from a military orphanage into a public school: tailored suits had now replaced the quasi-military uniform, classical studies the utilitarian syllabus, fee-paying students (for the most part) the fee-waived orphans. Yet, through all its changes Wellington had carefully preserved its military character. As a new boy, Esmond was made aware of this by the cost of his education; an officer's son, his fees were considerably less than those of a civilian's. The official statistics were another indication of this character. These were read out every speech day and showed, quite clearly, that Wellington College supplied more officer recruits to the military academies than any other public school. Other, more frequent reminders of the military connection were contained within the school itself, which celebrated its famous namesake by naming its dormitories after the Duke's fellow officers at Waterloo, and by lining the walls of the inner quad with busts of the same heroes. But more than anything else Wellington College showed its colours in its regimental enthusiasm for balking progress.

T.C. Worsley, in 1931 a junior master at Wellington, describes the school at this time as 'philistine to a degree almost unimaginable in a great school'. 'There was no literary society, no political club, no acting, no extra class activity of any kind, except that it had a lively music master.... In almost every possible way it was thirty, forty, fifty years behind the times.' Edmond's dormitory tutor, Rupert Horsley, echoes Worsley's criticisms. 'The masters were just as restricted as the boys', he recalls. 'During my first three years at College I regarded it as a prison.'

'I have had an opportunity lately of seeing the parents of several boys at Wellington,' wrote the school's vice-president, the Earl of Derby, to Malim in 1925 (six years before Esmond's entry), 'and I find from them that on the whole the school is not popular with the boys.' Derby had, naturally, tried to find out the reason for this:

One parent I think put his (or rather her) finger on the spot. She said that the boys are too well looked after. They never seem to have a moment to themselves the whole day long.... I do not feel that I know enough about the school routine ... to really offer an opinion as to the reason I have given is a right one, or whether indeed it is justifiable even to suggest it, but I wish you would think it over.

In his reply to Derby's letter Malim attributed the tight timetable to two causes. The first – 'the complexity of the modern curriculum which has come to include OTC, Physical Training, Boxing, Fencing, Wireless, Debating, etc., etc.' – can be discounted as no more than straw-clutching. The second explanation is more interesting. This was, in the headmaster's words, 'the deliberate intention of keeping the boys busy to keep them out of mischief'. Unfortunately, Malim does not expand upon this point ('I won't write you a long discussion of it now'). Nevertheless, it can be assumed that Derby was well aware that by 'mischief' Malim was referring, at least in part, to that great public-school taboo: sex.

Homosexuality may be a fact of life; it is not one which the public school cares to dwell upon. There is good reason for this: homosexual practice is an inevitable result of isolating pubescent boys from the opposite sex and the only way to counter it is to abolish the boarding system or to introduce co-education. Other than this there is no remedy, despite the many elaborate restraints.

During the period of its history covered by this narrative Wellington's way of controlling 'mischief' was to impose the tightest checks upon its students' time and movement. 'Needless to say,' wrote Worsley, 'the suspicion, and the counter-measures, had the opposite effect to that intended. Squalid discoveries of sexual misdemeanours were constantly coming to light: and the inhuman ritual of banishment to the sanatorium, roped playboxes, and the summoning of weeping parents was all too common an occurrence.'

Concluding his reply to Lord Derby's letter, Malim confessed to being disturbed by the vice-president's words. 'In my experience', he wrote, 'there were in all schools some boys who are glad to leave; but it is not desirable that they should be the majority.' Derby's letter had come as a revelation to the headmaster, the first of many during his last decade at Wellington; and they all pointed to the same thing: Malim was out of touch with his school.

For all his qualities as a teacher and administrator, Malim was too aloof to be an effective headmaster. He was a patrician figure set apart from the everyday life of the school, the control of which was assumed by an oligarchy of old guard, reactionary masters. The leader of this small but powerful clique, the power in the land when Esmond entered Wellington, was the infamous H.J.B.Wanstall. '[He] looks at every boy as if he suspected he was going to have a baby,' one of the masters had joked in commenting on Wanstall's perverse interest in the boys' behaviour. But Wanstall was no joke. Rupert Horsley recalls: 'There always seemed to be a line of boys outside his room awaiting punishment. They had to press a little button and when the red light went on they went inside and received their beating.... He was a horrible man; a sadist.'

The suspicion emanating from Wanstall was 'all pervasive', writes T.C.Worsley:

... it was palpable in the atmosphere, and it was nasty. It was the origin of the Old Guards' opposition to every liberal improvement. And I, incompetent as I was to pronounce on these sexual questions, was none the less convinced – and not merely from a shallow knowledge of psycho-analytic theory – that his suspicious nature was itself some form of perversion and that it was connected with his unbridled passion for beating.

Esmond's entry into Wellington, in September 1931, had coincided with a battle: a battle being waged within the school's own staff-room between the reactionary clique led by Wanstall and a group of more liberal-minded colleagues who, in petitioning for reform, had challenged the former's ascendancy. One member of the reforming faction was Worsley (later literary editor of the *New Statesman*) who arrived at Wellington in 1929, aged twenty-two. In *Flannelled Fool*, his revelatory account of the school between 1929 and 1936, Worsley recounts the many squabbles of the time: 'we began now a period of outfighting which was working up slowly toward a final confrontation', he writes, in terms suggestive of Armageddon. He was, in fact, referring to the heated discourse on the merits of the school cap which took place during Esmond's second term at Wellington.

There were several reasons why the reforming faction wanted the school cap abolished: it was too often a scruffy, unenhancing appendage to the school uniform; it was a weapon used by the school bullies; it was an object of worry, especially among the younger members of the school, who were always misplacing it or having it stolen. But more objectionable still, the school cap, with its various colours to denote dormitory, was a symbol of Wellington's system of petty rivalries and group bigotry. After debating upon the cap problem among themselves, the reforming faction eventually raised the issue at a staff meeting. The occasion, a stormy one, once again highlighted the headmaster's serious detachment from his school.

Reluctant to tackle the larger issue of dormitory rivalries, the reformers began their supplication by focusing only upon the minor iniquities of the school cap. When, however, it became clear that their arguments carried little weight with Malim, and that their motion was in danger of being temporized out of existence, Worsley, as the group's spokesman, let fly with the major grievance:

Did the master, or any of us, fully understand why there was such opposition to abolishing those wretched caps? It wasn't tradition or care for the old customs. It was this ludicrous jealousy felt by the different Tutors for each others' Dormitories.... As long as caps were still being worn, any Tutor could tell at any distance whether his boys were associating with someone else's; and he could rush across to stop it ... as the Master knew....

37

Needless to say, Malim did not know, had not a clue even what Worsley was talking about. As far as he was concerned 'a boy in any Dormitory might talk to any other boy in the school at any time he wished.... Didn't they invite their friends up to visit them in their Dormitories? He had always imagined that they had.' Surrounded on all sides by blank faces (that boys should enter other boys' dormitories had 'struck even the reformers as positively revolutionary'), Malim continued:

Kindly understand Worsley, that I have made no such rule about associations between boys in different Dormitories. I have never heard of it, and I don't want to hear of it.... And if that is what this ridiculous hubbub over caps is all about, if that is the misunderstanding on which the wearing of caps is based, we had better abolish them at once.

'Such', writes Worsley, 'was the sort of momentous issue on which we were expending our energies more and more. They seem trivial enough today, but they were symptoms of a real struggle going on not merely within the confines of the College.'

'Public Schools are undoubtedly changing', Malim wrote in his introduction to the 1931–2 *Wellington Year Book*, 'whether for the better or worse depends upon one's point of view.'

We do not wear caps any longer inside the College grounds, it is true. This may be a nuisance to those who wish to recognize a boy more easily, and a break with tradition that is not very old, but it is not necessarily decadent. All and sundry may now wear grey flannel trousers all the year round, this was previously the privilege of the school and dormitory prefects, but not a grey trouser was to be seen in College on a boy 30 years ago, except in the summer term. Whether we work and play harder than we used to seems doubtful, but the main difference we notice from earlier times is that we have more activities and a wider outlook and in this we do but reflect the outside world, so that it can hardly be prevented. If the country as a whole is going to the dogs, we are going with it, but not otherwise.

Malim was aware of a new era beginning at Wellington. He may not have been overjoyed by this prospect but he was prepared for it. Others, less prescient than the headmaster, remained oblivious, at least for the moment, to the changing environment.

'The advantage of having the discipline which existed in this school was as important in civilian life as it was in military life', intoned the Duke of Connaught in his 1931 speech-day address to College (an account of which follows Malim's message in the *Year Book*). It was the old boy's perennial sermon on honour, duty and jingoism and was, as always, well received by the Wellington audience, among whom was the thirteen-year-old Esmond Romilly, nervously awaiting the prize-giving ceremony.... 'Middle School Recitation, Third Block, to Esmond Marcus David Romilly,' Malim announced, as the squat but animated Esmond appeared on the podium to receive his prize, his first and last at Wellington College.

Esmond's tutor – Mr Rupert Horsley:

Looking through the Murray lists for that period I should say he was the only boy with any real talent at anything academically. I remember well one of his essays being brought to me. Very mature indeed; at least two years in advance of his age. He was not an academic type at all, you understand; not precise or earnest enough, didn't care for detail, just the passion. He was a very passionate boy . . . I think leaving school was the best thing Esmond could have done. Wellington could offer him little – he was a self-starter.

5
Another World

Esmond took white roses to Whitehall to deposit on King
Charles I's tomb. Found no one there, told by Verger
at St Martin-in-the-Fields that it was wrong date.
Esmond sobbed, would be at school on 30th. In the afternoon E. and I shot off airguns in the garden for two
hours at distant birds and men on the church.

GILES's diary entry, 1 January 1931

'I was keenly interested in politics while I was still at Newlands',
Esmond wrote in *Out of Bounds*.

Not only was I a Tory, but I was also something far more romantic,
a Jacobite. I worked out on a piece of paper during a geography
hour that King George was an impostor, as Prince Rupprecht of
Bavaria had a superior claim to the throne. When writing out the
kings and queens on a genealogical table, instead of 'Old Pretender'
and 'Young Pretender' I would write 'James III' and 'Charles III'.
I was also intensely proud of my Scottish ancestry, and here I rather
let my imagination run away with me. According to my accounts
to the other boys, I must have been descended from every king and
duke and earl that ever lived.

When Esmond entered Wellington in 1931 he was still a Jacobite,
the faith accompanying him from Newlands along with a large Ogilvy
tartan rug, symbol of his affinity with the Stuart claim. This was draped
across the Romilly bed where it became the subject of some interest,
some criticism and, in the second term, a 'violent quarrel'. The quarrel,
according to Esmond, was his last memory of his interest in Jacobitism;
the rug remained in his possession, but was no more than a token
gesture to this his first cause. There were, after all, more than enough
contemporary causes to capture his imagination, like, for instance, that
of Sir Oswald Mosley's New Party.

The New Party had been formed by Mosley in March 1931 as an instrument for enacting those policies of nationalization and employment previously rejected by his colleagues in the Labour Government. At first this venture generated some interest and attracted both Labour and Conservative supporters unimpressed by their parties' softly softly approach to the Depression. But Mosley's group never posed a real threat to the major parties, and its impetus soon waned.

In October 1931, only weeks after the General Election put paid to the New Party's future plans, Nellie Romilly took her two sons to tea with the Mosleys and Harold Nicolson, and introduced Sir Oswald to one of his youngest supporters.

I cannot claim to have seen the birth of British Fascism,* [Esmond wrote] but I can claim to have seen the death of the 'New Party'. I remember how sorry I was when Harold Nicolson told us that they would be unable to continue the production of their weekly bulletin, *Action*. I read *Action* keenly, and had distributed a few copies to friends at Wellington.

Was Esmond oblivious then to the New Party's fascist leanings? More than likely he was excited by them. Fascism couched in such dynamic terms as 'action' and 'progress' must have had a heady appeal to a thirteen-year-old boy until recently enmeshed in the swashbuckling world of the Jacobites. When, in an Easter vacation eighteen months later, Esmond read his first copy of the *Daily Worker* the same emotive forces were again at work. 'I did not learn much Communism', Esmond admitted; but he did learn 'that there was another world as well as the one in which I lived'. This was not Communism's only attraction, of course, but sad to say the others were no more doctrinal, centring for the most part on thoughts of the prestige to be gained by flaunting the new belief back at school. Esmond:

At first I had thought that being a 'Communist' might gain for me added respect and even popularity at Wellington. I know a good many people who longed to achieve a reputation by this means. Very few succeeded, for, as with me, the colossal conceit which accompanied their pose absolutely undid any effect that originality might have achieved.

Giles had fallen into a similar trap himself nine months previously, when in the summer term of 1932 he had entered Wellington's Classical

* The British Union of Fascists was formed by Mosley in October 1932.

vi. As one of the younger boys in the Upper School, Giles adopted Communism as a prop to distract attention from a nervous performance. 'I "became" a Communist and an atheist', he wrote, 'without in the least considering what it means to "be" either ... I was hopelessly ignorant and up-in-the-air ... I tried to give the impression of knowing everything about everything, while knowing nothing about anything.'

The family learned, somewhat dramatically, of Giles's conversion in the 1932 summer vacation. Esmond:

We were all in the drawing-room after breakfast and discussing 'plans'. I think Giles must have said something about going to Russia, for we were soon on to the subject of Bolshevism. My brother hotly defended his adopted creed with a vehemence that was hardly justified by knowledge. My mother – as dramatic as ever – inquired whether he would be prepared to shoot his mother and father. The answer was 'Yes' and the rest may well be left to the imagination.

Uncle Winston thought it a great joke that Giles had turned 'Red'. He called his two nephews the 'Red Rose' and the 'White Rose' – the 'White Rose' being an allusion to Esmond's Jacobite sympathies. But Churchill was mistaken: Esmond was no longer a Jacobite, and as for his colour, that he would probably have described as 'school grey'.

London Workers March Against Fascism

COMMUNIST PARTY & ILP
GIVE CALL FOR
FURTHER UNITED ACTION

A Pledge of
Solidarity

CALL TO EXTEND
UNITED FRONT*

These or similar headlines were read by Esmond at the beginning of his Easter vacation of 1933. The message – united action against Fascism – had appeared in the *Daily Worker* every day for the last

---

* Front-page headlines, the *Daily Worker*, 3 April 1933.

month, every day since the Communist International had released its manifesto calling for a joint Communist and socialist programme against Fascism. This writ had been prompted by the Reichstag fire of 27 February which virtually sealed the fate of the democratic process in Germany. Even as the Comintern's message went to print, German Communist and socialist leaders were in hiding or on the run, earmarked by the Nazis for the first concentration camps only months away.

Fascism was not the only burning issue of the day, as Esmond learned. There was also the matter of those Metropolitan Vickers' engineers, Thornton and MacDonald, who were languishing in a Moscow prison, awaiting trial on charges of sabotage and espionage. 'Trial Will be Just and Fair' ran the *Daily Worker* headline of 3 April. Colonel Romilly had read a different story. Stirred into unusual loquaciousness, he solemnly declaimed: 'I loathe and detest war, and I'm long past military age. But if they don't release those men, I shouldn't hesitate to volunteer for service.'

This outburst took place in Dieppe where the Romillys were again on holiday. Esmond said nothing but, no doubt, questioned his spur-of-the-moment decision to have the *Daily Worker* delivered to St Antoine every day during his stay.

Life was difficult that Easter. Esmond was bored; bored with his family, bored with Dieppe. The town which had once represented everything cosmopolitan and exciting had suddenly turned into a small parochial pumpkin. Esmond's holidays, once spent in a frenzy of outdoor activity, were now spent indoors in an inanimate stupor. Now and then he shook himself, climbed on his bike and made for town, but this was no more than a ritual cage-pacing and invariably led in a circle back to St Antoine – down the rue des Fontaines, left on to the rue du Faube de la Barre and thence down the rue de Sygogne, past the dilapidated château on the left, and on to the sea-front, past the redundant old casino and the half-built replacement; a right turn into the rue Duquesne, past the harbour and the stench of stagnant water, past the ferry; another right turn and into the centre of town: the Café des Tribuneaux to the left, the poignant sickly sweet smells of the rue de la Barre pâtisseries to the right; then back to the rue des Fontaines and an uphill climb to home, to slump once more into the chair and contemplate ... what? The ends of one's trousers perhaps, the ones you were told to turn up, the ones now torn and covered in grease. 'I suppose', Esmond wrote, 'this was the "difficult age".'

One result of Esmond's adolescent crisis was an unprecedented lack of confidence. 'Particularly,' he wrote, 'I was shy of meeting boys a year or two older than myself. With Giles's friends at Dieppe I developed a complex of "not being wanted", which was largely the result of the way I behaved.' One of 'Giles's friends' referred to by Esmond was another Wellingtonian, Henry Swanzy. In a letter to the author Mr Swanzy presents this account of life *chez* Romilly, Easter 1933:

It was astonishing to see all four together. Colonel Bertram was very small and sweet and silent, submerged I thought, by his formidable wife, and still living, so far as I could see at the Front with the Brigade of Guards – I remember his pleasure when he found I knew something about Field Marshal Robertson! Nellie, as you doubtless know, was like a very beautiful and rather untidy Persian cat, constantly smoking from a long cigarette holder, constantly talking about Winston Churchill.
'Winston Churchill started life without anything.'
'But surely it was something to have been born at Blenheim, with a father as famous as Lord Randolph?'
'Still he hadn't a sou and had to earn every penny for himself....'
She adored Giles, who, physically, took after his father, and was a feminine character, compared to Esmond, the naughty boy with his eager eyes and breathless voice. There were arguments between him and Nellie, but they always ended amicably.

'Rows', according to Esmond, were a feature of that Easter vacation. One of the worst occurred as a result of those stained trouser-bottoms. This one lasted a record ten hours, most were over and done with in thirty minutes.
'I was obsessed in freeing myself from my parents' authority,' he wrote, 'and indulged in all sorts of day dreams.' Most of these were promoted by his clandestine reading of the *Daily Worker*, through which he had taken the bold step of contacting 'some real live Communists'. In his enthusiasm he had even gone as far as to arrange a meeting with the same people in London at the end of the vacation. All was perfect, then Giles went and injured his foot while riding on the back of Esmond's *velomoteur* and had to stay in Dieppe to recuperate. Nellie, of course, wanted to stay with him. Esmond was told he was to go straight from Dieppe to school. Never one to take injustice lightly, Esmond made a stand: 'I was certainly not very good at self-control, and made such an appalling scene....' The plans were changed. Nellie accompanied Esmond back to London, where he managed to slip away and meet his Communists. Who these people were and where he met

them he doesn't say, but they did impress him, of that there is little doubt. Esmond returned to Wellington apostolized a supercharged convert bursting to spread the word.

Initially housed within the Murray annex, Esmond now occupied a room of his own within the main dormitory. A small rectangle, the room contained an iron bed, a rug, a desk and chair, a chest of drawers and a shelf conspicuous by its emptiness. There was also something called a 'hard-arse', a green baize-covered ledge jutting out from the far wall, a sort of fixture-cum-fitting. The room was painted green, so too was the corridor beyond; all the corridors and rooms were painted green – an 'underwater green' according to the submerged Giles.

Having surveyed both the interior and exterior scenes, Esmond crossed to his bed and began the sad business of unpacking his trunk – socks, shirts, pullover, spare tie, two copies of The Communist Manifesto, cricket boots, school greys, cake tin, 'various left-wing literature', picture of Uncle Winston and (relief, still intact) a porcelain bust of Lenin.

'When I went back to Wellington for the summer term, I took with me an odd collection of ideas,' wrote Esmond. The first of these was 'to swiftly convert at least twenty Wellingtonians to the creed'.

But his proselytizing was not a success. There were two reasons for this: firstly, he was ignorant of his audience and was trying to feed Communist slogans neat to people brought up on Daily Mail lemonade, and secondly, and more to the point, he hadn't a clue what he was talking about: 'It must be remembered that I had still not read a single Marxist tract.' In fact, the young prophet had somehow contrived to mix up Communism with pacifism – another popular religion of the period. It was quite some mistake, but one which not only Esmond was guilty of.

'Woozy minded Communists', that was the Daily Express' view of pacifists or, more particularly, its view of the Oxford pacifists. The 'woozy minded Communists, the jokers, the sexual indeterminates of Oxford', it bellowed on 13 February 1933, in its best sergeant-major manner.

The cause of this apoplectic outburst was the famous Oxford Union debate of 9 February, when the resolution 'this House will in no circumstances fight for its king and country' was carried by 275 votes to 153. Other newspapers joined in the harangue. The Daily Mail (a Wellington favourite) spoke of 'posturers and gestures', while the Daily Telegraph thought the motion 'Besmirching Oxford's Fair Fame'. Then Uncle Winston joined in: calling the motion (an address to the anti-socialist and anti-Communist Union) an 'abject, squalid, shameless avowal'. Things were hotting up. At the following Oxford Union meeting the president announced the arrival of 'two consignments of white feathers' – through the uproar, 'White feathers are therefore available for all members who voted for the motion last week, at a rate of two per member.' On 2 March, cousin Randolph appeared on the scene. As a life member of the Union he had gone down to Oxford for the day to see the blasphemy wiped from the books. The motion, to reverse the original resolution, was read out to a capacity audience and soundly defeated by 750 votes to 188. More caustic remarks from the Churchills. More fiery words from the Press. It was an incendiary year.

In the summer term, while still wrestling with bread-and-butter Communism, Esmond made his own gesture towards pacifism by joining a 'peace correspondence group'. But peace turned out to be the last thing his pen-pal, a French girl, had on her mind. The correspondence started off well enough with an interchange of views on pacifism and the class war, but soon branched off into 'free-love and birth control'. 'Finally,' writes Esmond, 'she informed me that she would meet me, and we would spend fascinating moments of "free, unrestrained intercourse"; she also took the occasion of enclosing photographs of herself in different postures, but they had little appeal for me. In a fit of annoyance and surprise, I tore all her letters up and burnt them. I regretted the action later.'

The radical neophyte was encountering reversals; his predicament that of the heady iconoclast, whose own image is more fragile than the one he sets out to break. More cracks followed.

In the middle of his anti-war fervour Esmond had to decide whether or not he was going to join the Officers Training Corps, the OTC. Zero hour arrived on 10 June 1933, his fifteenth birthday, when he was expected to write a 'C' (for Corps) next to his name on the form list. No 'C' appeared. The matter was referred to his tutor.

Several terms before this Giles had faced the same dilemma: should he join the 'Corps' or should he risk being 'different'. Undecided, he had first entered the OTC and had then undertaken the difficult task of getting himself released. Eventually, after many interviews with his tutor – a man steeped in the public-school spirit – Giles left the 'Corps'. Overjoyed, he wrote to a cousin thanking God he would never have to wear the king's uniform again. This gave rise to another of his mother's outbursts – 'Why, all that family [the Romillys] have fought and died for their country; how dared you, an impertinent little boy....'

Nevertheless, Giles had set a precedent and whatever Nellie's feelings, she abided by this democratic principle when Esmond's case was brought before his tutor. Nellie wrote to the tutor, Rupert Horsley, explaining that it was up to Esmond to make his own decision and Horsley, never a staunch upholder of the faith, let the matter rest. Much to Esmond's amazement and, doubtless, his indignation, he was spared without a fight.

In *Out of Bounds* Esmond wrote, 'I realize that I was, in fact, neither a hero nor a martyr in the affair but simply got out of many inconvenient and unpleasant hours.' This is, however, the sixteen-year-old author speaking, not the fifteen-year-old schoolboy. There was more than a little of the martyr lurking in the fifteen-year-old.

Esmond had escaped the OTC and that should have been the end of the issue. It wasn't. Some time during the summer term he had written a letter to the *Student Vanguard.** The letter, printed in the July issue (i.e. several weeks after he had successfully avoided serving in the 'Corps') read:

Dear Sir,

I cannot see the slightest ground of defence for the OTC as run in public schools. At this college the OTC is theoretically voluntary, but is actually entirely compulsory. Every boy is compelled to join the Corps at the age of fifteen, and must stay there until he leaves, or until his last year, when he may, as an alternative, join the Scout Troop.

The idea of being compelled to drill and wear uniforms at school must be repulsive to all but the most inflexible diehards....

Yours faithfully,
E. Romilly,
Wellington College.

The letter was brought to the attention of the much-harassed Rupert Horsley and the culprit was summoned. Esmond:

I suspected nothing when I entered the room and was greeted with the usual 'Good evening'. 'I just wanted to know whether you wrote that', he said, and produced a copy of the June/July number of the

* A left-wing periodical released in November 1932. First editorial: 'The *Student Vanguard* makes no pretence of impartiality. It is written by the students who are convinced that conditions in every section of social existence are more and more forcing a radical alteration which alone can remedy its many evils.'

Student Vanguard. I had not seen the copy, and did not even know that my letter had been published. So I remained politely interested while he turned over the pages of the correspondence columns. Suddenly I remembered the letter, as I saw it in front of me. My first feeling of horror at the consequences was at once overcome by the novelty of seeing my name in print, and I read the letter over several times to myself, feeling bitterly annoyed that I had not expressed myself better.

It was explained to Esmond that his crime did not lie in the syntax but in the content; he had told lies about Wellington College. An interview with the headmaster followed, 'my first "political interview"', he wrote with some pride. 'Altogether I had four while I was at Wellington.' On this occasion Malim was mildly amused – he soon wearied of smiling – and let Esmond off with writing an apology. The episode was over, the chapter just beginning.

The Romilly roller-coaster, the one which the children of Dieppe had so assiduously learned to avoid, was now gathering speed at Wellington. And like its fairground counterpart it turned and weaved an erratic course and came to rest only when it ran out of momentum. . . .

'Correspondence ("unsuitable correspondence")', wrote Esmond, 'was one of my greatest joys. I used to write up to all sorts of different organizations, with requests for circulars and newspapers. It seemed to open up a new field of life to me.' But the reformist Romilly was not content in finding his own anodyne, he was out to relieve society also, and in true quack fashion forced medicine down the throats of those not suffering from the illness.

One of the organizations written to during the summer term was a 'sinister' group known as 'The Friends of the Soviet Union' ('about which', according to Esmond, 'details can be found on reference to the Special Branch'). Enthralled with the information the group had sent him, Esmond dashed off a list of names of others who might benefit from the same literature. One of these names was that of the Wellington master, 'Mr Lincoln' (a pseudonym). Too late it occurred to him 'that it might have been more polite to have consulted Mr Lincoln first'. The master received his pamphlets – '"Impertinent little brat" was, I believe, the phrase used by Mr Lincoln at the time.'

This was Esmond's last political prank of the term. On the whole, his escapades had been treated lightly. Not all his confrontations with authority ended so painlessly, however. At the end of term he was caught chewing gum on the cricket field, for which abomination he was beaten. This was his second beating at Wellington; the first, for an offence known as 'Fines and General Slackness', occurred in his second term, and was related by the victim in graphic detail:

> With quaking heart I went upstairs. The whole dormitory was empty, and the doors of all the rooms along each side were closed. In the middle of the long passage there was a solitary table and chair, which looked very grim, like a preparation for some medieval torture. Feeling singularly unlike a noble martyr, I had – in accordance with the rules – to shout at the top of my voice: 'Dormitory please! Speak to Bumsbury please!' (the latter was the executioner). He stood by the table, with a cane in his hand. At my entry he laid the cane on the table, and proceeded to take off his jacket. The next three minutes were spent on a speech, in which he explained the necessity for this unpleasant scene – a totally inadequate explanation, as it seemed to me.... I was then required to mount upon the table, kneel on it, and grasp the chair in front. However, it took another minute before my position was quite satisfactory to the other performer. He then walked several yards down the dormitory, turned sharply, advanced at a sort of galloping trot, and hit me a shrewd and extremely painful blow on my left thigh. When he had repeated this procedure once, he was unlucky enough to break his weapon, and had to go back to his room to procure another. He stopped there to exchange a few remarks with the other prefects, who stood at his door watching the entertainment free of charge. I received another three strokes, in the course of which I was unable to restrain myself from emitting a few gasps. Having been dismissed, I descended from my perch, shouted out: 'Down to my Room, Please!' in a most unconvincing tone, and departed to relax in private in the lavatory.

In *Out of Bounds* Esmond had only one comment to make on the subject of corporal punishment at Wellington. 'It is', he remarked, 'the only possible form of punishment. A system built on force and fear must be maintained by force and fear.'

6
Dilemmas?

At the end of the 1933 summer term Esmond took advantage of a day's holiday to go down to London and visit a young Communist with whom he had been corresponding. The address given for the meeting was 4 Parton Street, WC1, home of the Parton Bookshop.

The name had a familiar ring to it. Some months previously he had written to the Bookshop in response to an advertisement for a 'lending library of contemporary Marxist literature'. There had been no reply. It was now 9 o'clock on the morning of the meeting and Esmond was again awaiting an answer. He rang the bell, and again:

After ringing the bell for about five minutes the door was opened by a young man in a rather jaded dressing-gown [this was the owner, David Archer]. I could not hear what he said, as his words seemed to break off in the middle of sentences; but I gathered that the person I had come to see was not up yet. We went into the bookshop. It was quite unlike any bookshop I had ever seen.

Esmond was beckoned into a young left-winger's paradise, the fruits bountifully scattered around him; for at the Bookshop the floor was as normal a place for books and pamphlets as the well-stocked but untidy shelves which lined its walls.

'The floor was covered with stray copies of the *Daily Worker*, *Russia Today*, *Communist International*, and other exciting literature of this sort', wrote Esmond, recapturing the first wide-eyed moments; while the large, centrally prominent table was laden with the red-backed classics of the Marx–Engels–Lenin Institute, and other expensive radical tomes. Completing this heady setting were the posters: Soviet propaganda scenes, depicting healthy bronzed workers on gleaming red tractors against backgrounds of fecund yellow cornfields.

No. 4 Parton Street functioned as both a bookshop and a lending library, but very few people paid attention to formalities: subscriptions were rarely paid, borrowed books rarely returned, while Archer, oblivious to ruin, was as likely to present a crisp new volume to the bright-eyed neophyte as to sell it to him.

Although often described as the 'archetype of people's bookshops', Archer's was in effect more a bourgeois charity than a Communist co-operative; the owner more the doting maiden aunt than the radical literary mole.

On coming down from Cambridge in 1932, the young, philanthropical David Archer had begun searching for some kind of social work to which he could devote his life. The Bookshop was presumably seen as a first step in this career: a library exposing the evils of society and, at the same time, offering what Archer then believed to be the only remedy. But the Parton Street premises were more than a book-shop-library; they were also a centre for young radical, intellectual and poet. By the time Esmond made his first appearance at the Bookshop in June 1933, the dynamic John Cornford was already an *habitué*, as were the young poets George Barker and David Gascoyne. T.E.Lawrence was another visitor – a private face out of place – so too was the young, retiring Alec Guinness. These were the talented and/or committed frequenters; there were also any number of impecunious hangers-on.

Archer was a sucker for the hard-luck story, consequently there were always people dossing down on one or both of the upstairs floors, or moping around the shop offering eclectic ideas on capitalism, revolution and the price of cigarettes; occasionally 'borrowing' the price of a cup of tea from the ever-open till. Stephen Spender, another Bookshop visitor:

> Archer's affairs were always in a total mess and he was constantly receiving donations to bail him out. He was a very amiable, very soft, intelligent, friendly, well-meaning person who did a great service to literature in a way – didn't he publish the first Dylan Thomas* – but he was a bit of a hopeless character who was easily taken advantage of by many of the boys. I think he was a bit in love with a lot of them.

Esmond's first meeting with his future landlord and employer got off to a good start. Having each discovered that the other was also

---

* *18 Poems*, Thomas' first publication, was published by the Parton Street Press in December 1934.

a Wellingtonian the two fell into a discussion of 'the changes in the Anglesea and the reputation of the Blucher', the conversation only coming to a halt on the appearance of the somnolent comrade whom Esmond had come to see.

From the Bookshop Esmond and friend moved on to Meg's Café – another Parton Street institution – where, over a leisurely 10 a.m. breakfast, Comrade Romilly gave Comrade X the low-down on the political situation at Wellington – the address delivered in a whisper, the other having warned him of the presence of 'splits'.

Parton Street had revived Esmond's flagging spirits. The Deptford Communist demonstration, attended at the beginning of the summer vacation, gave them a further boost, elevating him 'onto a plane of warm emotion, perhaps not altogether different from the effect produced on others by the sight of a Union Jack'.

The meeting had coincided with the Romillys' visit to Chartwell, Esmond stealing away from his opulent surroundings to join the seething throng:

> I clapped loudly at the speeches of the leaders as they exclaimed on the 'increasing reactionary role of modern capitalism finding its reflection in the rising tide of mass revolt under the disciplined leadership of the Communist Party', and I was glad to hear that it was not only the working classes who were to be allowed to participate in the smashing of Fascism, but that the 'broad masses of the petit-bourgeoisie and poorer peasantry, and the intellectuals' were to be thrown in as well.

Unfortunately, Esmond had more than the 'final conflict' to occupy his thoughts that summer. There was also the conflict raised by living 'materially in the one world, and spiritually in the other'. It was 'an absurd contradiction', and not one he could easily resolve:

> I would, as it were, be thinking out the tactics of the 'United Front' while enjoying all the blessings of the Capitalist system.... My parents saw the absurdity of my position without trying to help. Usually, in fact, they elaborately drew and overdrew the contradictions for me. If I was a Communist, they would say, surely I should be working with my fellow men. As a start, it would be suggested that I should do a little housework, the practical proposal being that I should make the beds and clean the boots and shoes.

His conscience was not, however, sufficiently troublesome to prevent him from attending a two-week Devonshire house-party at the end of the summer, entering into the party spirit and wolfing down quantities of delicious country food. These activities did not, of course, preclude political discussion – 'For what could be more pleasant than Communism in such an atmosphere – Communism discussed over really good roast chicken and Devonshire cream?' Nor was this remark made entirely tongue-in-cheek. 'Sometimes', wrote Esmond, probing the core of his rebellion, 'I would persuade myself that my desire to change the conditions of my life was due to intellectual understanding; whereas, really it was probably due simply to the combination of a wish for change and excitement, with irritation and boredom.' The Devonshire house-party was, in its way, as exciting and stimulating as a meeting of the CPGB Deptford Local and therefore equally to the young Romilly's piquant taste. Esmond never had any real qualms or anxieties about jumping back and forth between the 'two worlds', although he did complacently assume that if ever there were a clash between principles and way of living the former would win.

The house-party, described by Esmond in *Out of Bounds*, was at Clovelly Court, home of the Asquiths.* Betty Asquith (*née* Manners) was an old friend of Nellie Romilly, and the Romilly children had made frequent, pleasurable visits to Clovelly throughout their childhood, the pleasure being heightened by the four Asquith daughters, Jean, Mary, Christine and Sue. Jean was Esmond's favourite. He had fallen madly in love with her at the age of nine, serenading her to sleep every night for a week with the tortuous cries from an old harmonica. There were protests, but Esmond was deaf; not so the others in the house, including the loved one, who were driven nuts by the noise. Now, six years later, there was yet another tune to contend with. It was suffered with the tolerance of long-term liberals. 'We thought it was a "passing phase"', says Mary (the Hon. Mrs Keith Rous), 'and inflamed Giles and Esmond all the more by saying so.'

Whatever the conflict raging within Esmond during the summer months it appears to have resolved itself by the time he returned to school in September, when 'I told myself importantly, that my only purpose at Wellington from then onwards was as a propagandist, and I devoted myself to this end wholeheartedly'.

* Brigadier General Arthur Asquith, third son of the Liberal Prime Minister H.H. Asquith.

And yet – 'If there had been only one or two more boys of his ilk at school', his tutor, Rupert Horsley, believes, 'Esmond might have pursued an academic line.... He had no friends that I know of, just a little band of supporters. I think he was quite lonely.' Isolation was, unfortunately, the price paid for entertaining ideas outside the school mainstream. The young Communist John Cornford had lived on this island throughout much of his time at his own public school, Stowe – 'I'm beginning to feel rather badly the need for interesting people', 'I am distinctly bored by almost everyone' – and wrote often, and at length, to his parents to be allowed to study in the more conducive atmosphere of home. Not that Cornford's solution would have appealed to Esmond. Study was already anathema. As for living at home, he had felt for some time that the answer to his own problems lay a thousand miles away from the cloying embrace of Pimlico Road.

As Horsley noted, Wellington's self-styled subversive had begun forming a band of supporters, facing the problem familiar to all revolutionary leaders, that of attracting the society misfit. 'I managed to collect a small circle of adherents at Wellington,' he wrote. 'None of them were particularly inspiring. Unfortunately, moreover, by what cannot be described as purely a coincidence, they all happened to be singularly unpopular.'

On the whole his supporters turned out to be a liability, attracting opprobrium to the already unpopular Romilly, while falling far short of their leader's dictum: 'the more involved one was the better' – an involvement not only confined to extra-collegiate activities.

Like Esmond, the Wellington debating society was becoming increasingly politically involved. 'This year the debating society averaged three debates a term,' wrote the secretary in the 1933–4 *Wellington Year Book*, 'of which four were purely political.' On 15 October Esmond, for some time a keen interpolator at the school debates, was awarded the almost unheard-of privilege for a 'junior' of proposing the motion. On Sunday 15 October, recorded the society secretary in November's *Wellingtonian*,

... a debate was held in Mr Talboy's classroom, when E.M.D.Romilly proposed the motion that 'in the opinion of this house the political freedom of women is a sign of a civilized society'. The Hon. Proposer using such phrases as 'on reaching maturity doubtless, you see', spoke with confidence and sincerity. He quoted Mr Bernard Shaw and Miss Sylvia Pankhurst indiscriminately, and warned us against the Forces of Reaction. He instanced Germany as a country overwhelmed by a wave of Barbarism – munitions firms were financing the Nazis.

Such a country was clearly not civilized. And in Germany women were turned out of jobs and told that their place was in the home.

Despite the *non sequitur*, the secretary described this as a 'good speech'; not good enough, unfortunately, to win over the diehard reactionaries in the audience who, led by brother Giles, the opposition spokesman, defeated the motion twenty-nine votes to nine. Among the 'against' party were 'The Master' (a rare debater) and C.H. de Sausmarez Esq., a master who, that same term, had the unenviable task of instructing Esmond in political science.

A member of the extreme right-wing 'English Mistery' group (which advocated among other things the restoration of the monarchy into the body politic), Cecil de Sausmarez espoused his beliefs with a vehemence to match that of his young charge. 'He waged a relentless struggle', wrote Esmond, 'against the intellectuals, who always held him up to ridicule in the school debates. Unfortunately, he had not the slightest sense of humour, and always spoke as though he were in the midst of an "historic occasion".' Cecil de Sausmarez:

The portrait Esmond draws of me in *Out of Bounds* is not a favourable one [Esmond refers to Mr de Sausmarez as Mr Debrett]. This is not surprising as, at that time our politics were diametrically opposed. Nevertheless, our relationship was more cordial than the book suggests. He was in one of my classes on political theory and I remember being much impressed by his precocious ability to develop an argument as well as appalled by his atrocious handwriting. We much enjoyed arguing with each other – though neither of us was prepared to shift his ground – and nobody was more sorry than I when he did his bolt.

Several days after the 15 October debate, Malim summoned Romilly to his office to discuss his future and to propose that he remain at Wellington College – there had been talk of him joining a stockbroking firm at the end of the academic year – and try for an Oxbridge scholarship. Had this interview arisen from Malim witnessing Esmond's impressive maiden speech, or was it possibly part two of a plan, which included the previous debate, to integrate Romilly into the Wellington society? While recognizing Esmond's undoubted academic potential, the headmaster was surely equally intent on earthing a potentially dangerous live-wire.

As to Malim's query about the 'future', Esmond wrote: 'I am afraid that I did not worry myself sufficiently about the question. I believed then, as I had believed for some time, that I should neither stay at Wellington for another two years, nor go into the stockbroker's office. Though certainly, to all intents and purposes, there seemed no other choice.'

As Esmond 'did not feel strongly on the subject' Malim succeeded in persuading him to work for the scholarship. He would invite Colonel Romilly to the school, he told Esmond, to discuss the matter further. Thinking the interview was over Esmond made to leave, but was brought to a halt by another enquiry:

'By the way Romilly, how far are your Communist activities limited to yourself?'

I explained, to the best of my ability, that I had no 'Communist' activities, but was simply working in conjunction with the university anti-war movement.

'Well, I admit that I am puzzled,' he said, 'but I have received a letter from a very high official at Scotland Yard, whom I cannot mention by name, who says that there is a Red Group which is centering its attention on Wellington College.'

I replied that I knew nothing of any such 'Red Group', and that if there was such a one, its activities were certainly unconnected with myself. Mr Malim himself seemed to treat the affair as rather a joke.

'I wrote back to the official,' he said to me, 'saying that I thought he must be mistaken, and furthermore, that I did not consider Wellington College to be a very fertile field for Communist propaganda.'

Nevertheless, the official's words had awakened Malim to the need to keep an eye on Esmond's activities.

Rupert Horsley: 'I remember Malim coming to me and saying, "Look, Horsley, do try and stop the young Romilly interfering with the remembrance service on the 11th." So I had a word with Esmond about this and told him not to be unreasonable because it was not going to gain anything, it was just going to make a lot of fuss.'

The 1933 Armistice Day fell on a Saturday, the Anti-War Movement taking full advantage of this occurrence to organize demonstrations throughout the country. One of the most dramatic of these took place in Cambridge, where the Socialist Society and the Student Christian Movement collaborated in staging an anti-war parade through the centre of the city to the war memorial. 'To the victims of the Great War, from those who are determined to prevent similar crimes of imperialism' read the inscription on the marchers' wreath. That was the first casualty of the day (by order of the police department), others followed rapidly as the marchers were attacked by more belligerent elements along their route. The Press had a field day. In terms reminiscent of those used in describing the Oxford debate of the previous February, the demonstrators were denounced as 'young hooligans who had got what they deserved for desecrating a holy day'.

Meanwhile, back at Wellington College, agent Romilly was indulging in 'a little propaganda of a somewhat spectacular nature' of his own. Some days before Armistice Day Esmond had received a consignment of badges from the Anti-War Movement. These were now distributed among a group of supporters, who agreed to parade around the school on Saturday giving a practical demonstration of their beliefs. Not unexpectedly, 'the whole affair soon became a veritable battle royal' with 'frequent all-in fights in the quadrangles'. Esmond:

Unfortunately a good many of our supporters, believing themselves pacifists, acted in the spirit of their conviction. Others found feeling in their dormitories too strong for them and wisely decided that discretion was the better part of valour ... eventually, a group of us in my own dormitory found ourselves sufficiently strong, and little enough pacifist, to attempt a few reprisals. Accordingly, to the surprise of all who witnessed the unusual event, we waylaid one of our chief opponents (a 'tough' with a considerable reputation) and unceremoniously removed his poppy. This rash action proved very bad tactics in the revenge which was inevitable. Altogether, we succeeded on the whole in making ourselves conspicuous and unpopular. And this was by no means all.

Along with the parcel of badges, Esmond had also received a wad of 'Armistice' leaflets. On the Friday evening he and a friend had sneaked into the school chapel and inserted the sheets next to the hymn chosen for the Armistice service – Rudyard Kipling's 'O, Valiant Hearts'. Turning to the hymn on Saturday morning, the Wellington congregation confronted this statement: 'The rattle of rifles and the blare of bugles which precede and follow the two minutes' silence may be a fitting accompaniment to the war preparations of our government, but they are nothing but a hollow mockery of the dead we are supposed to revere.'

Ironically, the grunts and guffaws which accompanied the hymn had exactly the same effect as those rattling rifles and blaring bugles which the leaflets warned against. One master in particular, Cecil de Sausmarez, was absolutely livid with anger, and Esmond had to make him a personal apology for 'spoiling his Armistice Service'.

By Saturday evening the whole affair was out in the open. Rupert Horsley sent for the culprit. 'I shall never forget the expression on Mr [Horsley's] face when I went to see him that night,' wrote Esmond, 'it was a mixture of hopeless despair and philosophical resignation. He honestly thought that I would be expelled. And to him now fell the task of returning to report my action to the Headmaster.'

The following day the tutor informed him of Malim's decision: 'It was a question of "next time", but my activities were to be severely curtailed. I was required to give an undertaking that nothing of the sort would occur again, in addition to the equally clear understanding that if it did, I should forthwith cease to consider myself a member of the community of Wellington College.'

Of course, Esmond did not heed the warning and, although he professed at the time to have 'sympathized' with the tutor's predicament, this did not prevent him from placing the fretful Horsley in a similar position in the future.

'He was a lone wolf with a wolf's bite for any hand that fed him, and a wolf's snarl for anyone who reasoned with him'; thus the urbane T.C.Worsley summed up the fifteen-year-old Romilly, giving an indication of just how intolerant and intolerable Esmond was becoming.

On Monday 13 November, two days after the Armistice Day escapade, an agitated Nellie issued one of her many supplication-commands to her wayward son – 'It was really a masterpiece', wrote the impenitent offspring:

The first part was devoted to remarks chiefly about loyalty and my father. Then on a personal note: 'You have allowed yourself to be carried away by the flattery and adulation of people who are so far short of adherents in this country that they have to seek the services of irresponsible schoolboys.' My mother suspected, I think, that I had signed away my birthright to Moscow. 'Documents you may have signed and promises you may have made are not legal in a boy of fifteen and must be scrapped. You have now an opportunity to go to your tutor and tell him exactly what are your obligations.' I decided it was best to make no attempt at a reply, and needless to say I did not go and see my tutor.

7
A Bang! – Not a Whimper

We all acted at Christmas – even me! You will hardly
believe that. We (Sarah, Mary and myself) acted in a
short play by Gertrude Jennings called 'Mother of
Pearl'... I took the part of a dirty old tramp & enjoyed
it enormously.... Then there was a thriller called 'The
Hand in the Dark' in which Mrs Romilly, Sarah and
Esmond performed. They wrote it themselves & it really
was quite gruesome.

CLEMENTINE CHURCHILL, letter to a friend,
January 1934

Despite the obvious high spots, like the amateur dramatics, the
Chartwell Christmas had, for Esmond, lost its former magic. This was
mainly the result of his infatuation with the 'other world', it was also
to some extent the result of his parents' excessive solicitude for his
actions. Esmond:

At Christmas we spent a week at my uncle's house. I was arguing
one evening with one of the guests about politics, when my uncle
joined us for a moment. I heard him whispering to my companion.
The conversation was changed. I was amazed afterwards to find out
that my father had particularly asked that politics should not be
discussed with me as it had a bad effect. Apart from natural surprise
and indignation, I was also disappointed for I had much enjoyed the
few political arguments I had had with my uncle.

Back at Pimlico Road the situation grew steadily worse. Esmond
was now in the habit of spending his days at the proscribed Parton
Bookshop. He tried, of course, to keep these visits a secret from his
parents but their suspicions were aroused. Where had he been? What
had he done? He was fast running out of plausible explanations. The
situation finally blew up one afternoon when he had planned to

59

distribute some political leaflets with another Bookshop friend. Esmond:

Lunch that day went on for ages, and it was not difficult to see that there was 'something up'. Try as I might, I could not find any excuse for leaving the table. My father said he was going to some sort of entertainment at the time – I cannot remember now exactly what – but, anyway, my company was invited. Having expressed reluctance to provide it, I was naturally asked what I intended to do that afternoon. It was useless to say that I was going to a film or anything of that kind. So I said that I was going to an exhibition to do with Soviet Education, which I had seen advertised. My father was furious. And I was categorically forbidden to go to this or to 'any other of your Communist exhibitions'. Not only this, but I was informed moreover (and I was scarcely likely to forget) that every one of my activities was able to be checked and there were to be extremely serious consequences if I was disobedient ... I neither distributed leaflets nor went to the exhibition.

The time had come for a long talk. The next day the Colonel, in a conciliatory mood, took his son down to Brighton, where, once again, the subject of his future was broached. The options were still the same : he could either remain at Wellington and try for a university scholarship, or leave (at the end of the next term) and join the stockbroking company run by some friends of his father. At one time, Esmond admitted, he had been excited by the thought of joining the stockbrokers, sharing his mother's vision of 'from office boy to millionaire'. (Nellie had always been fond of telling stories of men who seemed to begin life as sellers of rabbit skins and rose to great heights.) But now the scheme had lost its attraction. In any case, he would be required to live at home, and 'I realized by this time that I disliked home life almost as much as that at school'.

While Esmond was musing, without any great interest, on the singularly unappetizing possibilities laid before him, the Colonel also took the opportunity to add that, whatever his choice, it had definitely to be understood that Communist activities must cease. This was a blow, but not one he was in any position to counter. He therefore gave his promise, while taking the order to 'be good' as an admonition to 'be careful'.

The problem, the immediate problem (was there ever any other?) : how to attend the 13 January FSS conference with impunity?

The FSS (the acronym of the disingenuous Federation of Student Societies) was a Marxist-oriented central bureau for left-wing university
activity. Formed in April 1933 by several of the more militant university groups, it grew rapidly, eclipsing the rival University Labour Federation (the limp Labour Party puppet), until, by the beginning of 1934,
it was in control of all but two of the university socialist-Communist
factions. In the winter of 1933, with the university dissemination
almost complete, the FSS began to turn its attention towards the public
schools, where it discerned an ever-growing radical market ready to
be captured and fed the party line. It was with this policy in mind
that the Federation sent the following circular to Esmond at the beginning of December 1933.

> The FSS now has contacts in several of the Public Schools and it
> is obvious that opposition to this system is crystallizing in a more
> definite form than ever before.... Action against such a system of
> education must be co-ordinated in all the schools. It must also be
> linked with the work of progressive students in the universities, and
> with the organized working class, who are the most effective, indeed
> the only allies in the fight for a live advancing culture. To provide
> this co-ordination the FSS is calling a conference in London on Janu-
> ary 13th (1934) We hope you will be able to come and bring anyone
> you think would be useful.

The meeting, held at the top of a Bloomsbury café, was divided into
two sessions. Esmond had no problems attending the morning session,
but over lunch became apprehensive about getting away for the afternoon sitting. 'Under no circumstances must I appear in the least hurried
or impatient,' he reasoned, 'but I remember that I almost wept tears
of vexation as the meal dragged on over drawing-room coffee, and my
father lighted his pipe, and my mother read the *Daily Express*, and
no one attempted to make any sort of move. At last I escaped, but
not without exciting considerable suspicion.'
In a letter to Jessica Mitford (December 1964), John Peet, another
Red schoolboy (later editor of the Berlin *Democratic German Report*)
recalled the events of the afternoon session, and the rift caused as
Esmond took over the meeting:

> The FSS had deputed a student to look after our meeting and see
> that it took the right decisions as previously decided by the FSS

leadership. Rules had to be drawn up, subscriptions decided on, a committee elected and perhaps the FSS would allow us a probationary period, to have a Public School page in *Student Vanguard*, the FSS periodical.

Most of us were so pleased to be set concrete tasks, and to find that there were quite a lot of other young people like us, and also so thrilled and impressed by the slightly conspirative air of the whole undertaking, that we were ready to vote on anything put forward by our student advisors.

But Esmond, by far the youngest member present, soon put an end to this acquiescence.... Setting up an organization was going at things the wrong way round, he said. What we needed, right now, was a magazine written by public schoolboys. If there was enough support for the magazine, then the readers could join an organization later. Then he set out with great eloquence and conviction the various points later made in the 'Out of Bounds' manifesto, issued in February 1934.

Esmond's speech threw the meeting into confusion. The student advisor was horrified to find things getting out of his control, and talked darkly of the need for revolutionary discipline. Most of us felt that Esmond made much better sense than the official line, but the magic words about 'discipline' worried us. Finally, we all agreed to support the officially-prepared resolutions, but then, shaking off the student advisor, and a couple of his satellites, we held a rump meeting at a tea-shop in Gray's Inn Road at which we promised Esmond our support.

Esmond had obviously been thinking about the magazine for some time to wax so eloquently on its format. It was only now, however, with the promise of support, that 'Out of Bounds' came to life.

As was his habit, and he was a creature of strict habits, Colonel Romilly had gone down to Hereford to pay his New Year respects to his childhood home. This meant a much more amenable Nellie Romilly. Esmond and Giles took advantage of the situation not only to set the magazine project in motion, but also to introduce their mother to some Parton Street comrades.

The introduction took place at Meg's, the Parton Street café, where the Romillys had gathered together a selection of the more presentable Bookshop members for their mother's perusal. Among this group was the mellifluous 'Peter Crew' (a pseudonym), a highly effective salesman, on whom Esmond now relied to sell his mother a few of the more moderate left-wing ideas. Crew succeeded 'beyond our wildest hopes'.

He was tactful, and highly flattering. Altogether, he completely captivated my mother. At the end of lunch, indeed, he relieved her of
half-crown, ostensibly to be devoted to the funds of the National
Hunger March Committee. He then produced pen and paper, and
dictated a letter, to be written by my mother, 'To the Editor of the
Daily Worker....' The gist of the letter was more or less as follows:
'I wish to express my entire sympathy with the cause of the unemployed, who have had their benefits cut, and I am glad that they
are availing themselves of a traditionally British method to voice
their grievances. I am therefore giving full support to the cause of
the National Hunger March.'* My mother wished to add at the end
– 'God Save the King!' no doubt to show that she was still sound
at heart. Crew dissuaded her from this by pointing out that it would
be an inappropriate comment.

Realizing that Crew was going to make as much publicity as possible
out of the statement from the sister of Mrs Winston Churchill, Esmond
thought it wise to retrieve the note. Crew resisted. An argument ensued,
the note finally being handed over to a neutral party, who promised
not to use it in any way. Nellie's infamy disappeared without trace,
much to her relief and her son's regret – 'I felt a mischievous desire
to retain the letter myself, for use in disputes of a political nature.
I saw it indeed, as an ideal trump card to be played at the right moment.'

Back at Wellington, the Romillys began drumming up support for the
magazine. They had ambitiously given themselves only several weeks
to produce the first issue and were desperate for contributions and
subscriptions.

Towards the end of January 1934 a manifesto was circulated to all
interested (and some not so interested) parties. On 2 February, in reply
to his letter of interest in the new venture, John Peet (the earlier FSS
splinterist) received a copy of the manifesto, along with this note:

'Murray', Wellington College,
Crowthorne, Berks. 2/2/34

Dear Comrade, (excuse paper)
Many thanks for your letter. I enclose some copies of the 'Out of

* An eighteen-contingent National Unemployed Workers' Movement (NUWM)-backed
hunger march was at that moment on its way to London.

63

Bounds' circular, which may interest people.

Yes, we are very badly in need of contributions, Articles, etc. very important.

One of the most important features of the paper is going to be 'news' of events (debates, controversies, teaching, etc.) in the different schools. This would be unsigned and un 'written up'. So can you guarantee to send us news of events at Bootham?

The paper will be attractively printed (32 pages) [Archer must have already been talked into publishing the magazine] but will cost 1/-. So I suppose you will sell a dozen or so.

Please get contributions, etc. in as soon as possible as we are very pressed for time (Closing date for 'latest' news is February 20th)....

And the manifesto:

'Out of Bounds' is a new paper dealing with the public schools and their relations to the outside world. The greater part of its material will be drawn from the schools and will relate directly to events in the schools. It will appear twice each term, price one shilling. The first number will appear in March.

Disintegration affects in our period the whole of our society. It affects profoundly the public school, showing itself in:

(1) Confusion of thought in face of modern problems.

(2) A deliberate attempt on the part of the schools to exclude themselves from genuine contact with political and cultural realities.

(3) The positive and blatant use of the public schools as a weapon in the cause of reaction.

(4) The opportunities offered to the Fascist to exploit the situation.

But in the outside world the very conditions which produce these tendencies have created more and more widely among all healthy and virile elements a realization of the inherent viciousness, economic and cultural, of our society. And in the public schools, as in the universities, the fight to free us from this system has already begun and is steadily growing. 'Out of Bounds' will openly champion the forces of progress against the forces of reaction on every front, from compulsory military training to propagandist teaching....

By the time, however, that John Peet received the Romilly letter much of the above – and more – was already public information.

The 'Out of Bounds' story broke on Thursday 25 January when the *Daily Telegraph* published 'three gently sarcastic paragraphs' in its 'London Diary'. This was followed by a request for an interview from the Press Association, which took place over the phone from Wellington, on Saturday 27 January, and was transcribed in the following day's *Sunday Graphic*. On Monday, William Hickey (Tom Driberg) mentioned Esmond in the 'These Names Make News' column of the *Daily Express*. The Romillys were fast becoming personalities.

On Tuesday, Rupert Horsley sent for Esmond and questioned him about the newspaper reports and his proposed publication. The interview was reported to the headmaster. On Thursday, Malim called for both Romillys and informed them that their magazine could only be published under the censorship of a senior master. On Friday:

RED MENACE
IN PUBLIC SCHOOLS

MOSCOW ATTEMPTS TO
CORRUPT BOYS

OFFICER'S SON SPONSORS
EXTREMIST JOURNAL

SCOTLAND YARD INQUIRY

The *Daily Mail* had stumbled upon the story: its sensational headlines (published on the day Esmond had penned his note to John Peet) being elaborated upon, no less sensationally, in the article which followed: 'This is a story', it began, 'which will first make you laugh and then make you think. For there is something very serious behind it – a new form of Communist propaganda which aims at corrupting our public schools.'

The article went on to quote extracts from Esmond's manifesto, linking it with 'well planned and costly' propaganda financed with Bolshevik funds, and contained this crushing statement from Malim: 'The circulars were issued without the authority of the headmaster of Wellington College and without his knowledge. Steps will be taken to see that the boys of Wellington are not in any way concerned with the production of any such paper.'

The Romillys were once more summoned to the Master's Lodge, where they received confirmation of the fate of their magazine. Malim had finally lost his temper with this uncompromising duo, although the younger Romilly took some solace in the fact that 'he was more annoyed with the *Daily Mail* than with us'. Others were less perspicacious. 'It was only necessary', wrote Esmond, 'for the *Mail* to say that "bitter indignation exists at Wellington College" for people to begin to imagine themselves "bitterly indignant", without questioning for a moment if this indignation was justified.'

Indeed one dormitory's indignation was such that it drew up a covenant proposing to deposit Esmond in the school lake, a proposal which achieved support even within his own dormitory, 'where although by no means popular, I was not actively disliked'.

On Saturday, under the heading 'Check on Red Propaganda', the *Daily Mail* ran a follow-up to its 'Red Menace' article, claiming even more evidence of insidious schoolboy organizations financed by Moscow (a reference to the public-school activities of the FSS). It was at this point that Esmond made his decision to leave:

It was Giles' idea in the first place. He suggested it casually one evening after chapel. I agreed that it was an excellent scheme. It seemed to me that I could have nothing to lose by leaving at this time. I was due to leave at the end of term, in any case, to go into a stockbroker's office [he had changed his mind once again]. The prospect did not fill me with any sort of pleasure, except that it entailed leaving Wellington.

On Monday 5 February he received this plea from a troubled Nellie:

I do hope that you will make a great effort to behave decently and quietly, for we have been unhappy about you. As you know, we cannot control your thoughts, but we do feel you are too young to hold forth on political ideas.... Loyalty too, you badly need, and if you can't give it to your country at least give it to your father, who has never let you or any of us down and whose name is a by-word of honour.... You are strong enough and clever enough to take yourself in hand and begin all over again. I don't consider you are mentally unbalanced, as the papers say, but have been completely carried away by flattery and love of the sound of your own voice. There is no community in the world except, as far as I know, Communists, who would flatter the young as I heard Crew flattering you, and I was glad when you rejected it.

His original plan was to leave on Saturday 10 February. This was then changed to Thursday, and, finally, to Friday morning. 'I realized that "running away" was going to be fairly difficult if I did not want to be hauled back early in the procedure.... It was all very worrying, but I was now quite certain that I was going and equally certain that once I had said goodbye to Wellington I was not going to be ignominiously dragged back.'

Again the question arose as to the future. Esmond's plan was simple – he would maintain himself by working at the Parton Bookshop (yet another Bookshop liability) and produce the first issue of 'Out of Bounds' in his spare time. And beyond that – 'beyond that I did not know where I would be heading. But this was enough.' Characteristic of Esmond's plans – and he was a constant planner – was the total absence of the long-term projection.

Thursday 8 February was a half-holiday at Wellington, allowing him to make final preparations for the Friday morning escape. While thus engaged the post arrived bringing yet another anxious missive from his mother.

Not wanting to be labelled *agent provocateur*, David Archer had wisely gone to see Nellie to inform her of the possibility of Esmond disappearing from College. Poor Nellie. 'I hope', she wrote, 'you will think twice before doing anything so gravely disloyal, and causing frightful pain and loss of money....'

> He [Archer] told me you dreaded going to the city office because you had heard that your time would be taken up doing gym. This is the purest nonsense and a figment of your imagination. You will actually have a great deal of leisure time. Your hours will be 9.30 to 4 with an hour for luncheon, and you will be required to go to bed at 10.30 with occasional exceptions.... He hinted that some of your friends are disappointed that you have not been expelled for your political activities, so that you could have been turned into a martyr. Well, they must be very short of martyrs, and I refuse to believe that you entertained such a cowardly and ignoble hope.

'Well, I did "think twice",' wrote Esmond. 'For about an hour on Thursday afternoon', but he realized that there was no real hope for an amicable compromise.

> I knew too well what would be the result. We should go over all the old ground again. My mother would be swayed first one way, then the other. She might well compromise. But with my father it was different. Certainly I knew that he would not be prepared to compromise. My mother had said that he considered I had broken my word to him. He would always think this until I gave up every sort of political activity and returned to the life of a dutiful son.

67

I knew I might be wrong, but I could not just give up all my ideas like that. In the end, I decided that my running away was justified.

That evening Esmond hurriedly packed his suitcase – to avoid suspicion this had been left until the last minute – and went to sleep dressed in school uniform, overcoat and mackintosh. At 5 a.m. he prised himself from the bed, snatched up suitcase and parcels, and with old Homburg firmly stuck to his head, trod a torch-lit path along the dormitory and down a flight of stairs to a ground-floor classroom. Here he was to meet his brother, who had 'most nobly volunteered to see me off at the station'; but owing to a mix-up Giles never arrived. Esmond waited half an hour then collected up his assorted effects, sidled out of the classroom window and made for the station where he caught the 6.35 train to Waterloo. By mid-morning he was in the Parton Bookshop shakily savouring his new life.

MR CHURCHILL'S NEPHEW
VANISHES

COLONEL'S SON
RUNS AWAY FROM SCHOOL

WINSTON'S RED NEPHEW

SECRET DASH OUT OF COLLEGE

The publicity which erupted out of Esmond's running away, strangely enough, took him completely by surprise: 'Perhaps I should have expected something of the sort, but I just had not. I was certainly never more astonished than when I read my mother's statements to the Press, many of them quoted in headlines.' *Daily Express* (Saturday 10 February 1934):

MR CHURCHILL'S NEPHEW
VANISHES
FROM PUBLIC SCHOOL

'UNDER THE INFLUENCE OF LONDON
COMMUNISTS' SAYS MOTHER

A fifteen-year-old boy, a nephew of Mr Winston Churchill, and said by his parents to be deeply under the influence of London Communists ran away yesterday from Wellington College. He sent two messages to his mother that he was safe in London but at a late hour last night had not returned home.... A telegram was sent to his mother (from school).

Mrs Romilly visited Scotland Yard where she made a statement in which she gave the names of Communist people who, she alleges, have been influencing her son with communist ideas. Mrs Romilly:

'One of his friends telephoned me this afternoon and said that Esmond was coming to see me this evening. Then later in the afternoon a note was pushed through the letter-box from Esmond himself. In this he said he understood that we were taking what he termed "legal measures" and therefore did not intend to come home at present. The talk of "legal measures" is, of course, absurd. The trouble with him is that he can think of nothing else but Communism. He is simply fanatical about it.'

The Sunday papers brought more headlines and further comments from Nellie who was now, it appears, trying to quell the excitement caused by her previous reports. This to the *Sunday Referee*:

'I am not an alarmist', she said last night.

'My son is missing and I have no doubt that I could find him and bring him home tomorrow. But what would be the good of coercion?

'The boy is only trying to express his sense of revolt.

'If he returns home he will be welcome. I should like to talk things over with him and see if we could hit upon some way to smooth out our differences.'

The same newspaper also carried an interview with Esmond – 'A Secret Talk to *Sunday Referee*'. It was the only interview he gave. By the time he had recovered enough of his composure to begin touting the story, its news value had already waned. Like that other *Daily Mail* villain, the Loch Ness Monster, the 'Red Menace' surfaced on a tidal wave of sensation only to sink, as quickly as it emerged, back into the murky depths of Fleet Street.

Meanwhile, back at Wellington College.... 'I remember', says Rupert Horsley, 'going over to the Headmaster's Lodge after breakfast to report that Romilly had disappeared. I must have walked in looking rather lugubrious because Malim looked up at me and said, "What, has Romilly gone away?" I said, "Yes". He said, "Thank God for that." He just hoped that that would be the end of the matter.'

69

It was a vain hope, the following weeks bringing a deluge of inquiries and accusations from anxious parents and dyspeptic governors. The school elders were particularly acerbic in their attacks, the vice-president, Lord Derby, believing the Romilly episode the result of unsound discipline, while HRH the Duke of Connaught (the Wellington president) waved a pontifical finger at socialist under-masters. Malim listened patiently to all the theories, and patiently sang the inquisitors' minds to rest. It was, indeed, largely due to the headmaster's reasonableness that the situation did not develop into a minor witch-hunt. Trevor Russell-Cobb, one of Esmond's Wellington supporters:

Malim was exceptionally good about the running-away business. He asked me to the Lodge and made a deal. He said we could both make life difficult for each other; however, if I promised not to indulge in any more Communist propaganda while at school the matter would be closed. It was a very civilized gesture. He even took Giles down to Brighton for the day to help him get over the incident.

Despite regarding himself as 'an impenitent Victorian' Malim proved to be a reasonable, even enlightened figure during the troubled years of the thirties – through the Romilly affair, and through the increasingly aggressive struggle taking place within the Wellington staff-room. In March 1934 this struggle intensified when twenty members of the Wellington staff signed a petition demanding the dismissal of the sadistic H.J.B.Wanstall.

Consciously or not the petitioners had timed their attack perfectly; it was only weeks since Romilly's disappearance and Malim was in no mood to risk another protracted incident. He complied, at least partially, with the demand: Wanstall was suspended. But any ideas on the reformers' part of a new era beginning at Wellington College were short-lived. There were soon rumours of Wanstall being ill, then of an operation. The less militant signatories softened. Wanstall returned to College and remained until 1943, when he was dismissed for tampering with one of the boys while beating him. Rupert Horsley:

Although the battle taking place in the early thirties didn't appear to be a victory for either side, events were to show that it was a victory for the liberal faction. The turning point came in the early forties – the school was never the same again. Of course this battle had nothing to do with Esmond's rebellion. In fact I think his running away was as much a reaction against his family as against the school.

I didn't know his father, but his mother was a florid London type, very opinionated, very domineering. Was his father alive?

8
Misdeal

The indignant rebel: ... seems to depend on a specific
quality, the gift of projective imagination, or empathy,
which compels [him] to regard an injustice inflicted on
others as an indignity to [himself], and vice versa, to
perceive an injustice to [himself] as part and symbol
of a general evil in society.

ARTHUR KOESTLER, *Arrow in the Blue*

'Esmond always had some bee in his bonnet,' wrote the Newlands' master, Mr Browne. Now it was the public schools, before, the Jacobites. And before that? It would appear that Esmond was born indignant, his rancour yet another bequest of those volatile Scottish genes. It would appear so, at least, were we not already familiar with several other aspects of the Romilly background.

Nancy sent the little boy downstairs to his father and she thought how sweet he looked in his blue home-made dressing-gown, now much too short and barely reaching his knees. She kissed him as he disappeared into the room and she closed the door. She went upstairs to talk to her daughter. 'Why does father want to talk to Tommy?' asked Sylvia. Nothing ever escaped her notice.

'Well, it's very unfair', she said, 'I've got something very important to tell father.' Nancy smiled.

In 1932 Nellie Romilly's novel *Misdeal* had been published and confirmed, it is to be supposed, several beliefs her younger son entertained as to his family: that his parents' marriage was a shallow pretence of a relationship ('they were like two wild animals penned in a cage'), that his overpowering mother had an emasculating effect on the family ('she was turning him [her husband] into cotton wool') and that the elder child, a boy (Esmond was converted into a girl) was 'her heart's delight'. The story may also have contained a few surprises. *Misdeal* is an account of Nancy Durane's unhappy marriage and her affair with

72

one Cyril Landon which, after several stormy years, ends with Cyril falling in love with Nancy's best friend. This breaks Nancy's heart, and our heroine fades fast. Her husband is summoned from his military post in India, but to no effect. Nancy dies. The doctor in attendance assumes the role of chorus: 'You can see that he [her husband] would literally die for her, but for years he so undermined her strength by his need for sympathy, and his inability to provide her with – not money, but with fun and laughter which is the very keynote of her character.'

There is no way of affirming the *Misdeal* affair, Nellie's papers being firmly incarcerated in the Romilly trust, but let us suppose that the affair, like the rest of the book, was based upon fact. According to *Misdeal* Nellie's relationship began soon after her marriage and certainly before Bertram Romilly returned to Egypt (India in *Misdeal*) as Military Governor of Galilee Province in 1919. Was it possible that the affair had begun before Esmond's birth, and had this thought occurred to him as he pored over *Misdeal*'s pages? In reading *Misdeal* had he experienced, rightly or wrongly, the ultimate reason for indignation?

'That's my family history,' Esmond had said to Anthony Robinson, as he relieved his house prefect of the new grey volume he had just picked up. 'At first he was reticent about my reading it,' Mr Robinson recalls, 'although he did let me look through it a few weeks later. I believe one of the children was a girl.' Anthony Robinson viewed *Misdeal* only weeks after its publication, when the book still had some novelty value for the fourteen-year-old Romilly, as letters to his mother testify. 12 June 1932:

I think *Misdeal* is absolutely marvellous. It would appeal to anyone with any imagination. But why couldn't it have ended a little happier – and yet the ending was one of the best parts of it....

And 26 June:

Two boys in dormitory have read Anna Gerstein's book; one – who holds the same views as Giles said: 'I can just imagine that sort of book being a best seller.' I thought this would amuse you.

Yet the novelty appears soon to have worn off. There is no evidence of Esmond mentioning the book again to either friends or family; not even his wife, Jessica Mitford, had been told of 'the Horrible Mrs Romilly's book (I always referred to Nellie as the Horrible Mrs R. as opposed to the Honourable Mrs R. – ME!).'

73

There are, of course, enough overt reasons for Esmond's silence without proposing deeper ones. The logical conclusion is that his mother's exposition of family life came to embarrass and offend him, and as such was one of several factors which contributed to his adolescent anger and sense of injustice. As for his reading anything more into the story, that remains pure speculation. That is where we leave *Misdeal*.

But before returning to the rebellion, it should be recalled that in February 1934 Esmond was not just concerned with escaping the stifling atmosphere of family and school life, he was equally anxious to enter the outside world and make his own contribution to the Left–Right fray now so evidently in progress.

On Tuesday 13 February 1934, five days after Esmond had run away from Wellington, the 'Red Menace' was swept from the headlines by stories of 'Fierce Fighting Behind The Barricades in Paris', 'Police Fight Strikers in Spain', and 'Streets of Vienna Swept by Machine-Gun Fire'. The first two headlines referred to the bloody general strikes that were bringing both France and Spain to a standstill; the third to a much more gruesome battle taking place within Austria, where Chancellor Dollfuss had outlawed the large Social-Democratic Party – 'I am telephoning this message from the centre of a battlefield', wrote the *Daily Express* man on the spot:

> Vienna is in darkness. Machine guns are still rattling in the working-class quarters of the city.
>
> Reports of wild fighting are coming in every few minutes from the cities of Linz and Graz. Twenty-six people are reported to have been killed and 200 wounded at Graz. Vienna has been in the throes of civil war since morning....

It was in this highly charged atmosphere that the equally highly charged Romilly now entered upon his new life.

9
Out of Bounds

It's farewell to the drawing-room's civilized cry
The professor's sensible whereto and why
The frock-coated diplomat's social aplomb
Now matters are settled with gas and with bomb.

W.H.AUDEN, 'Song for the New Year'

There was an unmistakable 1848 quality about the New Year of 1934, and it wasn't only the Press that had sensed it.

In February 1934 the hunger march organized by the NUWM was converging on London, and sending some shock-waves through Parliament. The Home Secretary spoke of 'grave disorder and public disturbances', the Attorney-General of 'bloodshed'; rumours were abroad of a government police conspiracy to stop the marchers reaching the capital; a National Council of Civil Liberties was formed, comprising some prominent left-wing MPs and writers, its aim: 'to preserve the citizens' rights' in a period of democratic decay.

'Has anybody who cares to walk to London the Constitutional right to demand to see me?' asked a regal Ramsay MacDonald, 'to take up my time whether I like it or not?' Clearly not, the NUWM's request for an audience with the Prime Minister being refused. Thus, on Wednesday 28 February 1934, the marchers arrived in London, availed themselves of their democratic right to address the Trafalgar Square pigeons, and returned home.

'Please send me all the stuff about the hunger march', wrote Giles on Sunday 11 February, in a letter to inform his brother of the situation at Wellington subsequent to his departure:

I think you would be disappointed by the general apathy. No traces of a sensation beyond people buying the *Express* and *Chronicle* in large quantities. No legal action is being taken against you – it was [Horsley's] fault for making me think so. But apparently all the ports are being watched to prevent you from leaving England. Mummie was down here yesterday, and completely punctured by Talboys and Malim; she arranged with [Horsley] for your clothes to be sent to Pimlico Road. It would make a good impression if you arranged to go and see her – there is no question of coercion. Malim is writing on your behalf to Daddy – Mummie thinks this will calm him enormously. The doors are still not shut in your face. . . .

Lawrence is down today and is going to do a lot of canvassing for the paper at Cambridge. In fact, he is going to send me an estimate of how many copies he can get sold, then we can arrange for a batch to go straight to him from the printers. We can make him an official agent unless you have already got someone else. . . . Finally, what about funds? I have nothing left but subscriptions (more roll in every day) and I presume that you have spent what you had. That means our capital is nil. . . .

Some of your statements to the Press amaze me, but I daresay you weren't responsible for them.

Having precariously negotiated the first traumatic days of freedom, Esmond settled down to the task in hand, energetically writing and collating articles for the magazine which, due to the 'Red Menace' affair, was now running behind schedule. On Thursday 22 February he wrote to his Boothams School contact, John Peet:

Dear Comrade,

I must apologise for being so long in writing to you again. But things have been rather rushed here lately, as you may imagine. Thanks very much for news etc., which was very useful. As the stuff you sent yourself – reviews of pamphlets etc. – may not be suitable for the first number, could you send more, if you have time, and get other people to contribute as well, particularly on some subject or other which is relevant to some aspect of Public School life? About how many copies can be sold at Boothams? (I imagine about a dozen.)

March 4 brought yet another communiqué – typed in violet on a postcard – informing Peet of an end of term conference to elect an editorial board – 'let me hear from you and have your views on the idea'. In the meantime there would be a temporary board 'consisting of the public school bureau of the FSS'. (In fact, the Romilly–FSS relationship, always a brittle one, broke completely some weeks later when, counter to earlier policy, the Federation began a schoolboy publication of its own.) The message ended, once again, with an estimate of the copies to be sold, now upped to '15 on a sale or return basis'.

John Peet received another two letters from Esmond before the first issue of 'Out of Bounds' was published on 25 March, each sanguinely increasing the number of copies Esmond 'imagined' his Boothams contact could handle. Peet eventually received twenty copies and sold them without difficulty, such was the publicity generated by the 'Red Menace'.

'BANNED IN UPPINGHAM — BANNED IN CHELTENHAM', the first issue of 'Out of Bounds' announced on its front cover, whetting the reader's appetite for what was to follow, which was an equally blunt editorial and statement of intentions. 'The public schools are sly creatures', Esmond wrote;

> They have a horror of publicity, of being in 'the news'. They like to remain powerfully behind the scenes, accepting their tremendous responsibilities, fulfilling their functions, but never discussing them. So they go on from year to year turning out the men who shall rule our empire and few people ever question their unique privileges and powers. And why? Because it is not done to wash one's dirty linen in public – it might be found that there was nothing to be called clean.

This over-emphatic, slightly ridiculous opening tirade was not, however, characteristic of the rest of the magazine, which offered a rich blend of politics, literature and public-school criticism. There was a letter section on life 'In Public Schools', and another on the OTC. And Phyllis Barker of Ashford High School wrote 'As The Twig is Bent', a criticism of the restrictive atmosphere at girls' schools. There were also humorous offerings, these provided by J.L.Irvine of Wellington, who sent-up the public-school ripping yarn with 'Derek (a mime)', and by H.W.Stubbs of Charterhouse (of whom more later) with 'Blackshirt Lament'. Gavin Ewart (another Wellington pupil) provided two poems, and Giles Romilly some criticism. Esmond's contributions were an article on the arms race, 'The World Around Us', and a reply to a 'Defence of Fascism', written by the leader of the Oundle School Fascist Youth Group, who had set out to prove that 'the ultimate end of the Fascist Movement is Liberty, Justice and Tranquillity for each and everyone' — 'the Liberty of the Concentration Camp, the Justice of the Jewish Pogrom, the Tranquillity of Imperialist War', retorted the heated editor.

The thirty-five page magazine ended with a review of the current left-wing literature and an advertisement for the Parton Bookshop. It was priced one shilling.

The *Daily Mail* warmed to the new material:

**'REDS' NEW ATTACK
BOYS' MAGAZINE MENACE
'CORRUPTING YOUTH'**
15-year-old Editor's Boast.

The *Daily Mail* recently called attention to renewed efforts to incul-
cate Communist and Bolshevik doctrines into the boys of the public
and secondary schools of the country. Fresh evidence of the determination of this Red attack is provided by the new number of 'Out
of Bounds', the schoolboys' magazine which, it is stated, is edited
by 15 year-old Esmond Romilly, who recently ran away from
Wellington College.

It boasts in large type that it has already been banned in
Uppingham and Cheltenham, and in an 'editorial' it is claimed, 'We
shall infuriate every schoolmaster over 30 (and some under) throughout England. We shall be deliberately corrupting youth.'

The *Mail* went on to quote some of the choicer pieces from the first
issue, leading its readership to the unavoidable conclusion that 'Out
of Bounds' was a Moscow export. Mainly, however, the Press viewed
the new magazine with leniency and even amusement.

Under the heading 'A Dreadful Production' the *Manchester Guardian*
commentator wrote:

Master Giles Romilly [sic], whose recent adventures when he ran
away from school provided some newspapers with a good, usable 'sensation' and most of us with plenty of harmless amusement, is further
distinguishing himself by editing a boys' magazine....

The work is faced with a caption in the most up-to-date tradition
of modern literary advertising: 'Banned in Uppingham, Banned in
Cheltenham' – which seems to indicate that Master Romilly has some
of his relative Mr Churchill's flair for immediate public appeal....

However, 'Out of Bounds', though Communist, is evidently determined to be fair, for we are given the chance of reading an entertaining 'Defence of Fascism' by someone who is described as the 'Leader'
of the 'Oundle School Fascist Youth Group'.

All of which seems to show that the state of ferment among our
youth must be more riotously heady than we ever imagined.

The above article, appearing on 11 April 1934, coincided with yet
another 'Dreadful Production', the 'Incitement to Disaffection' (or 'Sedi-

tion') bill. No satire was intended, however, in the *Guardian*'s headline 'Menaces of the Sedition Bill' – this new government measure really was a sinister piece of work.

Did this ambiguously worded bill really propose to outlaw all pacifist literature? The *Guardian* thought it did, and was supported by the National Council of Civil Liberties, which held an emergency meeting to consider its implications.

Not unnaturally, incitement to disaffection was also on the minds of those present at the 'Out of Bounds' conference which convened on Saturday 14 April at that home of clandestine meeting and seditious debate, Meg's Café. Here the sixteen delegates reiterated the call 'To fight Reaction (political and cultural), Fascism and Militarism in Public Schools' and passed a unanimous resolution 'condemning the National Government's Sedition Bill'. The delegates also elected a permanent editorial board, viz: Esmond and Giles Romilly (Wellington College), H P Bartlett (St Paul's), P Jeffries (University College School, London) and Miss M.Harland (North Collegiate School for Girls). These same faces appeared on the front cover of the next day's *Sunday Graphic*, framed by the headline 'War on "Play The Game You Cads!" Schoolboys' Plan To Put World Right.' The meeting had been advertised as 'secret', but at the last minute an anonymous caller had informed the Press. Fleet Street had its uses, provided you got to it before it got to you.

Although out of school barely two months, Esmond was growing up fast:

> The snotty-nosed roly-poly schoolboy was disappearing [writes John Peet] and being replaced by a young man, still rather short, who could easily have passed for a young undergraduate. He wore roughly the same clothes as before – shapeless tweed jacket and baggy grey flannels – but the not very clean white shirt had given way to a roll-neck pullover ('saves washing' explained E.R.). He was extremely self-assured. Living alone as a runaway had already greatly strengthened his pronounced self-confidence.

Now in London for the Easter vacation Peet found himself plunged headlong into a week of frenetic 'Out of Bounds' activity. This began with the Saturday afternoon conference. It continued on Sunday morning with a Hyde Park demonstration against the recent budget. John Peet:

For the demonstration, Esmond had persuaded a waitress at Meg's – an art student – to construct a banner and etch out the slogan: 'The Nationalist Government of Hunger Fascism and War'. We – Giles, Esmond and myself – then took this back to Pimlico Road and painted it (the Romilly parents were out for the evening). After the painting, the three of us sat in the drawing-room, drinking a bottle of Colonel Romilly's port. For the first time I heard Marlene Dietrich records, and Giles gave me a slim volume of Betjeman's early poems (Betjeman was still widely unknown at that time).

On Sunday morning the 'Out of Bounds' schoolboy contingent assembled at Mornington Crescent and there joined the rest of the north-west section of the demonstration to march down Oxford Street to Hyde Park. Here the speeches took place, Esmond being called upon to speak from one of the platforms as a 'student comrade'. He did so, swallowing back his initial panic, and thought, all in all, that 'the ordeal passed quite successfully'.

> In gallant trim the gilded vessel goes;
> Youth on the prow, and Pleasure at the helm.

This was the image evoked by Monday's *Guardian* in describing the Romilly protest. Yes, Youth was 'certainly on the prow in the case of Master Romilly. And if he should be inclined to protest that it is Duty rather than Pleasure at the helm, he can only be reminded, in the old phrase, that "the pleasure is ours". London must have enjoyed yesterday's progress even more than he did himself.'

Esmond took advantage of the new Press coverage, hawking quantities of 'Out of Bounds' around Piccadilly at the beginning of the week. Peet was again in attendance. He was also present when, on Wednesday, Esmond gathered together some eight or nine Out of Bounders to canvass for the Communist candidate, Ted Bramley, in the North Hammersmith by-election. John Peet:

Esmond decided we should do things in style. He had raised some money from somewhere, and hired a small Vauxhall car for the day. Whether he had a driving licence or not I cannot recall, but he certainly drove the car, decorated with big red election posies, all round Hammersmith.

Late at night, driving along King's Road, Chelsea, on our way back to Parton Street, we passed the barracks in which Sir Oswald Mosley at that time maintained his Blackshirts. On an impulse,

Esmond braked sharply, and said he would pop inside to pick up some Fascist propaganda. He returned promptly at a hurried trot pursued by four Blackshirts in full fig, shouting 'dirty Red' and 'go back to Russia'. Before Esmond could get the car started the Blackshirts began to rock it sideways, and we had visions of being the first heroic victims of British fascism; anti-climatically we managed to drive off without damage.

It emerged that Esmond had made the bad tactical mistake of striding into the Blackshirt den wearing a huge red-paper carnation, the election favour of the Communist Party candidate.

Four days later, on Sunday 22 April, Romilly and Peet once more clashed with Mosley's Blackshirts, this time at a British Union of Fascists meeting in the Albert Hall.

Since launching the BUF in October 1932 Mosley had used the mass meeting as a floor show to display the strength and discipline of the movement. As the meetings grew larger, however, more emphasis had been placed upon strength than discipline. At the Albert Hall meeting, attended by over 10,000 people, there were again disturbances as the now familiar chorus of hecklers was evicted by Mosley's troops.

> One – Two – Three – Four !
> What – are – the Fascists – for ?
> Lechery, Treachery, Hunger and War.

Romilly and Peet were not among the chanting throng. Having negotiated the Blackshirt cordon, 'on the strength of our obviously right voices', they began patrolling the upper circle as self-ordained 'observers from the National Council of Civil Liberties'. Not surprisingly, they were very soon evicted, albeit 'relatively gently'. At the massive and violent Olympia meeting held two months later, neither Esmond nor his new accomplice would escape so lightly.

'In our two minor brushes with British Fascism', writes John Peet, 'E.R. demonstrated what I regarded at the time as a total fearlessness (I was peeing my pants). Looking back, I concluded he was probably just as nervous as I was, but able to put on a perfect public school "play up and play the game" front.' Obviously there were aspects of his background which Esmond could not escape, as he had already discovered, and this may well have applied to the public-school code. Nevertheless, Peet was somewhat hasty in discounting his original theory – the fifteen-year-old Romilly really was a dauntingly fearless character.

The school vacation was over, all but the farewells, these waved vigorously early one spring morning to the Special departing Waterloo Station for Crowthorne and Wellington College.

> My dear old school goes back today
> Fumbling for tips and 'Goodbye old boy'
> Shall we give it a cheer?
> Let us pray for its members, past and present
> Let us remember how unpleasant
> Most of them were.*

Esmond continued to work in the Bookshop for £1 a week, but found this hardly an adequate means of support. Fortunately, the renewed interest from Fleet Street now enabled him to supplement his earnings with the fees for newspaper articles. On 28 April the *Sunday Referee* published an article titled 'A Hurry – Esmond Romilly (aged 15) Views the World', in which Esmond confidently set forth his generation's position within a depressed world:

People from universities and public schools today are not content to deplore the misery and waste that they see.

They ask – Why? What is the reason behind it all? And they are forced to the conclusion that there is something inherently wrong with the system under which we live; that the world is divided into a large class of exploited and a small clique of exploiters, that capitalism can offer them nothing – not even a job.

The youth has a clear choice, there can be no half-way house. Either they must side with the parasites and exploiters to 'make the world safe for plutocracy', or with the working class to smash the capitalist system and lay the foundations of a classless society.

Ten years ago those in the public schools were not affected by economic crises. Their parents or their relations probably held the strings to 'cushy' jobs. But there is a very different situation today. Anybody is glad to be offered a job; and this no doubt accounts in no small part for the changed outlook of modern youth.

A week later Esmond was once more in the news, this time with a humorous article on a recent sales-drive at Eton College. 'ESMOND ROMILLY "GATE CRASHES" ETON – Day of Comedy' ran the *Sunday*

* Gavin Ewart, 'The Old School', 'Out of Bounds', No. 2, June/July 1934.

Graphic's headlines, indicating that, whatever the problems inherent in society, one person at least was avoiding depression. And why, indeed, should he be depressed; he now had everything he had longed for, hadn't he? Or had his own outlook, like that of the modern youth of his article, also changed?

Having spent three months in the 'other world' Esmond had come to a dramatic conclusion: it was not what it had appeared when viewed through the telescope – 'perhaps I should be expressing it rather pompously', he wrote, 'if I said that I came into my first real contact with human people, and found not very much to respect or admire in this experience'. The truth is that Esmond had not dreamed of walking into the reality of left-wing Bohemia, he had dreamed of walking into its legend. Now, as he came face to face with the flaws behind the legend, he grew cynical.

In the sort of atmosphere where I lived [he continued], people were chiefly concerned in the study of themselves. One talked about politics and one talked about sex, but the most popular thing of all was to run these together and talk about oneself. As a conversational gambit, remarks about the weather were replaced by remarks about the general dreariness of life.

Politics were unreal. How could they be anything else, when the people themselves were unreal? That did not make anyone in the least less charming. But I suppose it is general experience that the lazy ne'er-do-well is often a more pleasant companion than the conscientious hard worker....

And then there were the 'coming young poets'. All their sins can be forgiven them if they talk the language of the 'class-struggle'. The politics of the latter are an endless source of conversation: 'What is Brockway's latest game?' The decision of the ILP Guild of Youth to affiliate to the Young Communist International – making history; the Trotskyists and the United Front; an endless flow of gossip and scandal. X is known to be a police-spy, Y is a snob. Z is that most awful of all things, a 'careerist'. So it goes on ... I was soon tired of London.

Shortly after returning to their schools in April, the 'Out of Bounds' delegates received a report of the Easter conference and a note outlining what was needed for the next issue, estimated to be released early in June. Once again the editor was sanguine in his estimation – the second issue of 'Out of Bounds' was not released until July, by which time Esmond himself was back at school, the world of the left-wing Bookshop having lost its earlier appeal.

Esmond returned to school on 9 June 1934; not to 'public' Wellington but to 'progressive' Bedales, Petersfield, Hampshire, an establishment of which he had long been an enthusiastic advocate: 'I remember at Wellington I used to have furious arguments with boys on the merits of co-education. Nearly everyone said: "It sounds all right, but it just doesn't work." I would retort by quoting the example of Bedales which had worked successfully for many years and showed every sign of continuing to do so.'

And yet, as 9 June approached, he had to admit that mixed with his enthusiasm was a 'certain apprehension at the idea of returning to school at all'; an apprehension exacerbated on 6 June by the arrival in London of Philip Toynbee.

'*June 7th* 1934: I have taken the most momentous decision of my life. May God be with me.' Thus wrote Toynbee, the 'Out of Bounds' Rugby agent, as his train quit the Midland station and sped towards London and the promise of a new, romantic life.*

In his memoir *Friends Apart* Toynbee has described the scene when he confronted Esmond for the first time:

A boy was leaving the shop as my taxi drew up in Parton Street, a short, square, dirty figure with a square white face and sweaty hair. 'I'm looking for Esmond Romilly', I said.

'Yes.'

He was instantly, dramatically, on his guard, conspiratorial, prepared for violent aggression or ingenious deceit. I thrilled and trembled more hysterically than ever.

'I'm Toynbee', I said, 'Toynbee of Rugby.'

Esmond looked sharply up and down the street, then opened the shop door and pushed me through it.

Esmond had a flair for the dramatic, for turning a schoolboy encounter into a highly charged confrontation between an ingenuous Holly Martins and a farouche Harry Lime. It was this romantic quality, infused into everything he did, which gave his character an air of both Committed and Comedian. At present the former character prevailed. Later, in December, Toynbee would encounter the latter, as Romilly,

---

* Mr Toynbee had got the date wrong! He had in fact taken the most momentous decision of his life on 6 June, the day before Mosley's Olympia meeting staged on 7 June 1934.

rapidly losing interest in his magazine, became a dissipated figure, kicking out wildly and to no purpose against abstract injustice.

Philip Toynbee remained in Parton Street for just two days before succumbing, not unwillingly, to the pressure to return to school. He had witnessed his host's way of life and saw that, for all its trappings of romantic bohemianism, it was at bottom an existence of real personal hardship and loneliness. It was also tainted by violence – not that this perturbed that 'terrifying figure' Romilly. It did, however, make Toynbee re-evaluate his own ability to stay afloat in such a sea – 'I was no Romilly, to keep my head indefinitely above the phosphorescent waters.'

On Thursday 7 June Mosley held his mammoth Olympia meeting. This event, which gave rise to a great outcry against the BUF's violent methods, was attended by Romilly and Toynbee who, in anticipation of the fight ahead, had bought knuckle-dusters at a Drury Lane ironmongers. 'We flexed our fingers. "A bit too loose here." "Not very comfortable on the thumb." We were expert knuckle-duster buyers.'*

Keyed-up and ready for action, the two boys infiltrated the large auditorium, where the Leader was making his imperial entry flanked by his black-clad entourage. The heckling began almost immediately, followed by the forceful evictions. In the general pandemonium and hysteria Romilly and Toynbee found themselves in the midst of a Blackshirt ruck, from whence they were propelled in opposite directions, Esmond to a relatively bruiseless exit, Toynbee, through a corridor of punching, kicking Blackshirts, to a side door where, sobbing and shaken, he was led by fellow hecklers to a makeshift first-aid post.

His wounds dressed, his tears forgotten, Toynbee returned to Parton Street in a blithe state of euphoria – 'For I believed that I had struck my first blow for the revolution, and that the revolution itself must surely follow.' But on entering the Bookshop he was brought abruptly back to earth by the sight of Esmond already engaged in writing an account of the meeting for 'some weekly magazine' – 'this stubborn realism', wrote his friend, 'was always to prove a corrective to his fantasies, and without it his picaresque existence would have been impossible'. Yet, once the serious side of the business was out of the way,

---

* In defending Blackshirt aggression at Olympia, Sir Oswald Mosley, in *My Life*, pp. 299–300, cites Toynbee's knuckle-duster account from *Friends Apart*. By the combined quirks of fate and the Mitford family Mosley and Romilly later became brothers-in-law : in October 1936 Mosley married Fascist Diana Mitford; eight months later, on 18 May 1937, Esmond married Diana's younger sister, the Communist Jessica.

Esmond was as eager as the other to fantasize on the recent events; and the two boys 'sat up for hours in the bedroom, recounting tirelessly, but not competitively, the details of our adventures. And our first hopes became more apocalyptic than ever. Surely we had heard already the mutter of machine-guns in the suburbs of a brooding Petrograd, and tomorrow....'

'Tomorrow', Friday 8 June 1934, Toynbee went back to Rugby (where he was formally expelled). The following day Esmond also returned to school, to Bedales.

In *Friends Apart* Philip Toynbee does not list Esmond's return to school as a reason for his own flight back to Rugby, but undoubtedly this proved a major factor in his argument for calling it a day. Esmond may have been a 'terrifying figure', but life in the 'other world' was infinitely more acceptable with him than without him.

10
Bedales and Bedlam

'This is a boy who can contribute nothing to this school and to whom this school can contribute nothing.' This was the substance of the Bedales headmaster Mr Badley's end-of-term report on Esmond, and formed the peroration to his academic career. In his own reports on the school Esmond was more complimentary, although he was hard-pressed to descry anything Messiah-like in a headmaster considered by another essayist to have looked not unlike Jesus Christ. 'He was not very reassuring or comforting at my first interview with him,' wrote Esmond. 'The only comments he made for some time were a series of "Umphs".' Mr Badley, a puritan at heart, was not at all certain that his school was quite progressive enough to accommodate his new charge.

O.L.Badley had founded Bedales in 1893, with a view to providing an education in which 'aptitude was put before mere knowledge', and 'the harmonious development of the body and mind' before the obtaining of honours in examinations. It was this ideal which had drawn Esmond to Bedales and it was this ideal which he lauded in his later accounts. 'What is the object of education?' he asked in the third issue of 'Out of Bounds'. 'Are one's years at school to be years in which one's mind is being trained and one's character developed as an individual? In which one is to be given, as far as possible, an impartial view of the world and all its problems? Or are they to be years in which one is trained with fixed ideas, and in fixed customs and prejudices, so that one may serve some particular section of the community?'

Esmond was back on his favourite hobby-horse. The article, a compar-ison of the Wellington and Bedales systems, makes no attempt at a general appraisal of both schools but confines itself to an attack on the iniquitous rules and regulations of the former. The vacuum-packed conclusion: Wellington perpetuates an anachronistic class of empire-builders, Bedales creates individuals. Alexander Lourie, a Bedalian contemporary of Esmond's, criticizes this view. While agreeing with

Esmond that Bedales was less restrictive than the public schools, he is less inclined to believe that the children were quite the liberated individuals of Esmond's article. 'It was a school of sportsmen and physical exercise', Mr Lourie recalls, and the sporting fraternity, like its Wellington counterpart, harboured a quizzical distrust of anything bookish or intellectual: 'Over fifty per cent of the children at the age of thirteen were illiterate. Their parents were usually very rich and progressively minded, and didn't mind too much whether their children were taught or not. Attending lessons at Bedales was optional, and few people bothered to learn. Esmond, as far as I can recall, was no exception.'

Whatever Esmond's attitude to settling down on entering Bedales, it soon became obvious that the school could provide no more than a brief, enjoyable escape from his other life. Having taken a large dose of the outside world, Esmond had discovered that there was no known emetic. The interlude was nevertheless an enlightening one, and not only for its insight into 'progressive' school education.

Although it is probable that Esmond had already been introduced to the society of the *demi-monde*,* his experience of girls his own age had up until now been confined mainly to vacations spent with cousins. The girls at Bedales were therefore a new, interesting, and at times diverting experience. One of the things, indeed, which Esmond found most amusing about the Bedales society was the internecine war played out between the older girls; a war complete with armed camps and communiqués – this to Esmond:

Well, haven't you ever seen the way she giggles and rolls her eyes at boys? Don't think I dislike her for it, but there's no doubt that she's an awful little flirt. Still, you won't be the first person. I've seen so many people before you become infatuated by her, then grow out of it soon enough. She's certainly pretty, but she's very shallow. For heaven's sake do some work now and don't go on with this conversation. I'm sure you only want it for your beastly book or magazine or something.

But Esmond was not merely interested in the young lady in question from a journalistic point of view; he had, to use the school vernacular, a 'crush' on her. The name of this Bedalian temptress was Angela Jeans and she was, according to Alexander Lourie, the prettiest girl in the

* In *Friends Apart* Philip Toynbee mentions passing a certain *boîte de nuit* in Dieppe which Esmond had recommended.

school. Unfortunately, like her less comely contemporaries, she had strict rules on the boundaries of propriety. Esmond:

> After three months of fast life in Bloomsbury I imagined I would find everything [at Bedales] run in a wonderful combined spirit of the Parton Bookshop – Freud and Marx. My first error was about co-education. My first week I got on well with a girl whom I'll call Mary. She passed me notes during school hours saying 'I quite like you', and we went for walks together. Overbold with this success, I delivered her a long lecture on what I was pleased to call the petit bourgeois morals of the school. She became very bored and said she was going to go out and play tennis with some healthier minds. I got up and grabbed her clumsily round the waist to give some practical point to my arguments and received a smart blow in the face. That was the end of that friendship.

Alexander Lourie has his own version of the final schism: 'Esmond was infatuated with Angela and went off to Petersfield to buy her the biggest box of chocolates he could find. Tracking her down back at school, he handed over the chocolates and asked her to go to bed with him. She slapped his face.'

'There were plenty of "affairs",' wrote Esmond knowingly, '... but they were so much a part of the daily life of the school that no-one took them seriously ... it was only when people got to the age of wanting something more than romantic friendships that they felt the shortcomings of the system as it worked at Bedales. Still, many people would consider this for the best.'

Girls were not Esmond's only distraction. The continuing affair with 'Out of Bounds' was also taking up much of his time. Fortunately, at Bedales, Sunday was a free day and provided they were back by 6, the older students were allowed to spend it as they pleased. Esmond often used these free days to travel up to the Bookshop to check on the magazine's progress, on occasion joined by one or more bold Bedalians interested in glimpsing the world of the 'Red Menace'. On one Sunday, however, the party, two boys and two girls, had heedlessly overstepped the curfew time and found themselves in the uncomfortable position of enduring Mr Badley's wrath, known to be as biblical as his beard. But why get into trouble at all, piped the group leader. All they needed was a 'really convincing story about how we had lost our way on the Downs'. The others were dubious, but Esmond, already warming to the subterfuge, was in persuasive mood.

Next morning the headmaster interviewed each member of the party separately. Esmond was last to enter the office.

Calmly and convincingly I told my story. Then the headmaster said, 'Now as you know, this school is run on what we call the honour system. Breaking the rules isn't what matters – it's telling the truth. Now I'd like to forget all about what you have just told me. All right? Now tell me what happened.'

Well, I held my ground and repeated the same story. He shook his head sadly and informed me that when he had brought up the question of the honour system with the other people they had all immediately admitted to the truth about going up to London. He said I was the first boy he had come across in a very long while to whom such an appeal had meant nothing.

'It is perhaps no exaggeration to call Esmond a pathological liar,' writes H.W.Stubbs, one of his 'Out of Bounds' supporters. Esmond, more modestly, allowed Wellington to take some of the credit: 'I challenge anyone to deny that the public school system produces the most competent liars. All boys are probably natural liars, but the discipline of the public school makes them hardened and sometimes ingenious ones.'

Esmond left Bedales (and formal education) at the end of the 1934 summer term, the leave-taking performed under yet another black cloud: 'I believe [Mr Badley] told my mother I was a hopeless case.'

At the beginning of July the second issue of 'Out of Bounds' appeared, sporting a new, improved formula. 'In the first issue of "Out of Bounds"', Esmond reminded the reader, 'we stated our policy on the cover, "Against Reaction in Public Schools". As the result of a conference held last April with delegates from sixteen schools, this must now read in full: "Against Reaction, Militarism and Fascism in Public Schools".' There followed articles on all four abominations, this by one 'T.P. of Rugby' (who was, of course, Philip Toynbee):

On June the seventh I had the interesting experience of accompanying a friend of mine to the meeting of the Fascists in Olympia ... I should state first of all that before the above date I considered myself a non-party man with considerable interest in both Fascism and Communism, but no definite leaning toward either. I am no longer in that position, and I hope this letter will show clearly why I am not....

Not all blood and thunder, the second issue also introduced 'The Sex Question', Giles Romilly writing 'Morning Glory (Sex in Public Schools)', and Phyllis Barker, of Ashford High School, 'Hero-Worship Adrift' – an account of the 'pashes' which develop in adolescence at girls' schools. 'Girls' Public Schools are notorious for "incidents",' the article begins, but tails off rapidly.* Gavin Ewart in his poem, 'The Old School' is bolder, one verse reading:

> So we were onanists, beds at night
> Used to respond with continual slight
> Creaks of their springs
> But this was love's face in a mirror
> That showed fatigue, not joy or terror,
> Eyes hollow rings.

'I wrote the poem just before going up to Cambridge,' Mr Ewart recalls, 'and thought no more about it. Then, in my first term, I received a letter from Malim saying he thought it best if I didn't visit the school for a few years. There was a lot of wrath aroused by the "sex" issue, I got some of the backlash.' Esmond:

The second issue, though it generally received less publicity than the first, came in for much more criticism and abuse. This was not due to political views this time, but to the outspokenness of one or two contributions on the subject of sex ... we received masses of letters, mostly from women (presumably mothers and aunts) asking us how we found it possible to print such 'filth'. Giles and I also heard with mixed feelings after the publication of this issue of a number of erstwhile friends and relatives whose doors we should never darken again.

The same issue also introduced a new name to the 'Out of Bounds' circle, R.E.D.Stanley, who contributed a full page advertisement for the pamphlet (his own) *That's Sedition – That Was*, a skit on the Government's 'Sedition' bill still before Parliament. Stanley had borrowed the

---

* As a result of this article and her contribution to the first issue of 'Out of Bounds', 'As The Twig is Bent', Miss Barker was expelled.

title for the publication from the petrol slogan – 'That's Shell – That Was' – the contents from the Prime Minister Ramsay MacDonald's early 'seditious' speeches. The advertising was his own: 'No Member of HM Forces Should Come Into Possession of This Pamphlet' was the warning brazenly displayed on the front cover.

Ruddy Stanley had a flair for the gimmick, the well-timed piece of satire. There was the anti-Fascist toilet paper for instance, hawked with the pamphlets up and down the city's main thoroughfares. The rolls carried a cartoon of Oswald Mosley, hand raised in blood-stained salute, and the caption 'Put Mosley on the Spot'. They cost 9d each, but only the first twelve sheets were inscribed. Stanley was a wide-boy, a totally unscrupulous character. Esmond was captivated.

The Stanley brothers, Ruddy and the laconic Sidney, had appeared on the scene sometime in the spring of 1934. Who knows how Esmond came into contact with this unlikely pair of literati? He may have met them at a CP demonstration (they were both fellow travellers) or they may have just turned up at Parton Street and offered their services. Perhaps they thought that there was a killing to be made out of 'Out of Bounds' – gratuitous action was not their style.

To Esmond the Stanleys represented, for a time at least, real working-class Communism. After several months of examining what he now regarded as the fake item, this in itself was enough to stimulate his interest. But the brothers had more than their working-classness to recommend them: they also had the romantic aura of people living precariously on society's fringe. This image, one which the Stanleys did much to perpetuate themselves, was completed by the camp-following Sonia, a sluttishly pretty East End (according to Sonia, 'East European') princess who evoked, at least as far as the young Out of Bounders were concerned, the giddy height of sexual emancipation. John Peet:

> She completely captivated someone of my own puritan background by chattering quite freely – and not, I think, salaciously – about all aspects of sex. This was a phenomenon I had not hitherto encountered. Also outside my experience was the way in which, when an assortment of Romillys, Stanleys, etc. dossed down in the room over the Parton Bookshop, Sonia stood there and stripped off, while everybody else was getting discreetly undressed under the blankets.

Under the outrageous tutelage of the Stanleys, Esmond's behaviour became wilder than ever. The foursome (Sonia in tow), now began a series of raids on the public schools, the Stanleys' jalopy plastered with lurid red posters proclaiming sensational 'Out of Bounds' disclosures.

92

The ostensible purpose of these sorties was to sell the magazine, but as often as not egregious anarchy took over, as during the following trip to the old school:

It occurred while I was at Bedales.... Some friends came down to see me from London one Sunday and we went over to Wellington to sell copies of 'Out of Bounds'. I myself sat discreetly in the back of the car as we drove round and round the college grounds looking for potential buyers. Unfortunately there were not many people accessible, and we decided against driving across the cricket field. However, we managed to sell thirty copies by driving up to single persons and asking them whether they were interested. For the most part we were well received; but driving past one particular house we were received with bricks and water. Soon, however, news of our visit reached the ears of authority. As we drove down the main drive, a group of masters collected there with the old school porter, who looked very fierce and military with his walrus moustache and game leg. He advanced into the middle of the road as we came along and raised his arm in our direction in a Fascist salute. We accelerated, and at the last minute he got out of the way. That was the end of this visit to Wellington.

John Peet, who had also fallen under the Stanleys' spell, happened to mention his new, intriguing acquaintances to his father, a Fleet Street journalist. Peet elder, equally intrigued, more suspicious, made some enquiries and received a letter from an East End judge who described Ruddy Stanley as a 'hardened criminal with a long police record'; his latest offence the stamping of 'Osram' on cheap Japanese light bulbs. John Peet questioned Ruddy about the light bulbs. He was treated in reply to a long involved story about how he had been framed and anyway he was expropriating the expropriators.

Several months later Esmond had first-hand experience of Ruddy Stanley's criminal activities when, bored with London, he fell in with the brothers, who had begun touring the country selling anti-Fascist toilet paper and other items in the local markets. This 'new and exciting experience' came to an end after six weeks when Ruddy was arrested for stealing petrol from a country garage.

'Out of Bounds', Vol. 1, No. 3, Winter:

We wish it to be known that neither S. Stanley, our Distributing Manager, nor R. Stanley, are any longer in any way connected with us. We have terminated our connection with these individuals, and cannot be held responsible for their actions.

After spending the summer at Pimlico Road (Giles was also at home preparing for a pre-Oxford trip to Munich) Esmond was by September back in the 'other world'. His new address, as if a reaffirmation of his true allegiance, was in Hackney, where he had found a bed and breakfast for 7s 6d a week. The money had come from his father. Realizing there was no hope of enticing his son back to the fold, having no wish to entice him back, he had provided him with a £1 a week allowance, the money paid through the family solicitors.

Esmond now had the opportunity to examine his future – an examination he had successfully avoided during the last eight months. It was a bleak outlook. There was still 'Out of Bounds', but the magazine took up little of his time and the now out-of-favour Parton Street even less. What then was there to do but spend the day wandering around every corner of the city – a circuitous route as representative of *ennui* as his outfit, grey flannel trousers and thick red polo-neck sweater, was of confusion.

And then, with nothing constructive to contain his energy, with a feeling of being once again penned in, Esmond turned characteristically to aggression. 'He was like a wild animal, very worked up and ready for a fight', recalls Alexander Lourie, his Bedales friend, who accompanied Esmond to Mosley's Hyde Park demonstration on 9 September. 'I realized then that we were not at all the same type of person.' By Christmas Esmond's behaviour, if anything, had become worse. Now at the height of his adolescent intolerance he was, according to Philip Toynbee, 'scruffier and wilder than ever; a juvenile delinquent'.

The autumn had been a barren period for Esmond. True, 'Out of Bounds' 3 had reached fruition in November, but the magazine was no longer any reason for celebration. Besides, did the articles 'War and Education', 'OTC', 'Against War and Fascism' and 'Anti-War Activities in Public Schools' really have anything new to say, or were they just re-runs of the original broadcast? Even the poems sounded the same, Gavin Ewart's 'Public School' no more than a tame repetition of his earlier, shriller harangues. Had 'Out of Bounds', at least as it stood, reached saturation level? Esmond thought it had and called for yet another conference to be held in January, in order to discuss 'the necessity of reorganization and enlargement on an altogether broader basis for the coming year'. That the conference never took place was yet further proof of the editor's declining fortunes. In January 1935 both he and his ideas for the forthcoming issues were under lock and key in the London borough of Battersea.

Still, whatever the gloom and despondency on the road to ruin, there was always the occasional bright spot.

At the beginning of December 1934, Esmond travelled down to Charterhouse for the day to meet his Carthusian supporters, led by the school's 'Out of Bounds' agent, H.W.Stubbs. For the occasion Esmond was asked to assume the name Bagley Wren, an acquaintance of Stubbs at Bradfield. Wearing a black Homburg and raincoat to give full import to his alias, the 'Out of Bounds' editor stepped out, at a diplomatically keen pace, on his tour of the school.

The first stop was the library and a meeting with the school librarian, 'a kindly old man with a phenomenal stammer and an encyclopaedic memory for school prosopography'.

'He asked me about football', gasped Esmond, at last freed from the ordeal, 'and for the life of me I couldn't remember whether Bradfield played rugger or soccer.' The Menace was right back in his element and loving every minute of it.

The tour continued, Esmond interested in everything, but especially, writes Mr Stubbs,

. . . our school jargon : football was 'turning-up', the evening confinement, reasonably enough, 'locking-in', but what really amused Esmond was to hear a mini-football practice described as a 'ball-up'. We conversely were impressed by his knowledge of the great world. He was then on strength at Parton Street, and he told us about his famous customers. These included a future poet laureate, who six years earlier had taught me Greek at prep. school. I mentioned that in a fit of fury he had once hit me over the head with a large lexicon.

Esmond exploded in laughter: 'Of course he's homosexual. Most of them are homosexual. You can always tell.'

The conversation moved on to the theatre. Some time previously Stubbs had sent 'Out of Bounds' a 'deplorable comedy sketch prophesying World War II'. Esmond now asked if a fringe theatre group in which he was involved could produce the sketch. Stubbs was excited :

a teenage sketch, produced on the boards of proto-Unity Theatre, getting my name known, leading towards a recognized position in the sub-culture, and in due course fame, of a kind, though certainly not a kind that was recognized in the stockbroker-belt world of Charterhouse – but a brief exultation was modified by com-

95

mon sense; even I could perceive that Esmond was essentially unreliable. Still, I was flattered, and could only agree, concealing my gladness with a tentative query whether I would be paid for it. Esmond hedged.

'Well, I'm afraid people on the Left have very little money.'

I hastily assured him that this did not matter. It was, I believe, the first time that I had heard the word 'Left' used in this sense.

Over tea and biscuits at the tuck-shop Esmond treated his audience to a rendition of another sketch which the proto-Unity group had recently staged:

God the Father was sitting in an armchair, when an angel came in and said, 'Excuse me, your Lordship. A gentleman at the door, says he's the Pope.'

'Pope? I've never heard of him. Where's the Son? He may be a friend of His.'

God the Son comes in, in white flannels, waving a tennis racket.

'Here, Son, here's a man who calls himself the Pope. Have you heard of him?'

'I don't think so, Dad. Better ask the Ghost, he knows everything.'

'I say, Ghost, old chap, have you ever heard of the Pope?'

'The Pope? Let me see – Good God, yes! Why he's the bastard who started the scandal about me and the Virgin Mary.'

'Are you an atheist?' Stubbs asked earnestly.

'I think I'd sooner not answer that question,' came the prompt reply.

Although he was always 'courtesy itself in our correspondence', Mr Stubbs believes, with reason, that Esmond had no high opinion of him:

Soon after the December visit I heard, from a peripatetic Current Affairs lecturer, a glowing apologia for Mussolini's Italy, and feeling that one ought to be fair I wrote a letter to 'Out of Bounds' saying that however much one disliked Mussolini's bellicosity, he had done something for the Italian standard of living. Esmond printed the letter and, of course, wiped the floor with it – his statistics blowing sky high the eulogies of Mussolini's apologist. I accepted the rebuke but Esmond was left with the idea that I was a fascist sympathizer (I heard this later from Oxford contacts) and I appear in Philip Toynbee's *Friends Apart* as 'Ledward of Charterhouse – no bloody good'.

Single-minded in his own actions, Esmond was intolerant of others' equivocations. Toynbee had found this out in the summer when he bowed out of Parton Street under a storm of obloquy. But Esmond's anger, as volatile as it was caustic, never boiled for long, and when the two boys met again in December there was no question of recrimination – 'He welcomed me without reproaches, and the warmth of his friendship reminded me that I felt much more than an alarmed respect. For Esmond could charm as well as bully, and he was loved as much as he was feared.'

Since leaving Parton Street in the summer, Toynbee had been confined to Ampleforth Abbey, where he began studying for an Oxford scholarship. Here, amidst the quietude of the Catholic cloisters, he had been thrown back upon his thoughts and these turned to the life he had briefly probed in June. 'It's hell', he wrote at the Abbey, 'to have wild oats all pressed down inside one. I know that I shall have to sow mine some day, and after that I may be the paragon I have to imitate now.'

Having won his scholarship, Toynbee was now keen to experience the kind of adventure he had promised himself during his months of enforced passivity. Esmond, always eager to encounter a fellow traveller, was a ready guide. 'We were perfectly agreed that what we needed was incident, action and experience for their own sake alone,' wrote Toynbee, 'and we set off to find them in the Corner House near Piccadilly Circus.' Esmond led the way, the eager novice tripped merrily behind.

The boys are in high spirits and ready for action. Two men proposition them. Esmond throws a bowl of sugar in their faces and a scuffle breaks out. They leave and head back to Esmond's room (now above a Greek restaurant in Shaftesbury Avenue), where he has a bottle of whisky. They are drunk, Esmond in violent mood, his companion in a bleary acquiescent stupor. They walk the streets shouting, upsetting dustbins, looking for trouble. Esmond hails a cab. 'Pimlico Road!'

Much banging and bell-ringing. No one appears. Esmond frenzied. Toynbee silent, possessed by a sobering thought : in the summer, while on holiday in Dieppe, he had visited Nellie and sympathized over her son's behaviour – a double cross which might, at any moment, come to light. A police car arrives. Nellie has panicked. She makes a charge. The boys are bundled into the car and taken to Bow Street Police Station, where they are separated and placed in cells. Toynbee has had his adventure – 'Esmond seldom failed in any task which he imposed upon himself or others.'

The *Daily Telegraph*, Monday 31 December 1934:

SCHOOLBOYS IN COURT

DRUNKENNESS CHARGE

ARRESTED AT 4.30 A.M.

Late on Saturday afternoon Theodore Philip Toynbee, 18, of St John's Wood, NW and another boy, aged 16, both described as scholars, appeared before Mr Hay Halkett at WESTMINSTER POLICE COURT charged with having been drunk and disorderly at Pimlico Road at 4.30 that morning. Both pleaded guilty and it was stated that the police surgeon had to be called to Toynbee. In answer to the magistrate Toynbee said he had been drinking whisky. He was allowed to write the name of his school.

'Disgraceful conduct,' said the magistrate, looking at the name of the school.

In fining Toynbee 6d and 10/6d costs, the magistrate said to the father [Professor Arnold Toynbee]: 'Take him away and give him a good talking-to and I should give him a good thrashing if I were you.'

It was stated that the other boy had given his parents a great deal of trouble.

The magistrate was handed a doctor's report, and after reading it said 'It is pretty bad.'

The boy's mother said that he was living on his own in Shaftesbury Avenue.

The magistrate: 'Don't you think you are as much to blame for a state of affairs like that? Do you expect a boy of 16 to behave himself alone in London?'

The mother: 'We have done all we could. He quite refuses to submit to any control. A little time back he returned and behaved well for a few weeks, and then went away again.'

The magistrate: 'This is the Communist.'

The boy was remanded to be dealt with at the juvenile court.

11
In Remand and Out of Bounds

The meals – bread and butter or bread and dripping – were inadequate, the work was monotonous, the atmosphere tense, and the inmates alternately anxious and depressed. These were the symptoms; the Ponton Road Remand Home's illness was rather more complex, as Esmond explained.

> The LCC Remand Home, as its name implies, is the residence for the most part of boys who are 'remanded in custody' for a few days, for a week, a fortnight, or a month. But these are not its only inmates. It is also the waiting-place for boys who have been sentenced to go to 'Approved Schools'.... The latter are overcrowded, and boys sometimes have to wait as long as three or four months before a vacancy can be found for them.... There are no young Anthony Trents – only petty and rather inefficient pilferers. 'Knockin' off a boike' was a common enough offence. There were also several who had committed the grave offence of being 'in want of care and protection'.

There were also the 'obvious "mental cases"'.

> They were teased mercilessly by the others who welcomed any such diversion, and they were cuffed about by the officers if they were slow in obeying orders. As 'cases' in the eyes of the magistrate, the superintendent, the psychologist, they, like everyone else, received individual attention. Inside we were all treated alike whether we were safe-breakers, house-breakers, bag-snatchers or just 'uncontrollables' – whether we had been up for immoral assault, or because we had nowhere else to go.

What emerges from Esmond's account of the Ponton Road institution is that it functioned not only as a remand home but as a long-term repository for young offenders and residual council-care children – a conclusion, incidentally, reached by the 1944 Committee of Inquiry, which recommended separate institutions for children under the age of eight, girls suffering from venereal disease, persons committed to approved schools, and persons under punitive detention. The Committee also recommended that more suitable and better-trained staff be employed in the homes and that the children and young persons be 'fully occupied with suitable activities' – a situation, according to the report, already in existence at Stanford House (Ponton Road's successor)* where the boys were 'most actively and contentedly employed at all sorts of work with their hands'.

At Ponton Road, Esmond noted, the only official activities, apart from keeping the place clean, were standing in line or marching up and down stairs. When not cleaning or drilling the boys spent their time 'moping', unless, of course (*pace* the 1944 report) they had official visitors to entertain. Esmond:

The greatest mockery of all was the 'inspection' that I once saw carried out. Four prosperous-looking individuals would be conducted around the building; I suppose they came from the LCC or the Home Office or some official body or other. I remember it was about three o'clock. We were most of us sitting about with nothing much to do, looking very depressed, obviously presenting a sight that was not very good for 'inspection'. Brusquely came the order:

'Look as if yer werkin'.' This was not so easy as it sounds. However, we managed, by unfolding clothes and folding them up again, by upsetting a stand of boots and putting them all back, by collecting up a lot of towels and pieces of soap and then redistributing them, to present a fair impression of industry.

'And see you look cheerful, too, or you'll hear about it afterwards.'

This was more difficult. One or two failed miserably in the attempt. They heard about it all right.

'I suppose', he wrote disingenuously, 'one could not blame the officers for losing their tempers often. They had an unpleasant enough time of it themselves. But they were not very inspiring people. And their fists provided the easiest enforcement of their orders.'

'Cuffs' were the order of the day at Ponton Road, they hung menacingly over the work, indigestibly over meals, and with providential certainty over the Sunday service, a spectacle described by Esmond in all its burlesque detail:

* The Ponton Road Remand Home was closed down in 1936.

... there was the service on Sundays – conducted by two earnest but bleak-looking young men, with stiff white collars, and very correct striped trousers. Prayers for meekness and humility would be interrupted by such un-christian utterances as : 'Stop that there, will yer ? Or I'll give you one to remember. If anyone wants to start fighting, let 'em come out 'ere, and I'll give someone a sock under the chin'....

Then at the end of the 'service', the missionary would come in and 'say a few words'. A man of about fifty, short and smug, his harangue would consist at first of a boost for himself. He, it appeared, had had the Call at the age of fifteen. Since that time, he had been drawing slowly closer to God. Others could follow where he had led. The two young men at his side were shining examples of devotion to God's cause. Should *we* not follow them. The faces of the latter showed sickly smiles. We remained impassive.... We were encouraged to stand out from the common rut. (The speaker raised his voice and his eloquence grew.) We must not heed the mockery of our companions. Was there one boy present who had the courage to stand out, and say that he was prepared to follow Jesus ?

A pause ... it was apparent that he was no longer speaking in metaphorical language.

Was there no-one? Was there not one boy who was prepared to stand up for Jesus ?

Two bag-snatchers rose leisurely at the back. The rest of the room began to follow suit. Most of us, it appeared, were prepared to stand up for Jesus. Rumour had it that refreshment of some kind was provided as a reward for the faithful.

There was such an atmosphere of degradation and depression about the place, thought Esmond, that not even the most impervious of residents could escape its grip.

'Oi ain't no blinkin' toff,' one of the boys had remarked, 'but oi reckon oim a bit more refoined than this lot.' It was a universal sentiment : 'Each one of us felt he must be a little better than the rest.'

Esmond spent eighteen days in the remand home before being released on a year's probation. His internment had seemed like eighteen weeks, he wrote ; even so he had remained 'fairly confident' of the outcome. 'My parents had been most kind about the whole case, and it seemed I should be allowed to return home.' (How many of his fellow boarders enjoyed such certainty ?)

In the event, however, Esmond did not return home but, pressed by his wealthy second cousin, Dorothy Allhusen, moved into her country house at Milton Lilbourne, Wiltshire; his only orders to relax and take the country air.

Mrs Henry Allhusen, 'Cousin Dorothy', was renowned for her hospitality. The daughter of society hostess Lady St Helier, she had continued in her mother's tradition and had become known as the first Edwardian hostess to introduce the week-end house-party. 'Do come Saturday to Monday.' Such notables as Somerset Maugham, Lord Beaverbrook, Sir George Alexander (the actor-manager) and the up-and-coming Winston Churchill had often heeded the call. All were made welcome; few could have been treated better than the sixteen-year-old Esmond.

Cousin Dorothy – a widow – enjoyed all shapes and sizes of company, but she reserved a special affection for her wayward relative. He was treated like a son, a second son, the first having died in childhood. For his own part, Esmond complied totally with the mother/son role-play, settling into the country house routine, magnanimously allowing his elder cousin to fuss over him. The remand home experience had not curbed his prodigality but it had instilled, at least for the time being, a healthy respect for home comforts.

Set in the heart of the English countryside, Havering House offered a salubrious atmosphere, good food and tranquillity, and this, for the moment, was exactly what the doctor, or rather, the publisher, had ordered. For in the autumn of 1934 Esmond and Giles had begun writing a book about their schooldays. Esmond's account, on ice since the New Year, was now resumed and, with no disturbances, save Cousin Dorothy's enquiries as to what he would like for his dinner, finished within the month. Life at Havering House was not all work, however. Eager to have the young man's company as long as possible, Dorothy Allhusen made sure that there was always plenty of young company on hand to distract him from unappetizing thoughts of the outside world.

Almost every week-end there was a house-party at the Wiltshire home, where Esmond, a king in exile, was presented with a selection of old and new faces for his amusement. One of the new party, yet another of Dorothy's cousins, was the twenty-two-year-old Peter Nevile. Despite the six-year gap in their ages, the two young men struck up an immediate friendship, and this continued when, in May, Esmond returned to bed-sit London. 'It was as if there was no age difference at all,' Peter Nevile has observed, 'in fact in many respects I felt the younger.' But what really sealed the friendship, and kept it intact despite many a hot-tempered argument, was the younger man's 'great charm':

I remember arriving at Havering House for a visit and walking into the drawing room to surprise Esmond reading a book – it could only have been the second or third time we had met. 'Peter, how nice to see you', he beamed, and jumped up and clenched my hand. This effusiveness was infectious and completely undermined my own natural aloofness. He had that wonderful ability – found in so few people – of making one feel the most interesting, most important person in the world.

This winning charm did not blind Nevile to other aspects of Esmond's character: 'He was excitable, unpredictable; he had a quick, furious temper.'

It was 6 May 1935: Jubilee Day, and all London was sinking in copious bunting and sugar icing. Romilly and Nevile were not among the merrymakers, they had gone down to Lymington for the day to sail Nevile's fourteen-foot boat along the coast.

The sea was rough, but they set out, Esmond eager to splice the main-brace and the like. Yet, despite his enthusiasm, he was not at all the 'able' seaman, and this fact soon became apparent to his friend: 'The sea was getting rougher and I was nervous lest we capsize. I began ordering Esmond around, obviously too forcefully for his liking, because he suddenly turned on me and said he was not going to do "another bloody thing" and he didn't "give a damn" whether we sank or not. He was incensed with anger. I managed to bring the boat to shore without his help.'

Back on dry land a heated argument broke out and this was in full flame when the two boarded a bus for London. The conductor appeared. Nevile asked for a single. '"You're going to have to pay for me too," Esmond snapped. "I'm broke." "That's your problem", I said. He was turfed off the bus in a raging temper. I dreaded our next meeting. Thankfully, the storm had blown over. He could fly into a temper at the drop of a hat, but he could equally quickly forgive and forget. He never bore a grudge.'

In the late spring Esmond moved into a small flat in Bury Street, wc1 ('a different room ...' wrote Philip Toynbee, 'but in spirit, in essence the same room ... the same drab but delightful sitting room somewhere though irrelevantly in the neighbourhood of the British Museum'.) The new place was unfurnished, Esmond fitting it out within a week with bed, table and chairs, and brown cord carpet bought from a nearby shop run by the blind. After everything had been delivered Esmond's landlady noticed several large chips in the stairs wall.

'The delivery men, I'm afraid', said the tenant apologetically.

'Never mind', replied the other benignly. 'It must have been them with the poorly sight.'

Peter Nevile believes that while Esmond was anxious to give the blind his trade, this was as much a practical as a charitable act: 'The blind gave excellent credit facilities, he didn't have to pay up for several months. This impressed Esmond, he probably thought he could get away with it.'

T.C.Worsley, who observed Esmond both at Wellington College and at the Bookshop, has written of him: 'He was not an attractive personality, a tough, ruthless, wholly unscrupulous, iron-hearted youth ... I never like Esmond though I could not help admiring the spirit of I-care-for-nobody which gave him such a single-minded will.' This was the verdict reached by a number of Esmond's contemporaries and many of his brother's friends. Gavin Ewart:

When I was seventeen I bought some records of Wagner; things like 'The Ride of the Valkyries', 'Prelude to Tristan', etc., recorded by the LSO on twelve inch 78s. One day in my room in London with Giles and Esmond, I said I was getting fed-up of the records and asked Giles if he wanted them. I had hardly finished saying this when Esmond chimed in, 'I'd like them, I'd like them. Give them to me.' So I did. It was only later that I realized it was not because he was interested in music at all, which would have been Giles's reason for accepting them, but because he simply wanted to sell them to make some money.... I think the effect he had upon me – and others – was that of someone who was very good value and entertaining and lively to talk to, but, at the same time, someone who was totally ruthless, not to be trusted. Giles was a much more sympathetic person, just so painfully indecisive.

In November 1934 Dylan Thomas (whom the poet George Barker has described as 'looking liker to a runaway schoolboy than Esmond Romilly') had arrived on the Parton Street scene, and formed his own equally critical opinion of Romilly. It was not Esmond's unscrupulousness which nettled the young Welsh poet, he too being an adherent of the end-justifies-the-means approach to living, but the 'bogus' working-classness of his left-wing stand.

Since I've been in London [wrote Thomas to a friend in February 1935] I've come into contact on a number of occasions with intellectual communism and communists. They are: Norton, editor of the *Daily*

Worker, Gorbin, proprietor of the youthful *Notoriety*, Esmond
Romilly, editor of the schoolboy communist monthly 'Out of Bounds',
and with all the pseudo-revolutionaries who shall be unmentionable.
I dislike all of them. Not so much as persons; most of them I assure
you would be quite kind to dumb animals; but as revolutionaries
and as communists or, born in wealthy middle-class or upper middle-
class homes, educated at expensive prep. schools, public schools and
universities, they have no idea of what they priggishly call 'the class
struggle', and no contact at all with either any of the real motives
or the real protagonists of the class struggle. They are bogus from
skull to navel.

Such criticism, levelled innumerable times against the poets, intellectuals and middle-class trendies who filled out the Communist Party
ranks during the mid-thirties,* is in many cases a valid one; not in
all cases, however, as Esmond himself noted. There was also 'the
genuine "committee man", the hard-working Marxist student, who dup-
licates leaflets in the early hours of the morning and eats a bun and
coffee for lunch'. Not that Esmond was in any sense a 'committee man',
but then neither was he Thomas' mountebank. Certainly he had at
one time spouted 'class struggle' cant as prodigiously and as glibly
as the next, but his stand, if not his ideas, had become more original
since then. He was now at pains to deny his commitment to anything,
the Communist Party included. Philip Toynbee (who joined the CP
on entering Oxford):

Of Esmond I soon despaired. He had watched communists from a
position close beside them and he never for a moment wavered in
his determination to remain a free-booting ally on the flank. His
attitude to my role as an unbending communist was one of teasing
amusement ... he was never, in any sense, a 'contact', and even if
I had succeeded in my half-hearted attempts on his independence
it is likely that the Party would have refused to accept him as a
member. Good communists always spoke of him with the shuddering
distaste of a nanny referring to the rough street-urchin playmate
of her charges.

By Easter the Romillys' book was in galleys. To celebrate this event,
and the forthcoming publication, Esmond, Giles and Peter Nevile spent

---

* Ironically, the middle-class youth involvement in the CP came at the Depression's
ebb, when its working-class support was waning. See John Stevenson and Chris Cooke,
The Slump, Jonathan Cape, 1977.

a week-end in Paris, where, in the spring sunshine, they read over and corrected the proofs. Peter Nevile recalls, 'We stayed in the Hôtel des Maréchaux in the rue de Moscou (which amused Dorothy Allhusen a great deal). The weather was very good and on a couple of evenings we sat outside a café at the Rond-Point drinking champagne cocktails. These were incredibly cheap, about 1s 6d each. We felt very worldly.' This cosmopolitan mood continued throughout a visit to Pigalle but was then shattered, at least for Esmond, when, coming home, a prostitute accosted him with, 'Hullo *bébé*, you want to come with me?' He flushed purple with embarrassment and rage, not because of the offer but because of the *bébé*. It was a stark reminder that, however worldly he felt, he was still only sixteen years old.

Out of Bounds: The Education of Giles Romilly and Esmond Romilly was published in June, and received some very favourable reviews. Even the Romillys' old enemy, the *Daily Mail*, had to concede that 'the young authors lack neither brains nor literary ability'. Indeed, most people who read the book, outside the 'Old Gang' faction, were impressed, not only by the two authors' talent but also by their objectivity. In the opinion of Mr Raymond Mortimer, writing for the *New Statesman*, 'a candid and surprisingly fair book' – a subject for 'an enchanting film'. Whether Nellie Romilly would have agreed with this analysis is a moot point. The publication may have given her the opportunity, not that she ever needed one, to sing the praises of her two brilliant boys, but what about those extracts from her letters? And worse, Esmond had also included an account of the meeting with Peter Crew and the half-crown donation to the hunger march. Still, of one thing she could rest assured, her husband was never likely to read the book and discover the treachery.

Out of Bounds sold well and went, in the same month, to a second edition. It came out at a time when the public-school system was under debate and this helped secure its success. Only the year before Graham Greene had edited *The Old School*, a collection of essays in which various literary figures discussed their secondary education. In his introduction Greene wrote, 'I regard this book rather as a premature memorial.... For there can be small doubt that the system which the book represents is doomed.' Hear! Hear! said the Romillys. But for once the novelist's insight was to fail him.

In June, timed to benefit from the book's publicity, the fourth and last issue of the magazine 'Out of Bounds' was released. The issue contained articles on old favourites: corporal punishment, co-education, and the OTC (the last by Giles who, for some reason, preferred this subject to an account of his months in Nazi Germany). It also contained

'An Open Letter to Freshmen' from the Federation of Student Societies, which began like a public information broadsheet and ended thus:

> You who are going to University have three paths before you. You may accept everything unquestionably and become a blind and philistine hanger-on of the present decaying social system. You may run down some delusive road of escape only to find at the end a sign board with big letters – 'Man must eat before he can think.' Or you may think for yourself and take your place among those who break through academic seclusion in order to destroy the rotten society that exists, and build a new and better world to take its place.

More disturbing still, at least to the mother and maiden aunt section of the readership, was the article on 'Masturbation', in which the writer, a doctor (or was it Esmond?), attacked some of the outrageous myths perpetuated by public-school housemasters and headmasters. 'To suggest that offspring can be affected,' writes the doctor, 'that lives are shattered, or that any blood is lost, is a wicked lie. Nor is there any truth in the madness ramp.' He goes on to discuss *Healthy Boyhood*, a booklet published in 1909, the tenets of which still had credence within the public schools, quoting the author:

> The private parts of the body are closely connected to the spine and the spine is closely connected to the brain. It follows, therefore, that if you meddle improperly with these parts your brain will suffer; and you will be unable to concentrate ... Should this be your case, if you have already been led astray, then kneel down as soon as you have read this, at the latest before you lie down tonight, and make a frank confession to God of what you have done.

In conclusion, the doctor writes, 'If Masters genuinely want to help a boy about masturbation they cannot start better than by recounting to him all their own early struggles. It should be pointed out that some form of auto-eroticism is absolutely inevitable except in a person with complete sexual anaesthesia, a very rare psychological condition.'

'Out of Bounds' No. 4 may have raised some eyebrows, it did not cause a sensation, and it would have taken nothing short of this to revive Esmond's flagging interest. There would be no issue five, and although a fifth number was advertised it is unlikely that Esmond ever seriously considered its production. 'Out of Bounds' was played out. 'The magazine died a natural death,' wrote its editor. There was no remorse. Esmond was too wrapped up in his new venture to mourn the old.

In May Esmond and a Parton Street friend, Roger Roughton, had opened up an agency for public-school news. 'Our idea', as Esmond explains it, 'was to become headquarters to all the interesting – and deprecatory – news about different schools all over the country, and sell this to the daily press.' The two partners set up office at 102 Shoe Lane, a cubby-hole adjacent to the new and grandiose *Daily Express* building, and paid 5s to be registered as 'Educational News and Features'. Forever sanguine, Esmond had placed £25 into the venture (his advance from Hamish Hamilton for *Out of Bounds*). This sum was matched by his partner, for whom money-wasting had become a full-time occupation.

Roughton, a minor poet and major dabbler, had recently inherited a substantial sum of money which he gave the impression of wanting to squander as fast and furiously as possible. Some of this money now went into 'Educational News and Features', but this was just a drop in the ocean compared with the sums he poured regularly into the CP and the even greater amounts sunk into a series of continental driving sprees.

On the surface self-confident and blasé, underneath Roughton was a tangled skein of confusion and contradiction. He was never certain whether he was looking for order or running away from it, a dilemma emblematic of his 1936 journal *Contemporary Poetry and Prose*, which tried to fuse Marxist polemic and surrealist fantasy. The magazine folded after nine issues, Roughton's Party politics finally getting the better of him.

> Cased in the careful armour that you wore
> Of wit and nonchalance, through which
> Few quizzed the concealed countenance of fear,
> You waited daily for the sky to fall.*

The sky fell in June 1941, when the twenty-five-year-old pacifist gassed himself in a Dublin flat.

Contemporary Poetry and Prose did achieve some success, albeit in recondite circles, the Romilly–Roughton enterprise (not their last) collapsed after three fallow months – a lame footnote to a page whose first and last word was 'incident'.

Reading Chronicle, Friday 28 June 1935:

**PROTEST MEETING ON
OTC 'INCIDENTS'**

* David Gascoyne, 'An Elegy – R.R. 1916–41'.

There was a further sequel to the recent pacifist propaganda 'incidents' at Reading School when, on Wednesday evening, a crowded meeting was held at the Labour Hall, Minster Street, Reading.

The meeting passed a strong resolution calling on organizations friendly to the cause of peace to request a full apology from the headmaster (Mr G.H.Keaton) and the governors for their 'unconstitutional action', and asking for an assurance 'that freedom of expression will be guaranteed to all the school'.

... Councillor J.Taylor took the chair and those supporting him included Mr J.E.Boulting* (representing the dismissed student, Deryk Davis), Dr S.Clifford (representing the Reading Peace Council), Mr Esmond Romilly (the young editor of 'Out of Bounds') and Councillor H.V.Kershey (representing the Labour Group on the Town Council)....

John Boulting:

The Reading School incident – a whetstone on which both the right and left combatants sharpened their swords – began when Deryk Davis, a sixth former, myself and two other Old Boys, Archibald Francis and John Hall, planned an attack on the annual Reading School field day. Davis and I had written this pamphlet 'Sanity or Savagery' which we intended to have dropped over the school cricket field as the official, a Major General Fortune, was inspecting the troops. This backfired when our pilot got the wind up, leaving Davis with the unenviable job of placing these highly emotional documents in all the school lockers on the morning of the parade. For this he was promptly given the sack.

Equally promptly the headmaster summoned the three Old Boys to the school and asked them to sign a statement in which they recognized they had no right to attack any institution in the school and apologized to the school governors, the headmaster and the boys for their action. 'Naturally,' Mr Boulting continued, 'we refused to sign this piece of impertinence, and immediately released the whole story to the Press. Both the *Guardian* and the *Star* gave space to it and questions were asked in the Commons. Flushed with success we called a meeting – Esmond Romilly, who phoned us to ask what was going on – was invited to speak.' The *Reading Chronicle*:

---

* John Boulting, along with brother Roy, was later to make his name in the British Film Industry producing larger-budget entertainments.

Mr Romilly, who was at Wellington, said he was most interested in that case because for the last year and a half he had been among those conducting agitation against the OTC in a large number of schools. He had no hesitation in saying that any headmaster, when he talked of the primary objects of the OTC as character formation and so forth, was being a hypocrite and a humbug. (Hear! hear!) The OTC in the majority of schools was 'entirely voluntary'. Membership in most was 99%, and that meant that the headmasters used their authority and every possible weapon in their power to sway boys to join.... The speaker mentioned that he had put anti-war leaflets in the Chapel hymn books at Wellington College on Armistice Day. (Applause.)

John Boulting:

The meeting was packed, and gained a lot of publicity which undoubtedly persuaded the headmaster to allow Davis to return to school. Esmond spoke for about half an hour, very quickly, with enormous power; highly persuasive. He got a terrific reception. Later, we went to a nearby pub and he entertained us for the rest of the evening with an account of his earlier 'Out of Bounds' experiences.

And so, after eighteen months of frenetic public-school activity, the 'Out of Bounds' chapter had come to a close. Esmond was barely seventeen, equal to anything and qualified for nothing. The question was: what could he possibly do next?

12
The Fine Art of Salesmanship

Having been educated up to the school certificate stage at a famous public school (Wellington College), having left rather rapidly and suddenly, and decided it was preferable to support myself on my own labour, having no specialized knowledge of any kind, and not being troubled with an overquantity of honesty or scrupulousness, it was inevitable that I should soon be selling somebody something. I belong to that very large class of unskilled labourers with a public-school accent.

Esmond Romilly, Boadilla

Esmond had become a silk stocking salesman, plying his wares at all the prosperous-looking houses on the road to Kent at one shilling a pair commission.

It was a physically taxing job, but one at which (having bought himself a hat) he was 'not altogether a failure'. Apart from an abundance of confidence and natural enthusiasm, Esmond was also blessed with that never-say-die attitude which is the mark of the successful door-to-door salesman. He was an actor too, and the new role afforded him any amount of scope for indulging his chameleon tendencies. 'As a commercial traveller', wrote Philip Toynbee, 'Esmond had, of course, developed his own unique method. Confronted at the door by a resolute parlour-maid, he would say "Captain Romilly" with a large hint of question in his voice. When he was told that nobody of that name was living in the house, he would push proudly through the door, tap his seventeen-year-old chest, and say: "I am Captain Romilly."'

It was in this trilbied guise that Esmond turned up at Christ Church College, Oxford, one November afternoon to visit his friend. The visit was part social, part business – Esmond wanted information on the girls' colleges, where he hoped to sell the stockings. 'It was impossible not to admire him,' wrote Toynbee, 'or not to feel shame-faced envy for a life so different from my own.' And yet, the undergraduate was not altogether at ease in the other's company. For one thing he was still smarting over Esmond's acerbic letter of the previous spring. This had come in reply to his own epistle in which he expatiated on the need for finding a new, 'nobler and more generous political faith' than Communism. Having just spent three weeks immersed in the realities of life at Ponton Road, Esmond was in no mood to read the thoughts of Chairman St Francis, and he had scathingly said so. 'I was bullshitting,' admits Toynbee. 'Esmond hated bullshit.' The letter was not, however, the only reason for Toynbee's agitation.

'Esmond represents rotten meat to you,' his mother had told him after the December drinking episode. He was amused by the remark, amused too by Esmond announcing himself over the phone as 'the rotten meat merchant, interesting consignment of old lights here for you, Mr Toynbee'. But there was truth in the statement and it irked. In Esmond's brusque and boisterous company Toynbee's own, more flexible character was bent into submission. 'Esmond depressed me a great deal', he wrote of the November meeting, 'because I kept adapting myself to him and losing myself.' Toynbee knew he would always lose himself when with Esmond; that the two met less than 'one quarter of one per cent' of Esmond's life, one surmises, is as much due to this realization as to the exigencies of Esmond's nomadic existence.

The silk stocking racket lasted two months. By December, Esmond had moved into the trade press, selling advertising space for a small London events diary.

'A good man can sell a bad proposition, but a bad man can't sell a good proposition' was Esmond's employer's maxim, and by his own standards Mr Girton was indeed a 'good man'. 'When I first went to work for him', Esmond wrote, 'I was – like everyone – very much impressed; I believed I would soon be making £500 a year, then £1,000 a year; the fact that for the present I was to work on commission only, for his profit, made no impression on my mind.' Nevertheless, the 'kind of selling where you ring up people's secretaries to know when you may call, and give someone lunch when they've advertised in your paper is much more fun than ringing doorbells in Kent'. It proved more rewarding too.

In March 1936 John Grierson launched *World Film News* with Hans Feld as editor, Marian Grierson as sub-editor and Esmond Romilly as advertising manager. Esmond's experience with the London events diary had gained him the job, that and his friendship with Lulu Watts, the WFN secretary. The post was nevertheless no sinecure. Like everyone else who worked for John Grierson Esmond was expected to perform at 110 per cent capacity.

Since the much-acclaimed documentary *Drifters* had been released in 1929, John Grierson had become a major force in the documentary movement, and a guru in the eyes of his young employees at the GPO film unit. Harry Watt, one of these young acolytes, explains the Grierson policy: 'He was trying to present the true image of the working man, not as the gross caricatures shown in the commercial cinema of bubbly gardeners or happy-go-lucky drunks. He wanted to change this snobbishness, to put the working man on the screen.... We believed in the Grierson policy totally. We thought it a new art form.' And the new art form needed an organ. This was the purpose of *World Film News*, to combine documentary criticism with that of the commercial cinema and thereby attract greater attention to the documentary movement. The magazine had its problems from the outset as Basil Wright, another member of the film unit, explains: 'We thought in our madness that we could make a going concern and remain independent. Grierson refused to give editorial advertising, and this is where most of the money comes from in film journals. We were always in debt.'

Esmond enjoyed his work at WFN, at least at first. He had imbibed the Grierson air of enthusiasm, and shared his boss's visions of success. The work was fun too, and through it he met many personalities from the film and literary worlds. Grierson had a flair for co-opting the skilled and the talented for next to nothing: among them W.H. Auden who, along with Benjamin Britten and Basil Wright, had recently completed the successful documentary *Night Mail*.

> This is the night mail crossing the border
> Bringing the cheque and the postal order....

Auden, already regarded as a leading exponent of his generation's discontent, was much admired by Esmond, who now took the opportunity to engage the poet in literary discussion. Auden suggested that they continue the riveting conversation later in his flat. Esmond, delighted, readily accepted, only to find that the poet had something more physical in mind. A Romilly rage ensued, in which he tossed all of Auden's clothes out of the window before locking the cowering figure in his own room. This is the story that gained currency at any rate. Part of it, at least, may be apocryphal. It seems unlikely that Esmond would have been so agitated about being propositioned: it could hardly have been an unusual event within his circle of acquaintances. Perhaps, however, he regarded the incident as a slight to his intelligence, for he was more sensitive than he generally allowed to his lack of formal education.

The Auden incident was not the only reason for neophytic disillusionment. Esmond was also working himself into an impassioned state against Grierson; his wrath, stifled for the present, finding vent many months later in the first pages of his book *Boadilla*:

The head of the unit was well known in Wardour Street and in Bloomsbury. I will call him MacIntosh. In the small circle of his employees and admirers he had assumed an almost superhuman position. Like Sir Oswald Mosley he was known as 'The Leader' or 'The Chief' ... I believe there are numbers of young men who long to work all day, carrying heavy cameras or opening doors, so that they may have a chance to learn the methods of the Chief.

All this I learned in the course of my first week: I learned it from the reverential way in which his name was mentioned; from the way in which faces lit up at a word of commendation from the great man or clouded with dismay at a rebuke. Mr MacIntosh had definite opinions about everything, and was at no loss to express them; these opinions were faithfully taken up by his disciples. Like another great man, he was often inclined to deliver a parable. A usual scene would present the Leader at the head of a table with some of the faithful; all would be silent, waiting for the Leader to speak. He would pick on a paragraph in the evening paper, read it out aloud, deliver a pungent comment, and then general conversation could begin.

The Leader was not only brilliant, he prided himself on being tough; that is to say, he would be ready to engage in talk with anyone over a pint of beer in 'public bars as well as the saloons'. When their work would take his unit – say to film the life of a little fishing village – he was the one to get together with the local characters. Like all great men, like all dictators, the Leader had his critics. There were those unkind enough to suggest that he used sometimes to run fast up three flights of stairs to give his face the right expression of bustle and important work on hand.

To Esmond, Grierson represented bullshit, and he inwardly railed against it. But as Basil Wright points out, 'He would have known Grierson only as a whirlwind that appeared in the office, put the fear of God into everyone, then disappeared. Grierson must have been very irritating to a person in Esmond's position, nevertheless he was not in any position to judge him.' Yet Romilly's criticism did not arise solely out of a dislike for Grierson's personality. He was equally critical of his policy.

114

Forsythe Hardy, Grierson's biographer, writes of his subject, 'His determination to see things only his way ... his impatience with opposing opinion (for him the unimaginative) was often understandably resented. He was often able to forget his own failures.... Others, whose eyes were not so firmly on tomorrow, did not forget so easily.' Esmond would have countered that it was Grierson's eyes that were not so firmly fixed on tomorrow.

My worst moment [he wrote in *Boadilla*] came when I realized a few of the economic facts of publishing. I reached the conclusion that the *Film Review* would always cost somebody a few thousands a year if we went on trying to launch it in a big way. I knew who would pay all right, and I liked him.* So I wrote a long report to prove that the paper had no chance of success.

The reply from all the disciples was unanimous: 'Nothing the Chief has ever put his hand to has ever failed!' Illusions of supermen were vanishing fast.

Esmond had been working for *World Film News* for four months when the Spanish Civil War broke out on 18 July 1936. At the time Toynbee was spending a few days with him in his Bury Street flat. The two read the news out together over a hurried breakfast, before Esmond dashed off to No. 9 Oxford Street, the WFN offices. 'These offices of his,' wrote Toynbee, 'these necessary bread-winning occupations, always made me feel that I was less grown-up than he was, more frivolous, pampered and irresponsible, and Esmond, of course, did everything that he could to underline this difference between us. Far from being allowed to think that I had some advantage over him in my continued education, he convinced me that to be an undergraduate was to be something childish and outmoded.' Or was it just sour grapes? It is indeed probable that at the time Esmond was more than a little envious of his friend, who, as an emissary of the British Student Party, was about to attend a series of CP conferences on the Continent. Meanwhile he was to continue in a position, which, despite its grand title, was turning out to be little more than that of a glorified office boy.

Esmond was a small fish at *World Film News*, and this, it must be contended, had irked him as much as, if not more than, the realization that the magazine was sentenced to an early death. Like his famous

* A reference to Basil Wright, who put up £3,000 to launch the magazine. *World Film News* folded in November 1938.

uncle, he had a resolute confidence in his own opinions and was never at peace while these were blowing ineffectually about in the wilderness.

In the summer of 1936, Morris Carstairs, later Vice-Chancellor of York University, then an undergraduate at Edinburgh, was spending his vacation as a summer help at *World Film News*. Carstairs had no high opinion of Romilly, his criticisms being much the same as those directed by Esmond against Grierson, namely that 'he had a considerable measure of arrogance, self-centredness and intolerance of the opinions of others (characteristics that we Scottish day-school students attributed to the public school English)'. Although neither paid much attention to the other, Carstairs noted that Romilly 'seemed moody, at times petulant, and in general thoroughly dissatisfied with the job he was doing ... there was a feeling of bottled-up energy waiting for an opportunity to explode'.

Basil Wright tells of the explosion:

I was in the office one afternoon when Esmond appeared looking very pale. I asked him what he wanted. 'Basil, I'm terribly sorry about this, but I've just knocked Hans Feld [the editor] down.' He had had an argument with Feld about something and had knocked him out. A great crisis took place and Esmond was made to apologise. I sympathised with him. Feld was a second-rate editor and must have been very annoying to work with – he left soon after this incident, under pressure.

Esmond remained with WFN but began looking, half-heartedly, for another job. Nothing turned up. There was the night-club idea but that had to be rejected when he realized that 'however much could be achieved on optimism, bluff and credit, a solid capital of £100 at least was vital.... A pity, as I had the whole thing planned from evasion of the law to the arrangement of the tables and position of the band.'

It was the beginning of October. The Civil War in Spain had been in progress nearly three months, his work at *World Film News* for over six months – the longest period he would ever maintain one job; both war and work preoccupied him. 'If this were a political book', wrote Esmond in *Boadilla*, 'I would explain what I think about the Spanish struggle, which would be reason enough for my wanting to take part in it.... But I do not think anybody ever does anything just for one clear-cut, logical (in this case – political) motive. However strongly I sympathized with the cause of the Spanish people, no doubt

116

Nellie Romilly in 1914, the year before her marriage

Bertram Romilly in 1915

LEFT TO RIGHT: Giles, Sarah Churchill, Esmond (with daisy chain) and Randolph Churchill, Chartwell, 1922

Esmond at Newlands, July 1927

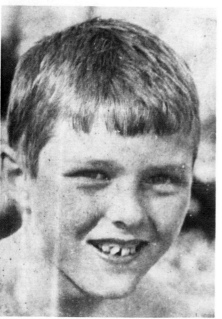

Esmond outside the Nevile
family house, summer 1935

Giles in Austria, 1935

Philip Toynbee at Oxford

Peter Nevile on holiday in southern France, Easter 1937

Esmond and Decca in their room at the Hôtel des Basques, Bayonne, April 1937

At Ascain, near St Jean de Luz, April 1937

OPPOSITE
ABOVE: On the beach near Calvi, summer 1938

BELOW: Staged shot for the *Washington Post*'s 'Baby Blue Bloods in Hobohemia' series, Washington, autumn 1939

Esmond and Decca at the
Roma Bar, Miami, December
1939

Esmond with his fellow
Observers, Canada, spring
1941

if my circumstances in London had been completely satisfactory, I should have gone no further than sympathy.'

Esmond's circumstances were not satisfactory and had not been so for some time. Spain provided yet another escape from the pedestrian and the routine; yet another trip into the 'other world' – not the world of the working class, although at one time the two had been synonymous, but the world of adventure. As for the altruistic reasons, Esmond was careful to play these down. Altruism smacked of emotion, smacked of sentiment. Esmond was shy of such disclosures and would almost prefer to appear callous than to express his inner thoughts – a reaction perhaps to his mother's excessive emotionalism. 'I guess we would refer to Esmond as being "macho"', says Stephen Spender, and although this image was never consciously maintained, it was still necessary from time to time to erect a dam against the more fluid elements within.

All was settled – thus were Esmond's plans made – he would leave for Spain on Saturday 19 October. He gave a week's notice at *World Film News* and on Saturday 12 October threw a last party in his Bury Street flat. Not that any of the guests were aware of its significance. Esmond was careful to inform no one of his intentions, 'for fear I should be ignominiously sent back'.

For the party Esmond had lined up an impressive array of young literary figures, among whom were Arthur Calder-Marshall and Cyril Connolly. The tall, wan David Gascoyne was also present, his own star very much in the ascendant after organizing (with others) the 1936 International Surrealist Exhibition and explaining in *A Short History of Surrealism* what it was all about. Esmond had visited the exhibition several times during the summer, its iconoclastic statements appealing to his own sense of the outrageous. Yet hard-line Communists had branded the event as decadent and élitist, and Gascoyne, a member of the CP, received much criticism over his strong surrealist leanings. Roger Roughton, another Party member, was exposed to similar abuse. His surrealist journal *Contemporary Poetry and Prose* had been running since May, and for six issues the young man, like a condemned heretic, had been feverishly denying devil-worship. Nevertheless, both Roughton and Gascoyne remained in the Party – such is the need for a religion – and Gascoyne's diary entry for 12 October records his attendance at a 'street-corner meeting in Twickenham' before going to a party at Esmond Romilly's.

Gascoyne stayed the night at Esmond's flat, and he and Esmond went to Sunday lunch at the Tottenham Court Road Corner House. In spite of the fact that he himself was going to Barcelona to do some propaganda work on behalf of the ILP, Gascoyne makes no mention of a conversation on the war. Holding firm to his resolution to silence, Esmond was obviously avoiding any reference to the conflict.

Sometime during the next week Esmond auctioned off his few items of furniture, the money, added to his last week's wages, bringing his travelling allowance to a princely £9. With this tucked 'safely' into his top pocket and with a few items contained within a haversack at his side, the eighteen-year-old boarded a train at Victoria Station and set off towards his war.

13
Spain

What's your proposal? To build the just city? I will
I agree. Or is it the suicide pact, the romantic
     Death? Very well, I accept, for
I am your choice, your decision. Yes, I am Spain.

                W. H. AUDEN, 'Spain'

'They clung like burrs to the long expresses that lurch/Through the unjust lands,' wrote Auden of his Civil War volunteers. Esmond's journey, less animated, was equally uncomfortable. 'My main memory of the journey', wrote Esmond – he had bought a bicycle in Dieppe and was pedalling towards Marseilles – 'is of the excessive cold of cycling at night.' Between Chartres and Orleans he had even considered turning back, but had drunk three or four brandies instead 'and felt marvellously drunk and warm and ready to go on for ever'.

The euphoria passed. Twenty-four hours later the cyclist was both cold and broke, the contents of his jacket – which, besides 600 francs, included his passport, Labour Party card and letters to facilitate his passage – lying somewhere on the road between Valence and Orange. The loss, a timely reminder of his practical deficiencies – the jacket had been carelessly draped over the bike's handlebars – went unheeded. He pushed on for Marseilles, covering the last 190 kilometres in one impassioned sitting.

Esmond remained in Marseilles a week before securing a passage on the *Mar Caspio* – a Spanish liner shuttling volunteers to Republican-held Valencia. On arriving in the French port he had just two francs in his pocket, but had quickly located a Catholic charity organization where – with Marseilles' other down-and-outs – he was able to spend a week free of charge.

The prospect of finding a boat bound for the Republic had looked bleak. For three days Esmond trod the foul docklands scanning the sleeping vessels for a glimpse of the red, yellow and purple ensign of the Republic, or skimming through the lists of incoming and outgoing vessels. But there were no Spanish arrivals and, with the exception of one tramp steamer bound for Rotterdam, no one was hiring hands. Rotterdam? He had almost considered signing on. Marseilles was no place to be without a sou.

'We passed a rough-looking sailors' bar. He fumbled in his pocket and then hurriedly pressed a two-franc piece in my hand: "Here, buy you sandwich, yes?" as he propelled me toward the bar, stepped away himself, seeming to want to show he was in a different class from its patrons.' Esmond had been in Marseilles a whole mendicant week when he ran into the little Frenchman. The man had approached him while he was eyeing the contents of a pâtisserie window and with much flourish had presented him with a bag of coconut macaroons. He was a friendly type, solicitous; Esmond told him of a strange incident which had occurred earlier that same day, when, standing on a street corner, he had been approached by a man who asked him to deliver a parcel to a nearby store and tell the shopkeeper to go to the devil. This he did, and earned himself two francs. The man had told him to meet him later if he was in need of further employment. He was killing time before the meeting when he bumped into his present companion.

My story sent him off into a torrent of words and chuckling: 'What sort zis man be, you know? No, p'raps he want zee boy, yes. Zey have much of zees type in zees town; and zey have men who get zee boy for zee rich one, or maybe it for zee Arabs.' Here followed a long description of the various tastes and attractions of Marseilles, with any amount of innuendo and personal inquiry thrown in. I began to think I had been unwise to come with him, instead of keeping the appointment; from his jests and chuckles, I could see he found it amusing that I pretended not to understand some of his remarks, but I think he meant well and understood all right that I hadn't any wish to be sold to the Arabs.

The Frenchman's approval, digested between bites of sandwich, was that Esmond meet the sailors as they came off ship and usher them to a cabaret-cum-brothel. For this he would receive one franc for every ten the sailors spent. It was while chewing over this offer that his boat came in.

It took two days to load up the *Mar Caspio* with its 600 volunteers. Esmond, one of the first on board, spent this time watching the arrivals as they were ferried to the ship by rowing boat. Most of the volunteers were French, although the Germans were almost as numerous. Esmond was the only Englishman aboard what had become a multi-national vessel. Outside the ship's dining room was a notice in French: 'Guard duties: 7–9 French, 9–11 Germans, 11–13 Italians, 13–15 Yugoslavians, 15–17 Belgians, 17–19 Poles, 19–21 Flemish, 21–23 Russians, 23–1 French....' Esmond joined the Polish group, striking up a friendship with a Polish émigré who since entering France had worked in the coalfields for seven years, and had done two years' military service. Nearly all the volunteers were working class. Most looked both tough and capable and Esmond was once again reminded of his own shortcomings – 'At the office in Marseilles they had asked me what military service I had done. I told them I had been in my school OTC. That wasn't true . . . but I was afraid they might not take me if I admitted this. I had not yet learned to put a true valuation on the numerous forms we filled in in Spain, or to make a guess at what became of them, and I was nervous of being found out. I determined to be a conscientious learner.'

The *Mar Caspio* weighed anchor at four o'clock in the morning and in a squall. Seasick for most of the day, by evening Esmond felt well enough to venture out on deck and gaze into the lights of Barcelona, now controlled by the city's worker committees. It was just like the Blackpool fun-fair. Only the order for ship's lights out 'gave meaning to the word "war". The rest was just a holiday.'

The holiday atmosphere continued in Valencia, at which the ship docked at 10 o'clock the next morning.

The procession stretched out of sight down the road – here and there a few ragged banners with slogans chalked in white – here and there a gap with a man marching by himself trying to get them to march in step. The crowd went with us, jostling along the pavements or walking in our ranks. A lot of vivas, and always the slogan '*No Pas-ar-an*', '*No Pasarán*', were the words one caught from the crowd's cheering. The Frenchmen, led by a cheer leader, shouted '*Vive le Front Populaire*', '*Vive la République*', then copied the crowd's '*No Pasarán*'.

Esmond had entered Spain in what Hugh Thomas, the Spanish Civil War historian, calls 'the heroic period of the Spanish Civil War', the period of vociferous idealism before the days of tight-lipped stoicism.

Tomorrow – a prescient poet might have written – the centralized control, but today the worker committee; tomorrow Stalinist subterfuge, but today Comintern aid; tomorrow an introduction to British hypocrisy but today a non-intervention agreement. Tomorrow the tragedy which will label glib even the least propagandist of elegies. But today, 'a huge cheering crowd, a hot and tiring march down interminable streets, slogans and posters and military flags and badges everywhere'.

There were words of welcome and speeches and a music-hall show and in the evening a magnificent supper accompanied by a cornucopia of local wine. The men had been warned beforehand about the strength of the vintage but few took note and by the time they bid farewell to the city – a valediction, if possible, more emotionally charged than the earlier welcome – almost everyone was showing the effects of the evening's Bacchanalia.

The train waited a long time in the station before moving off, and free kisses were given to anyone who leaned his head out. We learned new slogans: '*Viva las señoritas españolas*' and '*Viva Vino Blanco*'. In the first hour the train stopped at every little station on the way – and at each one there was the same crowd, the same friendly words, the same forest of clenched fists as we moved on. That was the agreeable part.

The men were now on their way to Albacete, where the International Brigade was already being organized. It was an unpleasant trip, despite the rousing send-off, and Esmond suffered from bouts of diarrhoea throughout the sweaty, overcrowded, painfully slow night. A grey dawn revealed the base which, in contrast to Valencia, was cold and bleak and cheerless.

A frown on the otherwise vacant face of La Mancha, Albacete had, by some oversight, been chosen to house the foreign volunteer force, while it awaited its call to the front. The call had still not arrived and a mood of petulant frustration had begun to diffuse the camp, inhaled by each new intake of recruits.

Having little to occupy his time Esmond began studying the literature on the barrack-room wall – a Russian newspaper reminded him that the plight of Leningrad in 1918 was greater than that of Madrid in 1936, a German axiom commanded him to 'exalt discipline', a French notice urged him not to render himself unfit for service by getting diseases in brothels. There was no training in the camp, only an early morning exercise period in which each unit worked out its own programme. Esmond's group spent this time playing leapfrog.

Separated from the Polish volunteers, Esmond had attached himself to a Russian contingent, only to discover that they were not Red revolutionaries but old White émigrés, anxious to prove their commitment to the new order and work their passage home. They were a sad group, the saddest of all being Nono – named after the inscription on his sweater, 'ss NONO' – who was old and fat and senile, and the continual butt of the others' jokes. Equally pathetic, but less innocuous, was 'the Little Latvian', an obsequious, shrew-like character, who had linked himself symbiotically to Romilly in the hope of gaining entry into an English group. Esmond had suffered four days of the Latvian's unction and Nono's gibbering when he ran into his first Englishmen.

The Tom Mann Centuria – it took its name from the legendary British labour leader – had just arrived from Barcelona where for the past two months it had been waiting to be drafted into the Aragon militia. Inactive and bored, the men had taken a vote to move south and join the International Column. All but the leader, Nat Cohen, were in favour. He had got a militia girl pregnant and had elected to stay in Barcelona to get married.

The new leader of the group was Lorrimer Birch, a twenty-three-year-old Cambridge scientist and ardent Party man, whose flair for organizing was counteracted by a pedantic display of Party propriety; a trait which did little to recommend him to the other men. He became leader because he was desperate to lead and because there were no other contenders for the position.

Esmond had moved in with the English group. '"Of course you'll have to be elected you know," said Birch, "before you actually join officially; but there won't be any difficulties about that."' At the official ingression later that evening Esmond took stock of the other volunteers: Sid Avener, 'a student from a London University'. Ray Cox, a Southampton clerk, the group's 'nice guy'. David Marshall, a dole-office assistant from Manchester. Bill Scott, an ex-IRA man. Donovan, also Irish, of no fixed views or abode. Philip (Jock) Gillan, a lorry driver from the Gorbals. Arnold Jeans, an East European (no one was sure of his nationality) – a six-passport 'mystery man'. Keith Scott-Watson, a fellow traveller (all the others, with the exception of Donovan, were Communists) with a public-school accent and street-wise cynicism. He was generally considered the group's eighth man. Despite his cynical gibes at 'the faithful', Esmond found him amusing, and the two struck up a friendship.

Since Esmond's arrival in Albacete there had been yet another intake of volunteers, amongst whom was rumoured to be a small contingent of British. This rumour had been circulating for two days when Birch received word that some Englishmen were drinking coffee in the Café de Albacete. Esmond had joked that they were probably more Latvians (the little Latvian had been indefatigable in his efforts to join the British group), 'But there they were, nine of them drinking coffee, when we arrived. A very different lot from our group, I thought. Older and tougher.'

The spokesman for the group was the broad, heavy-set Arthur Ovenden. He and his friend, the diminutive Harry (Tich) Addley had sold up their restaurant business in Dover to come to Spain. They were both veterans from the World War, and had had the foresight to bring their own boots and uniforms with them.

Joe Gough, a twenty-five-year-old out-of-work Vauxhall metal finisher, had met up with Ovenden (Babs) and Addley at the Brigade recruitment centre in Paris – this at the time when Esmond, oblivious to any formal organization, had been making his own way to Spain. Gough was an eccentric, with the eccentric's love of theatrics. Only the year before he had walked through Nazi Germany wearing Fascist badges and emblems captured from Luton (his home town) Blackshirts. His ambition was 'to return to Luton with a Spanish General's uniform and put the Public Assistance officials in their place'.

Martin Messer, like the other three men whom he met on the train to Marseilles, was a Communist. Norman, Messer's friend, 'hadn't got the same sort of credentials'. Both belonged to London's left-wing bohemian set and Esmond recalled seeing Messer from time to time in the Fitzroy Tavern, a notorious bohemian rendezvous.

Aussie, a thirty-year-old tramp who looked ten years older, and the shady, waif-like Jerry Fontana, an American deportee, debilitated by the heavy work of the French shipyards, joined the group in Marseilles. Chris Thornycroft, an 'Oxford student', whom Esmond at first found snobbish (an opinion, like most of his initial opinions, later re-evaluated) tagged on aboard ship. This left Marseilles four days behind the *Mar Caspio*, bringing another two thousand volunteers to the war.

The new men had already succumbed to the Albacete blues. 'What we've been doing here is waiting about and eating and then waiting about for the next bit of grub. Then they've started some jolly game of hauling ourselves out at six in the morning to go on parade and listen to some fat bastard gassing his head off in some language we don't understand. When someone tried to get us up this morning we just stayed fixed where we were.' Ovenden had vocalized everyone's sense of frustration: the feeling that they were guests at a war that was being fought and, if recent rumours were correct, lost without them.

On 18 July 1936 a massive dust cloud of discontent and enmity had enveloped the Spanish peninsula, which on settling had revealed a country split from north-east to south-west. To the east of this fissure, that is the industrial and anarchist Spain (this included the Basque territory) the country had remained Republican, while to the west, the Spain of the large estate and the Church-dominated pueblo, the people had embraced or had been bear-hugged by the rebel cause. This, then, is how the country stood at the beginning of November 1936, on the eve of the rebels' assault on Madrid.

A precarious headland of Republican loyalty in a sea of pro-rebel sentiment, Madrid had long awaited the attack. It came, finally, on 6 November, with a rebel push from the north-west. By the evening of the first day the insurgents were perched on the outskirts of the city, their general, Mola, confidently predicting the capital's imminent fall.

Madrid had fallen; that was the rumour now current at Albacete. Not that anyone attached too great an importance to the loss (it was only later that the capital's defence assumed its overwhelming psychological importance). 'We realized perfectly', wrote Esmond, 'that if Madrid fell the war would go on. I never even imagined we would go to Madrid. It was only one front out of many.' Nevertheless, the news had increased the volunteers' anxiety to quit the camp and join the fighting. Sensing the tension, André Marty, the Brigade's organizer, assembled the men in the main square on 7 November, and addressed them on the need for patience. Esmond took note: 'There are those [railed Marty] who are impatient, who wish to rush off to the front at once, untrained, without proper arms. I say those people who spread those ideas – though they mean well – they are criminals. We are preparing for war, not for massacre. When the first International Brigade goes into action, they will be properly trained men, with good rifles, a well-equipped corps.'* The men were to leave the town at once, Marty continued, not for the front but for a training camp (at Villa Franca). The address over, the commander had a special message for the British volunteers. Their comrades in the Thaelmann Battalion were willing and anxious

---

* The first International Brigade battalion entered Madrid and the war on 8 November, marching through the city centre to the roars and cheers of the crowd, and thence up Calle Princesa to the University City and the front lines.

that they should join their ranks. Having already made overtures to the German group, which they had voted for 17 to 1 over the French (Romilly being the only dissenting voice), the men accepted with 'three cheers for the Thaelmann and for the German comrades'. This salutation was returned, and the assembly discharged.

The volunteers did not quit the camp that day after all, but, kitted out with brown corduroy trousers, khaki coat and, to Esmond's dismay, a beltful of equipment, they returned to billets to await further orders.

The train conveying the 1,600-strong XII Brigade to the training camp pulled out of Albacete at midnight on 8 November, arriving at the Castilian pueblo of Villa Franca at six in the morning. The six hours had not passed without incident. To relieve the tedium of the journey Donovan had brought two bottles of wine, and these were being freely passed round the compartment when Jeans appeared with the message that anyone found drunk from then onward would be shot. Donovan saw this as a personal reproach – he had already been criticized by Jeans for his drinking habits – and became abusive. 'Jeans was rather apologetic about it all', Esmond noted, 'and said he thought his presence seemed to stir Donovan up so much that next time he'd send Birch along to give the orders.' It was just one of the several stormy scenes which occurred as eighteen men of different backgrounds, temperaments, and varying degrees of commitment settled down together. Esmond, too, had his critics. Arthur Ovenden was one: 'I didn't get on with Romilly to begin with. He was part of the Scott-Watson/Norman clique, and they got drunk quite a bit. This to me was tantamount to a breach of faith.'

Contrary to the forecasts of sixteen days' rigorous training, the Brigade remained in Villa Franca just twelve hours, practising the very latest German army tactics 'which always broke down because of bad coordination and because we could never understand the general plan'. This was disconcerting, so too were Esmond's attempts at rifle maintenance: 'My chief difficulty was with the firing pin – every time I tried to push it up it shot out and bruised my thumb, and I was relieved when Tich said: "Better leave that alone son, you don't want to muck about with oil and stuff".... I never once took my rifle to bits after this.'

Madrid had not fallen on 6 November but was still in the tenuous grip of the Republican militia. The XII Brigade received this news and the order to abandon manoeuvres in the afternoon of the first day. At six in the evening, amongst singing and raucous merriment, the men climbed aboard a convoy of lorries and set out for the capital. Esmond imbibed freely of the excitement, too freely, and was ill.

My face must have gone very green, because someone leaned forward to ask Paul [a group commander], who was sitting in front with the driver, to change places with me. It was better in front. Before we started they had distributed tins of fish and bread and pomegranates and the stink of all this food made me vomit.

As far as I could see on the road in front of us and behind was an endless stream of lorries; as we raced through the little villages on the way, crowds of old men and women and little girls collected in the squares. 'Salud! Salud!' they shouted. 'Salud! No Pasarán! No Pasarán!' It was a moving sight, but I was too occupied with my stomach to take any part in the frenzied cheering. At last I could contain myself no longer. The driver stopped at the side of the road and lorries roared past. Half an hour later the driver stopped for me again near a farmhouse. Six times altogether I stopped on that journey.

Fortunately, and not only for Esmond, for after six hours in the crowded draughty lorries everyone's spirit had sunk, the men were not being transported straight to the fighting. In the early hours of 10 November the lorries came to rest at the town of Chinchón which, lying 50 kilometres south-east of the capital, had become a makeshift barracks for the Madrid front. His stomach still performing contortions, Esmond went in search of a toilet. He stumbled into a bar, was given hot milk and lots of sympathy and began to feel much better.

The Brigade was in Chinchón two days, receiving another military address – this time from the Brigade's secretary, Hans Beimler – and, to Esmond's undisguised consternation, more equipment. That this equipment was the all-important ammunition bore no impression on a mind burdened by practical worries: 'The cartridges were stuffed into bandoliers, so that meant another difficulty getting them to fit into the pouches. Then they wanted us to take extra bandoliers of fifty cartridges to string over our shoulders. "Can't have too much of this stuff," said Joe. "Might need it, you know." He was laden up like a hedgehog. I had quite enough without any more. I could imagine nothing worse than carrying more lead on me.'

The XII Brigade was not sent to Madrid immediately, where the fighting was centred on the University City, but to the south of the capital where the Republican commanders were expecting an attack on the Madrid–Valencia highway.

On the morning of 12 November the Brigade lorries came to a halt at the village of Vaciamadrid, 5 miles to the south-west of Madrid. It was a beautiful sunny day, Esmond recalled, and this, combined with the setting, countryside 'resembling parts of the Sussex Downs', succeeded in defusing the term 'front'. The Thaelmann's orders, arriving with the mid-day heat, were to advance on a rebel-held village a mile to the west. The Battalion set off, was recalled, pointed in a different direction, and set off again. 'I imagine', wrote Esmond, 'this was all rather like an OTC Field Day – very hot, exhausting and disagreeable. I wished I had brought a flask of water but this would have meant something else to clank about my neck and get tied up in.'

Finding the village – Perales del Rio – unoccupied, the men relieved themselves of their equipment, ate some Serrano ham left by the previous occupants, and studied the next objective – a rebel-held 'fortress' a mile to the west. This fortress was in reality a Catholic monastery which, perched on the top of a great mound, Cerro de los Angeles (Hill of the Angels) afforded its occupiers – the Nationalist troops – a view of the Castilian plain in all directions. The XII Brigade troops had been dispatched to the north, west and east of the hill, from which points, and without an artillery back-up, they were to storm and take the monastery.

The British group had been ordered to make for a ridge within 400 yards of the monastery and mount their machine-gun. It was Esmond's first experience of being under fire.

Swish-swish-swish-swish; [the bullets] seemed to be rustling through the grass. We were in an open ploughed field. I worked like mad for several minutes, scrabbling up the earth in front with my hands. I don't know how long I stayed in the same position; it might have been ten minutes or half an hour.

'Who's that in front, hi there!'

I looked round, keeping my head well down. It was Bill Scott, about fifteen yards behind.

'This is a nasty spot to get caught,' he shouted. 'Who's that next to you?'

I shouted at the figure that was huddled up in the ground on my right. It was Jerry; he wasn't taking any chances by getting up to join in the conversation. I couldn't see anyone else from where I was, though I could hear voices in English and German. We waited for new orders. Just after the first enemy bullets a continual racket of firing had started over on our left. I began to feel cold.

'Think I'll have a pot', shouted Bill, and the next moment I heard a deafening explosion. This was his pot; then came a clink of a breech being shoved home and another shot. It was more disconcerting than the bullets over us, and I hoped he would soon stop. But it gave me an idea, and I decided myself to fire my first round.

'They're too far. You can't see a thing', said Bill.

Taking a hasty glance over my earth mound to make sure where the fort was, I pointed my rifle at an angle of forty-five degrees and pressed the trigger. The result was a click. Furious, I emptied the breech; but I had done everything right and another clip of cartridges produced no result.

'I expect they'll as like find half these rifles are dud by the time the day's over', said Bill.

At the ridge Esmond handed his rifle to Tich, who adjusted the firing pin and told him it would now work. The bullets continued to whistle overhead. Jeans appeared. As a fluent German speaker he had become *ipso facto* group leader. 'Maintain a continual machine-gun fire on the monastery', he told them; '. . . he paid no attention to the firing; every-one else was lying flat'.

Birch and Thornycroft assembled the machine-gun and trained it on the monastery walls. The gun spluttered into action – 'we were a bit surprised it worked' – dispensing its contents ineffectually into the ancient masonry. The return fire was more venomous.

We were suddenly in a hurricane of bullets. Birch went on a few minutes, then he and Kay and Marshall found it too hot to continue. I remembered I was supposed to be doing some 'protection'. Unfortunately, I could discern no figures at whom to direct my fire; I discharged five rounds, putting the sights at 1,000 metres – it was the first time I had fired a rifle in my life, but I had little time to reflect on the occasion; it seemed very unfair that the enemy now seemed to be able to see me but I could not see them.

There was a cry behind me. Ten yards behind the machine-gun two drums of ammunition lay on the ground, beside them was a German, clutching his leg and groaning.

Esmond helped the wounded man back across the field and handed him to a group of French who were making for Vaciamadrid. They had been engaged on the other side of the monastery and were telling stories of a complete rout. It was now dark. The firing had stopped. Esmond headed back in what he assumed to be the direction of the ridge.

The attack had been a fiasco. Without the support of artillery, the triangular affront by the Italian, German and French Battalions had been unable to get anywhere near the monastery-fortress. Esmond learned of this the next morning after spending a traumatic night wandering through a rugged no-man's land, looking first for his own group, then for the village, and finally, in a panic, for anyone at all on the same side.

What if I had got right round the other side of the fort? What if ... ? It had never occurred to me before that since the operation we had taken part in was an attack, and since [the village] had been unoccupied or occupied by the enemy until our arrival, there might well be some of the enemy anywhere around me. I suppose I must have assumed that as we were attacking the fort, they would be staying in that fort. But that was ridiculous; they would not be in it unless they had lines of communication with their other forces – all the country on one side was theirs. Suppose I was in this country now? Then came a more welcome idea – perhaps the fort was captured already. But the Frenchman's account didn't give much encouragement to this idea.

Everyone was in retreat. Esmond heard the news from Bill Scott, whom he stumbled upon later that night. 'We'd better be pushing back ourselves,' Scott had added, much to Esmond's relief. But the Irishman's sense of direction was, if anything, more execrable than Romilly's, and the two spent many hours feverishly pacing in all directions before locating a road and a straggling line of disconcerted volunteers. Scott-Watson was among the group. He had got caught up in the disastrous French attack on the west side of the monastery and 'had had an even more hectic time than we had'. Esmond told him he looked like 'a worried old nanny-goat'. He managed to laugh, but was clearly shaken. Later that night Esmond lost contact with him and when he arrived in Vaciamadrid – the village where the abortive manoeuvre had begun almost twenty-four hours previously – Scott-Watson was nowhere to be found. On a roll-call it was discovered that Donovan and Norman were missing too. Some weeks later the English group received a letter from Norman saying both he and Donovan had decided to return home. Scott-Watson had not gone so far, but, jumping a lorry, had made his way to Madrid, where he had run into the *Daily Express* correspondent, Sefton Delmer.

In his autobiography, *Trail Sinister*, Delmer recorded the meeting:

Keith Scott-Watson was a tall myopic Bloomsbury Bohemian, with a gift for sardonic irony, an enviable certainty that the world was

130

his, and a mop of flax blond hair which kept flopping into his spectacles. He had walked into the Telefonica one night as we were all lying around on the telephonists' unoccupied camp beds, waiting for our London calls to come through, while the Luftwaffe dropped their bombs around us outside.

I was tickled by the engaging simplicity of this young man as he stood there in his grey flannels, trenchcoat and rucksack, blinking into our dim candle-light, and asked, 'Is this where the correspondents work?' He explained with a lisp that he had come out to Spain to 'fight for freedom' but had changed his mind when he found it meant charging up hills against machine-guns, and could any of us give him a job.

14
Madrid! Madrid!

This is Madrid. It is fighting for Spain, for Humanity, for Justice, and, with the mantle of its blood, it shelters all human beings! Madrid! Madrid!

Radio broadcast by FERNANDO VÄLERA, a Republican deputy, 8 November 1936

However just a war may be, it must inevitably be a dirty and horrible thing. And when there is inefficiency and mismanagement over-enthusiasm turns to cynicism. Not that this is a bad thing. For while one realises how hopeless, how futile, how inefficient something is, one may still realize it is worth fighting for.

ESMOND ROMILLY, *Boadilla*

The XII Brigade was three days 'digging in' at Cerro de los Angeles, before being sent back to Chinchón for reorganization.

Back at the base the issue of desertion was raised. Jeans told the group that the German commander would have nothing more to do with them if either Norman or Scott-Watson were allowed to return. 'Both had been particular friends of mine,' wrote Esmond, 'but I took their exit very much for granted; I suppose because the conditions we were in made one adaptable to any change of one's friends or circumstances ... we spoke no more of them, but had a lot of wine, got suitably drunk, and felt we were all behaving as people just returned from the front should behave.'

An announcement that the XII Brigade was to move out immediately for Madrid cut short the festivities. There were murmurs of dissent and a meeting convened to discuss the cancellation of what most of the men considered a well-earned break. 'If we don't discuss this kind of thing, we might as well be fascists', said Bill Scott. Birch didn't agree and was furious throughout the meeting. Jeans, who 'looked tired

132

and said little', communicated the message. The Brigade moved out the next day.

In spite of the welcoming air-raid, Esmond was unimpressed by his first view of the capital. 'Madrid didn't look very exciting,' he commented, 'mostly tramlines and barricades. They had made it look like a part of London where the road is up and street mending is going on in a lot of places, with braziers heating the workmen's meals. It was an anti-climax.' Having withstood the first anxious hours of the rebel attack, Madrid had settled down to a business-as-usual Blitz stoicism.

On 17 November, and without any of the ceremony which attended the arrival of the first volunteer force a week earlier, the XII Brigade took up its reserve position on the edge of the University campus and awaited the order to join the attack. This came on a damp dawn mist, accompanied by a chilling whisper that Germany, Italy and Portugal recognised France's Government, which, according to their sources, had now established itself within Madrid. 'It was suggested', wrote Esmond, 'that our fight now would have a decisive effect on the future of international relations.'

The object of the exercise was to occupy a fortress (the Palacete de Moncloa) which, resting on the edge of the University campus, formed the rebels' furthest point of penetration. Esmond was one of a fourteen-man advance party who, having been sent to reconnoitre the area, reached the fortress and, encountering no resistance, established themselves inside :

Inside, Alex [a German commander] found heaped together the bodies of twenty Spanish government soldiers. The shell and bullet-hole marks showed the intensity of the rebels' attack. I cleaned the mud off my rifle.

I do not know how long we waited there; first one smack, then another; plaster fell from the walls as machine-gun bullets hit it. The fire was from our right, on the side of the reservoir [from their own lines]; the bullets all struck very high and we were well protected. The next thing was a series of heavy crashes. We saw the smoke from shell-bursts a hundred yards away, then a direct hit. Bricks, stones and earth buried four men; no-one was badly hurt. A battery of three of our own guns had begun a steady bombardment of the fort. Alex gave the order to retire.

In retiring the group found themselves in a cross-fire between the two camps. Two Germans were killed. The rest gained their own lines just in time to see the fort being reoccupied by the enemy.

Since Franco's troops had crossed the river Manzanares on 15 November, and anchored themselves within the University campus, a bloody and bizarre battle had been in progress, fought within and between the University buildings. There were no trenches; the front was an ever-changing kaleidoscope of advances and retreats between one department block and another. It was, in the words of Hugh Thomas, a 'macabre confusion', the destruction 'in strict accordance with the slogan of the founder of the Foreign Legion, Milan Astray – "Down with Intelligence"'.

Tich, a First World War sergeant in the Buffs, was disgusted. He had looked forward to a good professional war of attrition. Other members of the group began to feel the same way. Trench warfare had its benefits, not least of which was knowing where you were in relation to your enemy. Esmond recalled an incident two days after the first attack when 'a party of Germans brought back five "prisoners" in triumph and announced that their men had surrounded an enemy patrol. It was our own front line position they had practically surrounded, and their prisoners were men of the Garibaldi Battalion. The Germans were disappointed. The Italian leader told the interpreter that the next time his trench was sprayed with bullets by the Germans they would return the compliment . . . we placated the Italians by taking up extra rum rations for them at night.'

Esmond's group was involved in one more action before reoccupying their reserve position on 21 November. This was an attack on the Casa de Velasquez, which, standing 500 yards to the west of the Palacete, had become another focal point for the two armies' engagements. Esmond called it 'the White House'.

We reached the wall of the White House. It was a mad scramble. We kept near the road, and the bullets skimmed over harmlessly at first. Then there was a space of fifty yards, running all out, in threes. A few of the Germans dropped on the way – it was just like seeing people killed running in an American film. . . .

We entered a courtyard. It was a large farm, with a series of barns, workshops and armouries in separate apartments on either side. A deadly machine-gun fire from the second shed on our left made us stop; a party under Alex was storming the National Guard building on the right. A German pulled a mills bomb from his pocket, extracted the pin with his teeth; he stood up, bullets whistling past him, and hurled it in. We rushed in after the explosion. Four Moors had been firing from behind a dead horse. Now they were finished . . . In that farm the Moors left at least a hundred dead. Most were not killed by bullets – their bodies had been torn apart by shells, limbs blown off by hand grenades. The farm was fifty yards wide. Two mangy cows wandered aimlessly about. They were wounded, but their hides seemed too tough for the bullets. In the middle of the mud I watched a little blaze crackling away – two dead men were burning steadily.

The Thaelmann Battalion was now in possession of the White House but, with their lines of communication cut off by rebel machine-gunners, it was a precarious hold.

The commander asked for volunteers to form a line of dug-outs facing the rebel-held University buildings. Nine men, including Esmond, rushed out with spades, were pinned down by Fascist fire and recalled Esmond, the furthest from the White House, was the last to return.

The others made their journeys in stages, hopping down behind a tree every ten yards. I decided to run straight on, waiting would be awful. I didn't bother about the spade. A few yards from the road I missed my footing on the slippery ground, and fell head first. I heard Joe say: 'Looks as if he got one.' I thought so myself at first, but I had fallen into a large shell-hole.

'Where's my rifle?' I shouted. I groped out with my arm and got it. The shell-hole gave far more protection than my tree. I felt quite confident, and fired off five rounds.

... A few seconds later I thought my eardrum was broken – a deafening explosion seemed right on top. This must be another trench mortar. But it was one of our tanks which had come right up behind me.

The position at the White House was untenable, but while it remained daylight it was impossible to retreat. Esmond hoped it would soon be dark: 'I didn't want any more fighting today.' The men drank some soup and talked about morale while peering into the steady drizzle. The firing had stopped. 'I was surprised that the walls and doors did not fall in,' wrote Esmond, 'but each little bit of building was burning separately. Nobody took any notice of them. The burning, with the overpowering stench inside the house, gave an atmosphere of unhealthiness and decadence.' Later, the commander gave the order to retreat. Under cover of darkness the men crept back to their lines, the rebel troops crept back to the White House. The battle was becoming a perverse ritual.

135

On Saturday 21 November the British group, now back in reserve, was visited by Sefton Delmer. 'There was no missing them', writes Delmer in *Trail Sinister*. 'They stood out from the Germans like a schoolboy team from the Blues. Their cheerfulness was magnificent. But somehow compared with those barrel-chested Germans they looked smaller and younger and less self-assured.' Esmond records this meeting in *Boadilla*, he also records that the aura of cheerfulness was provided by Joe, who was 'entirely in his element!' 'We've got nothing to complain of here except the Russian grub and the Fritzies now and again', Joe told the journalist. Birch scowled but, undeterred, Joe continued, relating how he was going to walk down Luton High Street after the war with his row of medals for the benefit of the Public Assistance officer. Delmer told the group that Scott-Watson was working for him in Madrid. Esmond sent his best wishes. Delmer left with the promise to send the men cigarettes, chocolate and newspapers.

Delmer's article, 'British Storm Troop Defend Madrid', was published in Monday's *Express*. 'I don't think I have ever seen a finer body of men,' the journalist eulogized, 'all of them with the real fighting enthusiasm unquenched by the continual bombing, shelling, machine gun and tank attacks.'

The article made no reference to Esmond Romilly; that minor scoop belonged to Monday's *Star* which, under the heading 'SHOCK FOR MOTHER', told of Mrs Romilly's near-collapse when informed of her son's whereabouts by a *Star* reporter.

'We have been living in agony wondering what had become of him', she said. 'Please, please help me to get a message to him.'

With great emotion, her voice broken by sobs, she dictated a message, conveying her love and that of her husband to their son.

'The Star' reporter took it down, and a few moments later wired it to Esmond Romilly in Madrid.

'Are you Baldwin's nephew?' an incredulous Arnold Jeans asked. This came two weeks later. The War Office had received a series of telegrams enquiring about Esmond Romilly. Esmond explained the situation and was told that if he wanted to return to England he could do so. He declined. The subject was not raised again.

The Thaelmann Battalion had been dug-in in its rear-guard position for five days when they learned through the mad confusion of a retreating Garibaldi Battalion that Franco's troops had penetrated their front lines. The men, about 200 in all, crowded into the shallow trenches and awaited the attack:

... it started with two men falling dead from close range bullets in a dug-out nearby. Then the real hailstorm of lead came at us. I was lying flat on my stomach. We shoved in clip after clip of cartridges until the breeches and barrels of our guns were red hot. I never took aim. I never looked up to see what I was firing at. I never heard the order to open fire. I never saw the enemy – never knew for certain where they were – these things were talked over afterwards. My head was in a whirl – I was almost drunk with the smell of powder. I remember a young Spaniard next to me, wondering what he was doing and how he got there; but there was no time to work it all out. It was a mad scramble – pressing my elbows into the earth, bruising them on the stones, to get my rifle to my shoulder, pressing the trigger, rasping back the bolt, then shoving it home, then on to my elbows again.

The rebel attack failed, beaten back by the Republican machine-gunners. Jock, Birch and Messer went out later as part of a cleaning-up party – '"Ah was goin' to have his beard and dress myself like a Moor to give ye all a fright," Jock told us. "Only Alex wouldna let me, he said you boys'd all be on the run at the first sight of that beard."'

On the following morning the Thaelmann reoccupied the White House, which had been left vacant by the Moors after the previous day's reversal. They remained here for three days, making two disastrous attacks on the heavily fortified Palacete before being relieved on the morning of the 27th. That same day, after a furious bombardment, the White House once more belonged to the Moors.

The British group was now awarded two days' leave. Clean underwear, shirts, sweaters and shaving equipment were handed out, and Esmond spruced himself up while Tich made a few running repairs to his uniform. Esmond was grateful for the help, while attributing it to no more than an ex-NCO's general abhorrence of untidiness. Later Babs Ovenden disabused him. '"No it wasn't that," said Babs. "Tich liked you a lot. What he said was, he realized what was a little thing to him, sewing a few buttons, was more of a thing to you."' Esmond – his worst dreams had come true – was generally regarded as the untidiest, most practically deficient member of the group. His latest mishap was to lose his haversack at the White House. He later calculated that he had lost something at every place he had stopped in Spain,

137

including a suitcase full of clothes and effects lost in Barcelona on the return journey.

Having been made presentable, Esmond took off for Madrid in search of Delmer, Scott-Watson and a free meal. Birch accompanied him, while making it clear that he would not be overjoyed to meet Scott-Watson again. (It was Birch who, two weeks earlier, had called for Scott-Watson's enforced return and trial for desertion.) He now began a harangue not only against the absentee members, but against the attitude of the remaining men. Esmond found such inflexibility trying – 'His single-aim sincerity amazed me. I could see he would never begin to allow himself sympathy with those who couldn't keep his own high standard.' Apart from Birch, Esmond thought the group was looking noticeably bruised by the fighting, even 'Babs and Tich and Jock and Joe all looked less tough now; Jeans was the only person I could place with Birch, and of the two he had less of the inhuman about him'.

Catching up with Delmer in the Hotel Gran Via, the two volunteers were invited to several brandies, a hot bath and dinner. Over dinner the journalist introduced them to a delegation of MPs engaged in preparing a report on the war. They pulled up seats and were treated to brandies and 'any amount of war reminiscences', one Conservative MP becoming 'very eloquent in expounding his ideas on how General Franco could have cut the Valencian road – or, rather, how he could have cut it himself, had he had a company of cavalry'.

As it was by now too late to return to base, the garrulous MP invited them to spend the night in his room. They accepted, only to be kept awake all night fending off his amorous advances. In the morning Esmond – in a rage – threatened him with public exposure, unless, on his return to England, he openly supported the Republican cause. The MP agreed and kept his word. So too did Esmond; in this he had no choice. Birch, his only witness, was killed three weeks later at Boadilla.

A letter to Peter Nevile. Sunday 29 November:

                                            Frente de Madrid.

Dear Peter,

This is a note to tell you I've found a whole lot of blood and violent destruction all around. This is a pretty good argument for Huxley pacifism, but not quite as strong as the struggle itself. Before I left England, I read that Madrid would fall in a day or two. It is certain now that it can never fall. . . .

We are now having 2 days' rest after 12 days' action in the front lines (no trenches here). Yesterday we met the British parliamentary delegation – absolute useless idiots, though I scrounged a good deal from them, including 3 boxes of chocolates from the Liberal Party.

How's this for publicity –

12 days vigorous action, including bombing, machine-gunning, hand grenades, tanks, shelling. At last a much needed rest: coffee, butter, jam, a terrific reception by the civil population – one thing needed: a cup of Horlicks.

Why not ask Thompson's to send Horlicks in quantity to the English Section, Thaelmann Battalion, 12th International Brigade? Also send Rowntree's chocolate – wouldn't it be good publicity?*

During the action our company started with 120 men, present strength 37. So you see I think this is Adieu.

It was a melodramatic note and not something that Esmond would have wanted to be reminded of. It was, nevertheless, a true indication of his feelings on the eve of his return to the battle front. Both the XI and XII International Brigades had been involved in the University City fighting, and both had sustained heavy losses. Miraculously, no one in Esmond's group had been killed, although it had shrunk considerably from its original force of eighteen. Norman, Donovan and Keith Scott-Watson had disappeared after the first action. David Marshall had left at the same time, with a bullet wound to his foot. Later, on reaching Madrid, the group had lost Bill Scott, who had retired to hospital with kidney trouble, and Chris Thornycroft, retained at base as a mechanic. The latest loss was Jerry Fontana, who on the night before the group's return to the University City had calmly announced that he was 'quitting', and had made off for the capital.

The British group reoccupied their old dug-outs 200 yards from the White House and settled down to a 'routine of eating, sleeping, improving the dug-outs and communication trenches, watching the air-raids and listening to the heavy pounding of the big guns behind and in front'. The worst enemy was now the weather, the night temperatures often falling way below freezing. Esmond recalled 'a rainstorm that was worse than an artillery bombardment. After that we never recovered our good spirits and began to talk of being relieved.'

On Friday 4 December Romilly's section was shipped out to the Playa de Madrid, a country club on the outskirts of the capital, for a few days' rest. This was almost immediately cut short and once again

* Peter Nevile was working for the advertising agency J. Walter Thompson, which at the time was mounting an advertising campaign for Rowntree.

Esmond found himself back at the University City, swapping fire with an opposite number in the White House. On 9 December the group returned to the country club. They were not on leave, Jeans told them, but in reserve. A large Nationalist advance was expected at any moment. He cautioned them not to do anything silly, and some leave would be arranged shortly. 'But we were impatient,' wrote Esmond, 'so we did something silly.'

The opportunity for taking 'French leave' presented itself the next day, when the whole unit was transported into Madrid for a bath. Esmond, Joe, Aussie and Jerry (he had been harried by the Madrid authorities into returning) jumped lorry in Plaza España and made a bee-line for the Hotel Gran Via and the British journalists. The rest of the day was spent carousing. They returned to the Playa de Madrid in the early hours of the morning to find their quarters deserted and all their equipment missing.

The Battalion was now quartered twenty miles north of Madrid, in the Duke of Alba's magnificent country house at Las Rosas. The anxious four arrived at eight in the morning and were immediately placed under arrest.

Jock, Babs and Messer came to see them. 'No visitors allowed', one of the German guards interceded. They left. 'Joe's face flushed. "The f— b—s", he muttered. "Ask him who he's getting his orders from, and who told him to say that."' A Spaniard arrived and offered the prisoners cigarettes. He too was told to leave. A slanging match developed, conducted in French, Esmond translating Joe's stream of abuse and adding 'a good deal more of my own'. Then more guards were called. . . .

'The whole thing', wrote Esmond, 'lasted perhaps two minutes from the time the Spaniard had given us the cigarettes. At the end of it we were under double guard, the guards had all loaded their rifles, and Joe's lip was bleeding profusely where someone had struck him with the butt of a rifle.'

Later, an enquiry was held into the incident, and all four detainees were released. But the British group considered that Joe had been roughly treated, and called for a separate hearing. The discussion began heatedly, but the wound was eventually soothed by the placating, friendly words of the two company commanders, Walter and Herbert – a popular double act – and the British and their German hosts returned to an amicable if, at times, confused co-existence.

Three days were spent at Las Rosas, ostensibly on manoeuvres, although the men were given plenty of free time to make up for their earlier lack of leave. On the second day Esmond and Joe gained permission to go for a long walk.

We took wine and rolls of bread with us, and were given fried eggs at a little farm. Sometimes there were aeroplanes in the sky, but they did not disturb the serenity of the day. We walked through the woods of El Pardo, skirted Fuencarral, and got briskly down country lanes to the peaceful little town of Aravaca. On one side the country rolled on flatly past the green–brown plain of Madrid – it was small beside the towering snow-capped peaks of the Guadarrama mountains behind us. We forgot the war. It was cold and dark when we trudged up the last half-mile from El Pardo to the gravel drive of the castle.

Initially wary of the vociferous, eccentric Joe, Esmond had come to regard him as a close friend 'Like Tich,' Bobo Ovenden recalled, 'Joe Gough was very kind to Esmond and helped him keep his gear in order. He became a favourite uncle. It was a terrible shock for Esmond when he saw Joe get killed at Boadilla.'

Jerry Fontana was leaving to work in a Barcelona armaments factory. The American had become a liability and the Thaelmann commanders wanted to be rid of him. Esmond was sorry to see him go – 'his wise-cracking, tolerant individualism was a relief from the eternal grimness of the war. And Jerry had no politics, that was an important thing.' Jerry left the group on Sunday morning (13 December). The same evening the Battalion moved to Majadahonda, and from there, on the morning of 14 December, to Boadilla del Monte, where the long-awaited rebel offensive was already in progress.

'It was a lovely day', Esmond wrote, forgetting that the same phrase had formed the prelude to the earlier disaster at the Hill of the Angels. 'Joe and I were in quite an hysterical mood, roaring with laughter at each other's jokes ... I felt it was going to be like our manoeuvres at the castle [Las Rosas], I had thoroughly enjoyed those.'

The Battalion alighted two kilometres north of Boadilla. Esmond, now a company runner, and Lorrimer Birch entered the town with orders to locate the front.

Boadilla was in ruins, and on the brink of falling to the enemy. Esmond found the front – a semi-circular ridge defining the town's eastern perimeter – but could see no sign of firing. 'A Spanish Captain told us they had fought a rearguard action all night. Their losses had been terrible. He pointed back to the village. "In front of that road you have come along there is nothing."'

141

Romilly and Birch bore the news back to their own lines. The bombardment was still intense, and it was a relief to be away from it – 'it had given me almost the most nasty feeling in my stomach I have ever had'. By evening the rebel forces had captured the town, the Republican troops occupying a ridge to the north, where for the next three days they went through the familiar, distasteful motions of digging in. 'For me', wrote Esmond, 'the most important incident [of this period] was when someone called my name, and I saw John Cornford with his head bandaged.'

Cornford – a prominent member of the Cambridge socialists – had arrived in Spain in August and had fought in the early battles around Huesca before returning to England to recruit some fellow students to the cause. This group was now fighting as a machine-gun unit with the Commune de Paris Battalion. On the day that Boadilla fell, Cornford's group had been fighting a rear-guard action. Their two machine-guns were the last to leave the town. Cornford was what Esmond termed a 'Real Communist' – 'a serious person, a rigid disciplinarian, a member of the Communist Party, interested in all aspects of warfare, and lacking in any such selfish motive as fear or reckless courage'. He was killed two weeks later, on the day after his twenty-first birthday, while fighting with the British Battalion at Cordoba.

An ever-increasing case of neuralgia was affecting Esmond's spirit. This was so bad on the fourth morning that it even hurt to get up. After eating some breakfast and swallowing two aspirins with a cup of brandy he felt somewhat better, but continued to view the world from under furrowed brow. At 7 a.m. the big guns began pounding away from Boadilla, signalling an enemy advance which everyone knew would come that day. The bombardment continued all morning, gradually infiltrated by rifle fire which by 10 a.m. was flying in volleys and at close range. Esmond's head was splitting. '"Don't like those bullets boy," said Joe. "You keep your head down. Did you see that one, slap into that tree there, might have got my fingers; sounds like something wrong this time in the morning."'

Jock Gillan was the first British casualty, shot in the neck by a close-range sniper. Everyone watched as he was loaded on to a stretcher and borne away. 'All this is very clear,' wrote Esmond, 'Jock being wounded, Jock being taken back, Birch talking about the sniper and cursing Sid. All these things belong to another existence – they happened before that orderly life of ours which I regarded as everlasting because it was so strongly present, before that finished.'

The front line had collapsed; panic-stricken Spanish troops were crowding into the second line dug-outs. Through the clamour, Esmond heard the order for the Thaelmann to advance. A German patrol disappeared over the ridge and into the ilex trees below. Romilly's group followed, shouting to the men to their left to join them. But these had now received new orders and remained in their trenches. Esmond:

All the English were together – we were separated from the rest. Jeans was in front with Tich and Birch close behind him, Babs was close to Sid, then Joe and I, who had decided to keep together whatever happened, and Ray Cox behind us – we were a solid mass. I had no idea where we were going or what was happening. I don't think we went along for more than five minutes, just beyond the protection of the ridge to the right, when we had to stop and lie down on account of the hail of bullets that came over.

'I don't know where Oswald is', I heard Jeans saying. 'He must be ahead of us somewhere with a whole patrol. Where are the other zugs?'

All this is still quite clear – I can picture it today. We sat and lay on the grass slope, or crouched behind the trees; we talked about what was happening. It might have been a Group Meeting.

The bullets were getting unpleasant. They were coming from the ridge the Spaniards had evacuated – that must be it; if we kept behind the trees, we were safe. We returned the fire.

Then Tich and Birch were leaning over Jeans' body.

'We can't do anything', I heard someone say, and then, 'We've got to get him out of here, you pull his feet down, Lorrie, I'll get hold of the head.'

I sat up and saw Jeans' face under a pool of blood. They were trying to get his helmet off. 'Cut the strap, Lorrie, with your bayonet', I heard. It was Tich, groping over to hold up the chin of the man lying still on the grass. 'That bullet must have come from the left, where our own trenches are; we're under cross-fire.'

When I looked up and spoke to Joe I turned my head. That was just incidental – it wasn't because he had not answered. Joe was kneeling on the grass, his gun pointed on to the ground through his hands. I could touch him with my arm. I tried not to look at his head – it was sunk forward on his chest. I felt I was in the presence of something horrifying. I didn't think about Joe being dead – I just thought it was all wrong Joe's head being like that. I picked it up. Then there were more bullets, and I lay flat again – that was instinctive. Perhaps I was there three minutes.

143

Tich and Birch were still arguing over Jeans. I heard someone say, 'He's finished', but all the time I was quite calm. I kept saying to myself, 'All right, Joe's killed, that's finished, absolutely settled, that's all right, Joe's killed, that's the end of that', till the words screamed in my ears. All that is clear. Afterwards is not so plain.

Tich was shouting out: 'Get back, all of you, quick as you can', and Ray was sitting in front of a tree firing when he crumpled up and collapsed. These are blurred images. Then my own name being called, 'Here, Romilly, here, quick man, run all out', and I rushed through a hail of bullets to a bank where Babs was lying. After that we were together all the time. I went on saying, 'I must find Walter and tell him Joe is dead.'

Babs Ovenden:

Romilly was almost crying. It was a terrible experience for him. He had said to me before, 'Being here is ridiculous, sooner or later we're all going to be killed', and, of course, he must have thought this was the end.

It was a shambles. Everyone who was left was running away – no officers, nobody in command. We got up and ran like hell for fifty or sixty yards and dropped behind another ridge. We did this a few times. A German from the Edgar Andre Battalion appeared, cursing everyone for running away. Of course you couldn't blame anybody, we only thought we were an army. Then we saw a group of Spaniards led by two girls. I shouted to them to stop. They wouldn't. I thought, we've got to make some kind of resistance or we're all going to be killed, so I hit one of the girls with the butt of my rifle. The rest stopped and we divided them into groups of five. 'When the enemy comes fire a magazine and retreat', I said. This went on for hours. Walter arrived on a tank and I told him there was no command here. 'You're in command', he said and went away.

The retreat had stopped – Walter, Babs and a 'big fat English doctor' receiving most of the credit for this. 'The frantic rush from ridge to ridge,' wrote Esmond, 'the frantic wild firing into the air, the frantic rush to go faster than those tanks was ended. Companies and groups and nationalities were all mixed up, but order ensued at last.'

Esmond and Babs had met up with Aussie, who, having been left putting on his boots, had joined a German group and fought with them. The three men scraped a shallow protection and made themselves as

144

comfortable as possible. A 'thin greasy soup was handed out and tepid cocoa'. Just before midnight the roll was called :

[Walter] called out each name and paused, till the suspense was unbearable. Oswald and his patrol of fifteen men were every one of them missing.... The commander crossed their names all with the same word :

'*Gefallen*'.

From the 1st and 2nd Zugs, fifteen men called out the answer, '*Hier !*' Forty-three did not answer.

'Third Zug.' Three Germans answered '*Hier*' before he came to the English Group.

Addley – no answer, no information	'*gefallen*'.
Avener – killed	'*gefullen*'.
Birch – killed	'*gefallen*'.
Cox – killed	'*gefallen*'.

The suspense was still there; we knew they were killed, but yet we did not believe it. It was as if this was their last chance to plead before the final death sentence of the word written against their names.

Gillan – wounded	
Gough – killed	'*gefallen*'.
Jeans – killed	'*gefallen*'.
Messer – no answer, missing	'*gefallen*'.

There had been nothing to break the chain of those answers – we were all at the end of the alphabet.

Esmond's Spanish Civil War ended there. Five days later he and Babs Ovenden left the trenches outside Boadilla and returned to Albacete. Here the xv Brigade, with the recently formed British Battalion, was in training. Neither contemplated joining it, neither was in a fit mental or physical condition to sustain another dose of civil warfare. Esmond was now suffering from dysentery and had to spend two days in a Barcelona hospital before continuing his journey back to England, which he entered on 3 January 1937. Scotland Yard was there to meet him.

15
Elopement

Why should Scotland Yard focus so much attention on the eighteen-year-old Romilly? The answer is simply that with his propensity for publicity Esmond was easy to keep tabs on. Despite all the rumours of police spies and 'splits', Scotland Yard's main informant was the Press, and the right-wing members of that estate had conveniently labelled Esmond 'subversive'. There was nothing subversive about fighting for the Spanish Republic, however, or even illegal, at least not in January 1937 (the ban on volunteers was not implemented until the end of February), and so, after undergoing the formalities of an interrogation, Esmond was released.

More assiduous in its questioning, Fleet Street was equally unsuccessful in its attempts at pinning him down. Under a picture of a gaunt, ill-looking Esmond entering a taxi-cab, the *Express* could only report that Romilly would say nothing 'until I have seen certain people'. These mysterious contacts Esmond was so intent on seeing were the families of his fallen comrades. He had just come back from seeing the Cox family in Southampton when he was visited, at Pimlico Road, by Philip Toynbee.

Meeting him for the first time since his return to England, Toynbee was immediately struck by his friend's transformation. 'For one thing he had suffered from dysentery in Spain, and this had thinned his face and slightened his broad body, but the change in his spirit was more remarkable than any change in his appearance.' Esmond was 'serious, quiet and reasonable'. He made no attempt to hide the realities of the situation or his own reaction to them. 'He told me', wrote Toynbee, 'about the awful disorganization in the International Column, of disgruntlement, harsh mutual criticism, disgraceful retreats, cold, uncongenial company and the rapid fading of romance. He told me of the terror of being machine-gunned from the air, and how the shells and bombs sickened one with long-accumulated fear.' He told him also that he was determined to return. As he said in an interview with the *Star*,

146

there was still 'work to be done', although not with a rifle.

Esmond was going back to Spain as a journalist. He had chosen the northern front – far away from Fleet Street's big guns, still deployed around Madrid – and had even pocketed a £10 advance from the *News Chronicle* for first refusal of his articles. The negotiations completed, he again fell ill and had to be admitted to King's College Hospital, where he remained for ten days. He left the hospital on 22 January and went down to Cousin Dorothy's, ostensibly to convalesce.

Jessica Mitford – Decca – has always believed that her meeting Esmond at Dorothy Allhusen's country house-party was purely fortuitous – 'I had the insane hope that he might be there. And there he was to my absolute joy. How rarely does life work out like that.' How rarely indeed, leading one to suppose that Esmond, leaving nothing to chance, had planned the whole thing. He knew from Peter Nevile and others that the nineteen-year-old Mitford girl had been making overtures about running away; he also knew that she had been enquiring, a little too ardently to be casual, after his own welfare. Given this highly promising information, given also that Esmond was, in Jessica Mitford's own words, 'a constant planner', it is unlikely that the arrangements were left to anyone so inept as Fate.

In normal circumstances of course – they were second cousins – Esmond and Decca would have met as children, but Decca's mother, Lady Redesdale, and Nellie Romilly had always taken pains to avoid each other's company. 'When my mother was first married', says Jessica Mitford, 'she was accosted by Nellie in Dieppe, who asked her for a loan of £10 to go to the Casino. Not only did my mother not lend her the money, much to her discredit she also split on her to Aunt Nattie [Lady Blanche]. Since then they had had very little to do with each other.'

This parental feud had not, however, prevented Decca from following the family bad boy's career, listening attentively for his latest outrage or heresy. Given the opportunity she too could be a 'Red Menace' instead of the 'Parlour Pink' or 'Ballroom Communist' of sister Nancy's cutting jibes.

Jessica Lucy Freeman Mitford was the fifth of Lord and Lady Redesdale's six children – a large, eccentric family, satirized (only slightly) in Nancy Mitford's whimsical novels. Decca was the family's self-styled Communist, Diana and Unity the charming-alarming fascists. The girls were undoubtedly 'silly' (their mother's favourite pejorative) but they were also disturbingly single-minded, their purposefulness already

147

leading them beyond drawing-room dramas and into the vast, tragic, political tableau of the outside world.

> Of course [Jessica Mitford wrote] I had been in love with Esmond for years, ever since I first heard of him. Although I had a strong belief that you can make anyone fall in love with you if you really concentrate on it – my older sisters had told me this was so, and I felt it must be true – now I was about to meet him I was full of doubts and misgivings.
>
> I thought gloomily of all the competition I must face from all his unknown women friends; I visualized Elizabeth Bergner-like waifs in the East End, glamorous older women in the left-wing movement, even brave guerilla fighters behind the lines in Spain. All of them beautifully thin, no doubt.
>
> I spent an unusually long time getting ready for dinner. In the pink glow cast by the pretty lampshades in my bedroom, I thought I really didn't look so bad.

And yet, at first sight, Esmond was not exactly what she had expected. He was short, she noted, and very thin, but his 'extraordinary charm' made up for his deficiencies of height and stature, and he did have 'very bright eyes and amazingly long eyelashes'. The other guests, an American school-teacher and his wife, the Scotts, were equally impressed. They wanted to hear all about Esmond's Civil War experiences, but, to Decca's increasing admiration, the social lion refused to roar, channelling the conversation away from himself and on to British non-intervention.

At dinner – the cousins being seated together – Decca fired the question. When Esmond returned to Spain could he possibly take her with him? Yes, he could – he appeared to have been expecting the request – but they would talk about it later.

There were two golden rules to be observed in successful running away, the expert explained – he and Decca had stolen away after breakfast for a tête-à-tête. First, no one should be let in on the plans; second, one should allow oneself plenty of time in case of difficulties. Bearing this in mind, Decca suggested forging a letter from some friends (the Pagets) who were staying in Austria, inviting her to spend two weeks with them. Esmond was enthusiastic, but pointed out that it was better to have the invitation issue from Dieppe, that way she would be right on course for Spain, with half the trip paid for by her parents. The invitation was drafted. On Monday they travelled back to London together, arranging, provided 'Muv' (Lady Redesdale) was amenable to the Dieppe trip, to meet later to process Decca's papers.

As plans were already in motion for a spring world cruise on which she was to accompany her cousin, Dora Stanley (a pseudonym), Decca was concerned that her mother might veto a pre-cruise adventure to Dieppe. In the event, however, 'Muv' proved surprisingly amenable and Decca was able to report, in a rushed communiqué to Pimlico Road, that all was well. They arranged to meet on Wednesday afternoon (3 February) and attend to business.

With a Press card and a letter from the *News Chronicle* outlining his assignment, Esmond had no problems obtaining his visa. Decca's position — she was posing as Esmond's secretary — was more delicate. Miss Mitford would have to place a special request before the department's Señor Lopez, whom she would find at the Spanish Embassy in Paris.

The Paris trip posed no serious problem, Esmond insisted — just a few hours' delay in their journey south. Meanwhile, there were other, more pressing, matters to be taken care of. Letter to Peter Nevile (Friday 5 February 1937):

This will confirm our conversation of yesterday in which I agreed to appoint you as my sole agent for the sale of any news items, articles, photographs or other material which I may cable, telephone, mail or otherwise transmit to you from Spain, France or any country other than England.

I hereby give you full permission to arrange the sale of such material on any terms which you may consider desirable. . . .

Esmond added that 'no material of mine may be published in the London *Daily Express* or the London *Daily Mail'*, but thought better of this clause and put a line through it. Observing his own guide to successful running away he made no mention of Decca.

According to the forged note, Decca was expected in Dieppe on Sunday 8 February. Thus on Sunday morning a little band of Redesdales gathered at Victoria Station to see 'Little D' off. Esmond watched the ceremony from a distant carriage. They arrived in Paris on Sunday evening, and spent the night in the highly favoured Hôtel des Maréchaux on the rue de Moscou. On Monday morning Decca once again presented her request to the Spanish Embassy officials, and was told that her Señor Lopez had been recalled to London. Their only course of action, Esmond argued, was to catch up with the elusive Lopez and extract the visa. Decca agreed. She was already falling into the role of willing junior partner which she would assume throughout their life together.

At Dieppe they had several hours to kill before boarding the boat. Esmond suggested taking a walk. Decca thought she detected a worried mien, 'which made me worried because I thought he had had second thoughts about the whole thing. Then he said, "There's something I've got to talk over with you." I thought, Oh damn, he thinks I'm just another stupid deb and doesn't want me around. And then he said, "I'm afraid I've fallen in love with you." And that was sort of that. Of course I was delighted.'

The couple spent the night in Dieppe to celebrate their engagement and took the Tuesday evening boat back to Eastbourne. At 6.30 on Wednesday morning Peter Nevile was awoken and handed the news, along with instructions on how and when to deliver it to the Redesdales. To Esmond's and Decca's surprise he appeared annoyed, nor did he cheer up when he read the elopement note. 'My Darling Muv,' the note began, 'by the time you get this I shall be married to Esmond Romilly.' She had met him at Cousin Dorothy's, she wrote, but hadn't mentioned this because she thought her mother would disapprove of him:

> ... but I'm sure you wouldn't if you knew him. You can't think how happy I am. Peter Nevile (TEM 9301) knows us both and will explain the whole thing. Esmond has got a very good job as a journalist so I expect we will be in Spain and will have a mass of dough. There is no danger *at all* where we are going, but there might be if you tried to do anything to get me back or stop me doing what I want to. I'm sure you won't do this as we are naturally on the Government side and I don't want all Bobo's [Unity's] associates to be connected with me. Of course, you know how strongly I feel about this. Do remember that I *won't* be in any danger and it will be terrific fun. You will honestly *adore* Esmond when you know him so please don't be put off by all the secrecy, the only reason for it was because I wanted to go to Spain with him and thought you might try and stop me.

The same evening, and still without Decca's visa – Señor Lopez had continued to elude them – Esmond and Decca set off once again for Spain. By Friday morning they were in Bayonne. The Basque Consul at Bayonne, Señor Oruezabala, was sympathetic. The plight of the young freedom fighter and his girl appealed to his Spanish blood. But he could do nothing so diplomatically drastic as commit his approbation to paper. They did gain his unwritten approval, however, and he promised to keep his eyes open for 'friendly' ships.

On Saturday 13 February Esmond wrote to Peter Nevile with instructions on how to send money – 'say up to £25 of the first lot [from the articles] that comes in' – to Bilbao for which they were about to leave. He added that they were getting married as soon as possible. 'I'll send you a cable when we do.' But Saturday's plan had obviously foundered, for on Monday Esmond was still in Bayonne, and writing:

Dear Peter,
This is rather important – we have been delayed a day or two owing to difficulties of transport. Decca sent a wire to her mother and is writing at length by the same post to explain she won't be back till the end of the week as she's gone on tour south with the Pagets to the South of France. So do keep in close touch to see if this story has gone down all right (note, don't always ring up on the same person) and be careful not to deliver that letter till absolutely necessary.

I sent the *Sunday Chronicle* a very good story about the refugees living in a disused military hospital here – whose homes are at Irun and San Sebastian. But by now you'll have been in touch with them to know if they want it. The point is, cash is very short so, if you can, do manage a loan . . . .

Re. the marriage etc., don't make too much sort of publicity when it's announced – simply that we're officially engaged. OK?

Cash urgent.

The situation becoming critical, Esmond stepped up his appeals to the Basque Consulate. There was no shortage of boats, he was told. The problem was that the Bayonne area had now become Spain's diplomatic centre, and there were too many officials and their paid snoops for captains to risk illegal and non-profitable transportations. Esmond was advised to take a trip to Bordeaux, where a 'friendly' ship might be leaving within the next few days.

From Bordeaux, Friday 19 February, Esmond wrote again to Peter Nevile. 'We're off today by cargo boat (private this!) from here. But, of course, when you see Lady Redesdale give her the impression we've been here years and married already, etc. . . .' As for the publicity – a continuing preoccupation – 'do it from your own angle entirely, i.e. what you know etc. and all that! Really, that is the best. No statements from here.'

151

The cargo boat, the ss *Marklyn*, weighed anchor at midnight, and in a squall. Decca was immediately seasick and remained so throughout the three-day trip. Her condition was not so acute, however, that she was oblivious to her companion's sympathy. 'Esmond was worried about me and brought drinks of water, which I immediately threw up, too weak by now to make an effort to reach the basin. I was vividly and gratefully aware, however, of his concern – a side of Esmond not often seen in those days, and certainly not apparent in the long journeyings of the past few weeks about France and England.'

Jessica Mitford admits to having felt 'very strange emotions' during those first weeks:

Of course I would never confide these feelings to Esmond. He was very unsympathetic in those days, and was not about to take any nonsense from anyone, me included. He could be delightful company, though, and he had me doubled up with laughter for much of the time.... I never had any real misgivings about having run away with him. Really, if it hadn't been for Esmond where would I be now? In a loony-bin, I guess.

And what of Esmond's feelings? Even allowing for his adroitness in adapting himself to any situation, this new state of affairs must have been a little unsettling. Were those long, confused peregrinations of the first few days, for example, really necessary, or were they the confused ramblings of a young man in love? Had the 'Red Menace' become a marshmallow? Decca remained unconvinced; as she percipiently points out, no matter how unsettling the new experience it was not about to change overnight a personality weaned on the 'organized brutality of Wellington, the viciousness of the remand home, the rough and tumble of life in London'.

The Basque Foreign Secretary was at the port officially to welcome the journalist and his secretary to his country and to invite them to a performance which, being English, he was sure they would like. Esmond and Decca accepted enthusiastically. The boxing lasted four hours – 'we could only hope', wrote Decca, 'that the Foreign Minister attributed our stony silence to the well-known English characteristic of stoicism'.

Secure, or so he imagined, in Basque territory, Esmond instructed Peter Nevile to deliver the elopement note to the Redesdales. Nevile had referred to this mission as 'bearding the Nazi baron in his den', but found, on executing the assignment, that the invective was provided not by Lord Redesdale but by his wife and formidable daughters. Diana Mitford even went as far as to suggest that Nevile be publicly horse-whipped, and entrusted the task to brother Tom. As always the Redesdale son kept a low profile and said little.

Nancy Mitford's husband, Peter Rodd, was more forthcoming. Known to Evelyn Waugh readers as the irrepressible, wily Basil Seale of *Black Mischief* and *Put Out More Flags*, Rodd once again demonstrated that masterly deviousness which has earned him his place among the twentieth century's anti-heroes. 'Make her a Ward in Chancery', he advised, eruditely filling the family in with the details. By making Decca a Ward in Chancery the Redesdales would be transferring their own responsibility for their daughter's estate to the High Court. Any breach of the new guardian's jurisdiction would then result not in angry parental protestations but in possible imprisonment. It only remained to locate Esmond and release the news.

Meanwhile, in Dieppe, where she and her husband were holidaying, Nellie Romilly had received a rare letter from her son. He and Decca Mitford had met and fallen in love at Dorothy Allhusen's, he wrote, and were now on their way to Spain, Decca acting as his secretary.

> I expect by the time you get this [he continued] we'll have been married in Spain, as of course we've been unofficially so since we left, and we're intending to have three children.
>
> Of course her family loathe the name etc. of me so I think if you ever meet Lady Redesdale you might perhaps pour some whitewash on me. Also I'm sure you'll impress on her the folly of doing anything to get her back, as (a) She will be my wife by Spanish law (b) You know all about her sister and Hitler and it wouldn't be a very nice thing to have that advertised, anyway you know all about this already ....

As they knew, Nellie wrote to the Redesdales, Esmond had always been 'very fierce and the letter is quite fierce in his obvious wish to keep and protect Decca as his wife'.

She had had a very difficult time with him since he was fifteen – 'He has shown such independence that I have had to school myself not to be anxious about him as most mothers would be about anyone so young.' But when he had returned from Spain he seemed very much changed for the better; much more affectionate – 'tho' it is impossible to say that he has ever given me any sort of unselfish love'. He had been very ill and had to go to hospital. She had visited him every day and he had talked, it seemed, quite openly about his life and prospects. He wanted to return to Spain and report on the war, which he felt would be 'an honourable means of earning a living'. He had been so open, for once, that she had not suspected that anything was afoot. On the Sunday he left he asked her not to see him off at the station – 'He said he hoped I would not be hurt. I laughed and said, "I suppose you are being seen off by some woman friend." He looked sheepish and did not deny it.'

She understood what Sydney (Lady Redesdale) must be going through. Up until now she had been the chief sufferer from his naughtiness. 'But for all his faults Esmond was a man thro' and thro'; really as brave as a tiger and very self-reliant.' She knew only too well, of course, that he could not appeal to any mother as a husband for her child. Did the Redesdales want to get Decca back forcibly? She and Bertram were anxious to do all that they wished in the matter. She only hoped that the Press didn't get hold of the story. They were already ringing up Pimlico Road for information on his whereabouts. They might suddenly start pulling a stunt like 'Where is Esmond Romilly?' which was one of their favourite tricks when she withheld information.

As Nellie Romilly feared, the Press had got word of the story. The *Daily Express* had heard a rumour that one of the Redesdale's daughters had run away to Spain with Esmond Romilly, and would Lord Redesdale like to make a comment? His Lordship had nothing to say on the matter. The *Express* understood but perhaps if given a few details it could use its own network to locate the girl. The anxious parents capitulated. The story, 'PEER'S DAUGHTER ELOPES TO SPAIN', appeared on the front page the next morning. Peter Nevile to Esmond, Monday 1 March:

> You will be interested in seeing the front page of this morning's *Daily Express*. Unfortunately it had happened exactly as I thought it would happen. I told [Lord Redesdale] that as the Press would get hold of the story anyway it would be much better for me to give it to them at once, in which case they would not only get all the details correct but we should have been able to make some money out of the thing – which you are probably quite in need of. However he was adamant that I should not tell the press anything about it and I felt it was the least I could do. The result is, as you see – not only have we lost the chance of making £10 or £15 out of it but the story is hopelessly incorrect.

Despite its guile in gaining the story the *Express*, as Peter Nevile pointed out, had got it 'hopelessly incorrect'. They had even named the wrong girl, a careless slip which led to the Honourable Deborah Mitford (the injured party) bringing a libel suit against the newspaper – settled out of court – for £1,000.

Undeterred by Monday's mishap, the *Express* was back again on Tuesday with episode two of the elopement saga, this time with a guest appearance from Esmond's erstwhile comrade-in-arms, Keith Scott-Watson. Scott-Watson told the *Express* that he had treated the runaways to champagne and *foie gras* sandwiches at a West End restaurant before seeing them off to Spain. From Bayonne they had written to say they were going by 'fruit steamer through the mined seas of Bilbao'. Since then, he concluded dramatically, he had not heard from them.

Realizing the news value had by no means peaked, Peter Nevile released, on the same day, the authentic 'SECRETS OF THE ELOPEMENT' to the *Star*: an account designed to refute 'the fantastic tales that were abroad about these two people'. The article carried Esmond £20 – less his agent's twenty per cent commission. As always the money was 'urgently needed'.

By now all the popular dailies were involved in the elopement race, the field headed by the *Daily Mirror* (Wednesday 3 March) with 'Couple Trapped in a Peak Hut: Peer's Daughter and Her Fiancé?' It was left to the patrician *Daily Telegraph* to divulge the couple's true whereabouts, this gleaned from Señor Oruezabala, the Basque Consul.

'I can assure you', Senor Euzkadie [sic]* said to me, 'that they are both safe and well.

Letters may be sent to me and I will forward them. Whether Mr Romilly and Miss Freeman-Mitford have been married in Spain I cannot say, but in such troubled times it is quite possible that the authorities would not insist on the formalities normally required for the marriage of foreigners.'

Telephoning to gauge Lady Redesdale's reaction to a Mitford–Romilly romance, the *Telegraph* was told, 'I have heard nothing about a love affair ... I think she just wanted to go for the excitement and the adventure.'

The British Consulate in Bilbao had received a telegram from the Foreign Secretary, Anthony Eden. 'FIND JESSICA MITFORD AND PERSUADE HER TO RETURN.' In the absence of the Consul – he had moved,

---

* Euskadi is the Basques' name for their country.

along with the other foreign diplomats to Bayonne – the Spanish Proconsul delivered the message. He would need to draft a reply, he told the young couple. Esmond obligingly provided one: 'HAVE FOUND JESSICA MITFORD. IMPOSSIBLE TO PERSUADE HER TO RETURN.' The Proconsul left, assured that he had handled the affair 'in the very highest traditions of British diplomacy'.

Two days later Decca received another message, this time from the British Ambassador, Sir Henry Chilton, stationed at Hendaye: the Hon. Peter Rodd and Mrs Rodd were arriving in Bilbao on Tuesday morning (9 March). Could she be at the port to meet them? Decca went along to receive the family envoys, but found only the Consul, a Mr Stephenson who had returned on HMS *Echo* with the instructions to deliver Miss Mitford, by fair means or foul, into safe hands.

Failing to entice the young lady aboard the *Echo* (he had tried tempting her with a description of a delicious lunch cooked in her honour), Stephenson put the matter squarely to Esmond:

Stephenson told me [Esmond to Peter Nevile] that he had received instructions from the Ambassador of Great Britain in Hendaye to use 'all means' to make Decca leave Spain. In the course of this he said, 'It is a dirty game I have to play, I am afraid.' Then it was obvious that D. had to leave to avoid embarrassing the Basque Government – what he threatened. I decided to leave with her.

They boarded HMS *Echo* the next morning, Esmond fulminating against the British Government's base tactics.

Others too were expressing their concern over the Government's action. Mr George Hicks, socialist MP for Woolwich East, wanted to know 'why a British destroyer was placed at the disposal of the British Consul at Bilbao in order to enable him to persuade Miss Freeman-Mitford to return home from Spain, at a considerable public expense, for purely personal affairs?' Lord Stanley, Parliamentary Secretary to the Admiralty, replied that there was 'no foundation whatever for the assumption. The destroyer had gone from St Jean de Luz to Bilbao in the ordinary course of routine and returned to repatriate Spanish refugees.'

HMS *Echo* arrived at St Jean de Luz on Wednesday afternoon with 157 people on board, including Esmond and Decca. Fleet Street and the Rodds were on hand to greet them. The *Daily Telegraph*, Thursday 11 March:

When the *Echo* arrived the Hon. Peter Rennell Rodd and Mrs Rennell Rodd, brother-in-law and sister of Miss Freeman-Mitford, went to meet her in a motor-boat. They returned shortly afterwards with Miss Freeman-Mitford, who was smiling and cheerful, and Mr Romilly, who was in an angry mood.

Mr Romilly prevented journalists from approaching Miss Freeman-Mitford. When he was asked what Miss Freeman-Mitford's plans were, he said: 'She will go and grow beetroots for the rest of her life.'

After dining at a local hotel the party left St Jean de Luz and is expected to go straight to London.

The party did not go straight to London, but to Bayonne where, after a frictional leave-taking, the Rodds continued alone.

That family is amazing [Esmond to Peter Nevile, 14 March]. Everybody talks about how 'Muv' is comforting 'Farve' and how 'Farve' is making tea for 'Muv', and Debbo [Deborah] has had a wretched time, and how Bobo [Unity] and Diana are being so wonderful and the climax comes when I am met by Mr Peter Rodd at Saint-Jean-de-Luz and have a lecture on general principles, and his wife remarks that, after all, even when poor Aunt Tina died they soon got over their crying ... I'm afraid you seem to have had the worst of all this, but really the whole outfit is impossible.

Still pursued by the Press – or, rather, by one particularly adhesive member of that profession, Charing of the *Daily Express*, Esmond and Decca had taken refuge in the Basque delegation building at Las Mimosas. 'If you don't stop following us I'll punch you on the nose', Esmond told the journalist. This message was subsequently translated for the *Express* readers as 'I am with the girl I love'. Such attention was not only embarrassing, it was also prejudicial to Esmond's marriage suit, especially when the correspondents wrote that he and Decca were trying to get back to Spain, or (Charing again) that they had already been married under the Tree of Guernica – a Basque symbol for freedom.

'Please make a point of contradicting any reports that we are trying now to return to Spain', wrote Esmond to Nevile on 14 March in a letter asking for the address of the Redesdales' solicitors. 'If, by the way, they start trying to get Decca deported from France, etc., would you communicate to the Press that Lady R. gave me her promise that this would not be done – a condition of which was that I said she could keep in touch with D. by letter.' It was a peevish, empty gesture on Esmond's part, and indicated just how hopeless the situation appeared to be. What Esmond did not know, however, was that extradition proceedings might take months, even years to implement. This fact had recently been made known to Lady Redesdale, who, acting on the premise that not even the precocious Romilly was conversant with such matters, set off for Bayonne to make one final maternal plea.

Lady Redesdale remained in Bayonne for two days, just long enough to discover that her daughter was as redoubtable as her defiant suitor.

Telegram to Peter Nevile, 22 March:

LADY REDESDALE RETURNED LONDON THIS MORNING AFTER VISIT FRANCE TO SEE DAUGHTER AND PROSPECTIVE SON STOP NO CHANGE OUR PLANS STOP LADY HOPED TAKE DAUGHTER BACK BUT INTERVIEW AMICABLE STOP DONT PUBLISH THIS AS IF DIRECT WIRE FROM ME STOP CASH RATHER NECESSARY — ESMOND.

Realizing that a continuation of the contest would prove pointlessly wounding to both parties, Lady Redesdale had given in, and had persuaded her husband to withdraw his objections to the marriage. This decision was then communicated to the family solicitors, and later that week to the lovers themselves. On 'Friday (Good) 26th March', Esmond wrote again to his friend:

It now appears that Lord and Lady Redesdale are no longer opposed to the idea of marriage, in fact he seems to have given in in view of all that has happened. But of course, it doesn't rest with him to give permission now but with the judge ... you might kind of tickle the imagination and purse of the *News Chronicle–Star* outfit by letting them know that when and if Lord R. does withdraw his objections they will know all about plans for a presumably 'respectable' marriage.... On the whole I think this might be given right away to the *Chron.* as it can't do any harm, provided it's not presented with too many details as though a 'story' sold to the press. You see what I mean. Then we combine the proper attitude to this 'hateful publicity' with a little more filthy lucre don't you think?

It was a perky letter, and with good reason. Esmond had also heard that Giles, a member of the International Brigades since December, was alive and well, and working as an interpreter at Albacete – 'a terrific relief as you may have read that the English have had enormous casualties on the Jarama front'.

The news that Decca's legal guardian, Justice Luxmoor, had consented to her marrying came two weeks later, accompanied by a note

158

from Lord Redesdale 'to say [Esmond to Peter Nevile] she will not get a penny from him while she is with me (i.e. married or unmarried). That does not affect plans, of course; that we may be married here or in England in September, observing the conventions of a reasonable period of engagement... re. the marriage story, you can say if you like that D. said "So we'll probably be married about September, I suppose." I said "Everything is going to be ever so respectable now."'

16
Spring Wedding

Esmond had begun supplying Reuters with daily news bulletins gleaned from Bilbao radio broadcasts and the south-coast newspaper *Sud Ouest* – 'they [Reuters] have nothing better themselves'. The radio broadcasts were translated from Spanish into French by Monsieur Erramuzpé, the proprietor of the Hôtel des Basques, with whom Esmond and Decca had taken up residence. Esmond then converted these bulletins into English and delivered them to the news agency – his weekly fee covering the price of the couple's board and lodging at the hotel.

He was still sending items to the *News Chronicle*, but the newspaper was more interested in the personal story spin-offs – like a ten-part serial on famous elopements and 'What it Means to Be a Ward in Chancery' – than in Romilly's own journalistic contributions. 'I'm afraid', he wrote to Peter Nevile, 'it looks like all the stories you gave to the *News Chronicle* have been dumped in the wastepaper basket. This is all rather mortifying as of course they would have helped me perhaps to get a job later on.' Equally mortifying was the Foreign Office's refusal to sanction his Spanish visa, which he had been counting on to gain some first-hand accounts of Franco's recent push into the Basque Country.

His scope limited, Esmond continued to scratch around locally for tit-bits tossed from the Spanish table, and on 4 April came up with what seemed, at first, to be 'a very good story about The British Ambassador to Spain supporting the rebels'. The Military Governor of the Spanish province of Bidassoa, the Francoist Troncoso, was, it appeared, a frequent visitor to the Château Bordaberry, residence of the British Ambassador, Sir Henry Chilton. This in itself was rather intriguing, as 'Troncoso has no diplomatic work which would bring him normally into contact with the Ambassador'. But now there was a report that while the two men had been strolling in the Château's gardens after a lunchtime engagement, Troncoso had taken the opportunity to indulge in a little propaganda. Coming across a group of Basque refugees playing pelota by arrangement on the Ambassador's fronton court, the Governor delivered this *ex cathedra* message: '"The war is lost for you", he said. "Everyone with sense should go against the Reds, and with Franco. That is the side where England stands: I have just had lunch with the British Ambassador; there he is, he will not contradict me. Only Russia is on your side. I advise you to return to Spain." The Ambassador said nothing.'

On investigating the report further, Esmond discovered that Sir Henry was in fact at a diplomatically safe distance when Troncoso had made his speech. Reluctantly, the story was scrapped. Coming on the eve of the 'Bilbao Blockade' it did, however, cast a revealing light on British/Spanish Nationalist relations.

On 6 April, seven days after the start of Franco's northern campaign, the Admiralty received a report that the Nationalists had mounted an effective blockade on the port of Bilbao. Acting on this information, the British Government requested all merchant ships in the area to repair to St Jean de Luz and await further instructions. This unprecedented action immediately caused a storm within the Commons. Why, asked Clement Attlee, had merchant ships been denied – in contravention of their rights – the protection of the Royal Navy? And why was the Government so certain that there was a blockade at all, when the Basque Government had continually denied this? Was its information supplied by 'those curious people our consular agents, who seemed so silent on the question of Italian troop landings?'

From St Jean de Luz on 13 April Esmond reported that the situation was relatively quiet: a laconic '"What's the British Navy for?" and "My potatoes are ruined with all this mucking about", that's about all.' But as cargoes began to putrefy in ships' holds, the merchantmen became more animated; one captain in particular, a Welshman known as Potato Jones, enthralling the Press with his sea-dog repartee and allusions to 'secret plans'. Nor was the Welshman boasting – at least not about the plans; a scheme had indeed been devised by the merchantmen and the Basque Consulate to run the blockade, and Esmond Romilly – on friendly terms with the Basque Consul – was acting as go-between.

The eighteen-year-old was now in possession of the biggest scoop of the day, and the other journalists were, as Jessica Mitford recalls, 'fit to be tied'. Esmond to Peter Nevile, 16 April:

I rang up Cliff [Norman Cliff, editor of the *News Chronicle*] last night re some exclusive story over the ships. I have acted as interpreter between the merchant vessels and the Basque Consulate. When the ships arrive safe, I can give the full story of how we planned out in a cafe in St Jean de Luz the system of codes and signalling to the Government warships. The only story Reuter sends is what I give Holmes [Reuters' correspondent at Hendaye] – this is not a full one i.e. last night I didn't tell him about the insurance and the bonus to the captains.

The first ship to make the Basque run was the *Seven Seas Spray*, which set out on the night of 17 April with (as if in some Victorian narrative prose epic) Captain Roberts and his daughter at the helm. At eight the next morning it docked at Bilbao, welcomed by a large, hungry crowd with cries of 'Long live the British sailors! Long live Liberty.' No mines, no enemy ships; there was no blockade. The information, it was subsequently revealed, had been passed to the Admiralty by Sir Henry Chilton, his informant none other than the Military Governor, Troncoso. The Royal Navy had, it emerged, supported this story, while making no attempt to check its validity.

'Now that I have perhaps done something for you,' wrote Lady Redesdale to Esmond on 14 April (a reference to withdrawing her objection to the marriage),

will you do something for me, and that is arrange to get married now in Bayonne?... I know you will realize that old as I am I cannot agree with the unconventional idea of you living with Decca not married to her, and would never in a thousand years get used to such an idea, it seems to me entirely wrong, and I very much wish to see the end of this state of affairs.

In magnanimous mood, Esmond consented to the proposal, and began to make arrangements for a spring wedding. A week later Decca sent a telegram: 'SIXTEENTH MAY. HOPE CONVENIENT.' No, not really, came Lady Redesdale's reply, as she had promised to take Margaret Ogilvy (Decca's cousin) to her school in Florence, leaving London on 15 May. She would, of course, attend a 16 May wedding if there was no possibility of advancing it, but she would prefer an earlier date. It was not, perhaps, an unreasonable request, but Esmond, intolerant of matriarchal caprice and surfeited with Redesdale 'advice', chose to take umbrage.

Bayonne,
Friday, April 23.

Dear Lady Redesdale,

Decca has shown me her letter from you this morning. I must say at once that we have had not the slightest wish to interfere with your plans, and I know that Decca was always urging you to go on your previous cruise. Also we know ourselves how irritating it is to have one's plans spoiled.

At the moment, I am uncertain as to the exact date of our marriage, but I can't see how this can affect your plans for going on a cruise [sic].

There was also something else he would like to straighten out:

I have heard from two separate sources that thoroughly vile things have been said and believed about me by the Rodds to the effect that I was anxious to get money out of this affair – all the more impertinent because the only reason which Rodd could produce for Decca going back to England when we saw him at Saint Jean de Luz was, as he put it, 'that by doing so D. would get an allowance out of her father'.

I think you will realise that it would not be much good having a 'family' marriage here, in view of all this.

Wisely, Lady Redesdale adopted a placating tone in her next letter to her daughter. She realized now, she wrote, that her request for a change of date may have seemed 'ungracious' after Esmond had consented to an early wedding, but letter-writing was such an inadequate means of communicating, and could so easily lead to misunderstandings. As to those aspersions cast on Esmond's motives for eloping with Decca, she paid no attention to such rumours – 'In my experience it is just the contrary, he always says he can quite well get along, and I have told everyone this to whom I have spoken about it at all. Actually I admire this independent spirit very much.'

Appeased, Esmond wrote to apologize for his outbursts – 'I entirely agree, it is extremely stupid to take any notice of such things but one usually does at the time.' The wedding was not on 16 May as Decca had written but on Tuesday morning, 18 May.

The whole thing takes I think about ten minutes or so, and is performed by a slobbering old Swede, who – by some curious chance, represents His Britannic Majesty as well as Lloyds Limited in this town. So there is nothing much to it. But D. is very anxious you should come, and I very much hope you will if you haven't changed your plans.

The wedding, attended by both Lady Redesdale and Nellie Romilly, took place at 12 noon on Tuesday 18 May at the British Consulate, Bayonne; the ceremony was performed by the British Vice-consul, Mr Schoedling. For the occasion the groom sported an old brown suit, the bride a simple brown dress cut a little full to hide the slight pregnancy.

17
Settling Down

Esmond had begun writing a book, 'working steadily and lazily,' he told Peter Nevile, 'with a view to publication for the autumn season'. His wife told a different story. 'I used to watch Esmond', she wrote, 'as he worked furiously on *Boadilla*, brown head bent over the typewriter, papers scattered all over the floor, wondering how much he minded being separated from the struggle in Spain.'

Holding herself partly responsible for Esmond's captivity in Bayonne, Decca was understandably sensitive – over-sensitive even – to her husband's moods. But his enmeshment in *Boadilla* is no indication that he had any serious misgivings about his decision not to return to the fight – a decision which, in any case, he made before meeting the future Mrs Romilly. 'This is ridiculous,' he had said to Babs Ovenden in Madrid, 'if we stay here sooner or later we're all going to be killed.' It was a stark realization and one which the writing of *Boadilla* served only to reinforce.

In the closing paragraphs of *Boadilla*, Esmond referred to the British Battalion, in training at Albacete when he had left Spain in December. 'I might have gone back and joined those men', he wrote, 'who are the real heroes of the Spanish struggle. But I didn't. I got married and lived happily instead.' As Esmond knew, the British Battalion had seen its first action at the Battle of Jarama on 12 February 1937, losing 375 of its 600 members on a mound of Spanish earth thereafter known as 'Suicide Hill'.

Most of the journalists had left for Bilbao, gone to report on the war now concentrated on the Basque Country. Denied a visa, Esmond remained in Bayonne to finish his book, and to follow the ever-worsening situation through the Bilbao radio broadcasts.

Held up for two weeks due to bad weather, Franco's war machine sprang again into action in mid-April with another series of rapid advances against the ill-prepared Basque defenders. Once again the German Condor Legion was used as a spectacular vanguard, often terrorizing the Basques into early retreats. On Monday 26 April – a market day – the Condor Legion attacked Guernica, bombing and machine-gunning the town from mid-afternoon until dusk veiled the decimated town centre; 1,654 people were killed in the bombing, a further 889 wounded. Lying thirty kilometres from the front line, Guernica had been chosen by the Nationalists as an experiment in 'total war'. 'We bombed it and bombed it, and *bueno* why not', a Nationalist staff-officer told a *Sunday Times* correspondent, his words giving impact to General Mola's flatulent threat to raze all the province of Viscaya to the ground.

'"*Alemanes! Criminales! Animales! Bestiales!*"' – Decca recalled one old lady's chant as the news of the bombing was broadcast into the Hôtel des Basques dining room. The woman was a refugee, one of the many already flooding into southern France to escape the Nationalist advance.

It took just two months for the Nationalist Army to overwhelm the Basques (Franco's troops entered Bilbao on 19 June 1937), revealing yet again the awful disparity between the two camps' weaponry; a disparity maintained by the lopsided implementation of the non-intervention accord. Already France had shown itself prepared to abandon an agreement which Italy and Germany were openly contravening. Even the axis powers themselves appeared, at times, to be indifferent to perpetuating the sham. Only Britain, setting a straight course towards appeasement, was intent on keeping the talks alive, and did so through another eighteen months of hostilities, proving, finally, too stubborn an opponent even for the tenacious Spanish Republic.

The Romillys did not leave Bayonne immediately after the Basque defeat but stayed on to take part in the July festival, an event, Esmond told Peter Nevile, 'just like *Fiesta* – everyone drunk after four days' revels.... Outside the hotel yesterday they let loose six fierce wild cows and everyone baited them and had their trousers ripped up. I watched, from a window, a proper bull fight in the afternoon and lively fire-work display and street dancing till 3 a.m. Another cowfight after lunch – perhaps I shall take part with anarchist handkerchief.'

Four months spent in the fringe of the Iberian peninsula had given Esmond a taste for the Spanish way of life; so much so indeed that he had even begun to mull over the possibilities of moving to pro-Republic Mexico. He put the idea to his wife, along with a plan to convert the couple's savings – a £50 advance from *Boadilla* – into a substantial three-figure travelling allowance. He had been thinking a great deal about *boule*, he announced – *boule* being a gambling game offering even worse odds than the prohibited (the Romillys were still minors) roulette.

When he spoke of boule [wrote Jessica Mitford] Esmond's face assumed the far-away expression of one seeing a vision of happiness; the look of a child on his way to his first circus, or a mother shown her new-born infant for the first time. It was a soft, radiant look, full of excitement and promise for the future, and one that I was to come to know well over the next few years.

A novice in dealing with her husband's beatific visions, Decca too became convinced of the plan's feasibility:

It was so extraordinarily simple and yet so absolutely sound! There is a choice of seven numbers in boule. We would pick a number, say 4, and put a very small amount on it – one franc to start with. Every time the 4 failed to come up, we would multiply our investment by 7 – to 49, to 343, to 2,401 and so on. Actually our potential fortune would increase in direct proportion to the failure of 4 to win, for eventually it would be bound to come up, and by that time we should have thousands and thousands of francs on it. . . .

And so the punters made their visit to the Dieppe Casino, staked their savings, and in 'two agonizing hours' lost the lot.

It was while sitting in an all-night café, addressing an impecunious future, Jessica Mitford wrote in *Hons and Rebels*, that the unlikely archangel Roger Roughton appeared and saved the day. He had recently acquired a four-storey property on the south bank of the Thames, he told them. An excellent place for a little informal gambling operation, Esmond suggested. Roughton agreed, and invited the down-and-outs, with hardly any prompting, to move in.

Originally a merchant millionaire's warehouse on the Thames old cinnamon wharf, No. 41 Rotherhithe Street had recently become, along with several of its renovated neighbours, a fashionable bohemian retreat. Its previous occupant, the writer Arthur Calder-Marshall, had passed the house on to Roughton when he left for Hollywood in June 1937. Roughton occupied the second and third storeys and rented the self-contained top floor to the Romillys. The ground floor – over forty feet long but only twelve feet wide at the Thames side and eight feet at the street side – functioned as both dining room and Saturday night gambling den.

Staying at Rotherhithe in September as a guest of Roger Roughton, the young poet Bernard Gutteridge recalls the events of one Saturday night session:

A whole cross-section of people were asked to the big dining room where there was food and ... wine. At the right moment the table was cleared, the green baize cloth laid and the boule wheel was placed at the top with Esmond as croupier. Beside him was a cardboard box which had once held a dozen bottles of wine but now contained 'the bank'.

Boule is a crippling game, with such high odds that even then it was forbidden at most casinos. I didn't know this and I imagine most of Esmond's guests that night were equally ignorant of their chances. As part of the premises I poured the wine. Two of the other non-gamblers were Gavin Ewart and a man called Easterbrook who wrote for the *News Chronicle* on farming (!) He smoked a battered pipe and leaned against the wall by the fire, quietly drinking and looking on. He must have known the odds.

When the party was over and the gamblers had been pushed off, the bank box was tilted up and all was counted. The profit after food and drink was just over £10. And that was good in those days for a week's housekeeping and beer in the pubs. I remember Esmond's cherubic grin, his hands gently clapping; then the boyish frown. 'We won't have that bloody Christopher Isherwood again', he said. 'He only bets in sixpences.'

Back from the States for two months at the beginning of 1938, Arthur Calder-Marshall also found himself drawn into a Rotherhithe gambling party, and discovered that Esmond had devised yet another means of making a profit from the enterprise: 'Bring a bottle', said the host, who thereupon secreted all bottles of gin and whisky within the grandfather clock in the corner, while continuing to serve beer.

Bernard Gutteridge, who remained at Rotherhithe Street for several days after the Saturday session, remembers Esmond as 'boisterous and full of zest'; his wife – who was now six months pregnant – as 'poorly but a good hostess'. His visit, he recalled, had coincided with Giles's twenty-first birthday, Esmond dashing off a telegram to 'the good boy of the family' who 'deserved all the rewards there might be', a teasing reference, for certain, to his brother's late, self-conscious delinquency.

The elder Romilly may have been, as Esmond wrote, the family's blue-eyed boy. It was not an image he was going out of his way to promote. Towards the end of the 1936 winter term Giles had peremptorily left Oxford and, in the company of Tony Hyndman, Stephen Spender's estranged secretary, had headed for the Spanish Civil War. The two volunteers had arrived on the Madrid front just in time to witness the last days of the Nationalists' campaign against the Spanish capital. For both men it was their first experience of firing, but it was the ex-guardsman, Hyndman, whose nerves shattered under the bombardment. Finding himself in the thick of the Jarama campaign, he retreated early to camp where he sat out the next three months refusing, on pain of death, to return to the front. In Spain as part of a writers' delegation in the spring of 1937, Stephen Spender took time off to plead the offender's case. After his many entreaties, the enervated Hyndman was released and allowed to return to England.

Giles too had had problems with the authorities who, discovering he was yet another of Churchill's nephews, were intent on keeping him away from the battle front. Determined, however, to continue his rebellion against life's cosseters, Giles had slipped away to fight with the British Battalion at Brunete. In August he was back in England, but, he insisted, only for a rest. He was determined to return to the war. Equally determined that her son should stay put, Nellie Romilly contacted Arthur Ovenden, then involved with clandestine volunteer recruitment, and asked him to prevent Giles from re-entering the Brigade. "'I'm not so worried about Esmond," she said, "I know he can take it, but Giles is different – and I think it would kill his father if anything were to happen to him.'"

For once in agreement with his mother, Esmond was also at pains to discourage his elder brother, whom he regarded as much more delicate than himself, from returning to fight. But Giles was no longer the effete malcontent of his Oxford days; he had changed, as Philip Toynbee observed, 'in quite the opposite direction from the change which had reduced and sobered Esmond. Giles's slender body had remarkably filled out; he looked healthier than ever before, and he had turned himself into a ruthless communist.'

Of course, Giles had taken it all too far. The Spanish Civil War had provided a reason for leaving Oxford, but what next? Insecure, he could not ignore or feed off the contradictions of a free-floating life style, as could his brother. He needed a belief, and Communism, while not being the answer to his problems, was at least a specious substitute. He plunged into the creed with an enthusiasm all the more zestful for its lack of conviction.

As a small neurotic boy at Wellington, Giles had been worried by his 'mental emptiness'.

The high marks I obtained in work did not satisfy me, because I could not think ... I liked to stroll out onto the drive on a sunny afternoon, or lie at night with my head on my hands, and say: 'Now I will think'. It distressed me that I could never find anything to think about. Vague generalities would come my way, of course, but nothing, I knew, that would not be quite trivial if put on paper. I became terrified of my own inadequacy. And yet, the more desperately I tried to think, the less I seemed able to.

The schoolboy's inanition had persisted long after Wellington College – an altogether too subtle ache to be treated by the prescriptions of Karl Marx.

Eventually Giles's self-imposed hardships caught up with him. He became ill and left his lodgings in working-class Poplar to return to Pimlico Road. Away from the East End, seeing the moral as well as physical poverty of his communist life style, Giles turned away from the Party and, with the help of the family's friend, Lord Beaverbrook, went to work for the *Daily Express*.* A fine, controlled writer, Giles had at least found an outlet, although an inadequate one, for his talents. His abilities were soon noted by his editors and he became, in 1938, Beaverbrook's man in Stockholm. Symbolically, the first winter of the war found him wading through the frozen north, as far away, one imagines, from that perfect hyperborean state as ever before.

Esmond had not followed his brother into the Communist Party. He had been impressed by the communists' efforts in defending Madrid, and had even told Philip Toynbee, on his return from Spain, that despite his many objections to the Party he would have to consider himself a communist. But away from the fighting, the old arguments prevailed: the CP was casuistic, petty and prevaricative; worse, it was dictatorial, the very antithesis of the rebel's personal philosophy. 'The Bermondsey Labour Party was much more to our liking', wrote Jessica Mitford;

---

* In marked contrast to its right-wing image, the *Express* employed many left-wing writers during the thirties, including Michael Foot.

more militant than Transport House, it continued its fund-raising campaign for the Spanish Republic, in defiance of the Government's non-intervention policy.

It was while attending a local Aid Spain meeting in September that Esmond bumped into an old friend, trying to enter the outlawed Brigades. 'Esmond was much more mature,' writes John Peet, 'thought it completely natural that I wanted to go to Spain, though he warned me it was going to be tough, and put me in touch with a cloak and dagger recruiter, through whom I rapidly entered the war.'

Appearing on the scene at the same time, Philip Toynbee was also impressed by the married Romilly; impressed, that is, by his complete immutability. 'When I saw him in October, 1937', wrote Toynbee, 'he had been back in England only a fortnight, but already he was planning an expedition to Mexico.' The plan again came to nothing; nevertheless it was characteristic of their meetings that they should take place in an atmosphere of leave-taking, making precarious a genuine but often tense relationship.

On this occasion, however, Toynbee felt none of the anxiety that had marred several earlier encounters with Esmond: 'I had never been so happy in his company or so sharply aware of how much I had been missing by his absence.' The friends drank beer and talked until 3 o'clock in the morning about the Civil War, about the elopement, about the young pregnant wife asleep above: 'The only thing to do with the English upper class', opined Esmond, 'is to marry into it.' A typical Romilly remark, it was cast out like a wrought-iron tenet then promptly forgotten. At Parton Street, at their first meeting, Esmond had confidentially told Toynbee that 'Craven A were the *only* cigarettes', and for several years he smoked nothing else. He was less inclined to take the latest philosophical gobbet to heart, however, concluding, reasonably, that Decca was probably the only member of her class who could possibly have contemplated married life with Esmond.

After so many months of brief, not always satisfactory meetings, and long uncommunicative separations, the Romilly–Toynbee friendship now entered a period of relative normality. In early November Esmond and Decca visited Toynbee at Christ Church, Oxford; the host, a sociable, popular figure amongst the college community, took them on a tour of his home turf.

I had been nervous before their arrival, [Toynbee admitted] for it was hard to envisage Esmond and Decca in this unfamiliar company, or to believe that either side would make the necessary concessions to the other. But I had underestimated Esmond's astute social sense (and Decca's impervious ease in any company); he took immediate soundings of the unknown situation and then, since he had come to Oxford for pleasure not for conflict, he made himself at home in it.

But contrary to this analysis, Toynbee's account of Esmond's visit reveals not a person at ease in his surroundings, but someone tense and excessive. When introduced to the philosopher, Isaiah Berlin, 'Esmond's appreciation', according to his friend, 'was as flamboyant as his disapproval; his laughter was raucous, and he would repeat a remark of Isaiah's which he had enjoyed as if to redouble his enjoyment.' This behaviour did not apparently offend Berlin, although other dons were somewhat 'surprised' by a young man, far more experienced than the average undergraduate, whose 'uncontrolled enthusiasm' was like that of 'a happy child of eight'.

On the second day of the trip the Romillys, with Philip Toynbee and the young don Frank Pakenham (later Lord Longford) as guides, took to the Oxford countryside. Esmond had hired an old car for the trip and was intent on getting his full mileage out of the vehicle. Returning to Oxford after an exhaustive day's touring, the foursome passed by the country estate, Buscot Park. Off guard, Pakenham chanced to admit an acquaintance with its owner, Lord Faringdon, a remark immediately pounced upon by Esmond, who insisted they pay the peer a social call.

The troupe piled into the country house where, to Esmond's undisguised delight, a week-end house-party was in full swing. Known as the Red Lord because of his socialist leanings, Lord Faringdon had gathered together a veritable *pot-pourri* of trades unionists, left-wingers and hungry aristocrats. Esmond felt there was an ingredient missing and asked Pakenham to solicit a dinner invitation from the host. He obliged, while excusing himself, wisely, from the evening's proceedings.

With the exception of the Romillys, Toynbee and several tweed-jacketed Labourites, everyone dressed for dinner. While this ceremony was taking place Esmond and Toynbee loosened up on the peer's whisky, greeting the returning guests with broad smiles and rosy good humour: '... they must have been surprised', wrote Toynbee, 'to find that Esmond and I had made it our duty to put them at their ease. While Esmond handed round the sherry, sometimes pausing to apologize and to take a glass himself, I held the olives and salted nuts. We felt benevolent, and wished everybody else to be happy.'

But lacking Toynbee's insight into the situation, the other guests might be excused for feeling slightly ill at ease in the presence of

Esmond's exuberance. Were they being confronted by a sparkling young wine or a more sinister concoction? It is doubtful whether Esmond himself knew; certainly his friend was beginning to question his benevolence. 'He was becoming more and more like some lusty barbarian invader being uneasily entertained in conquered and civilized territory.'

Toynbee was right to assert there was no malice in Esmond's actions – Esmond was not a spiteful or vindictive person. But he was excitable and too often truculent, especially when his primary impulses for gratification were being opposed. Taking stock of the situation, Lord Faringdon decided against a policy of confrontation, and when his drunken young guest asked if he and his pregnant wife could stay the night, he diplomatically acquiesced. Toynbee was then driven back to Oxford at breakneck speed, Esmond returning to take further advantage of his host's hospitality.

The Romillys were back in Oxford early the next morning, editing, augmenting, improving on the previous evening's events. Toynbee was delighted – 'feeling better than I have for ages', he wrote in his diary and, three days later, after an Oxford party: 'I really don't belong to these people, nice though so many of them are. I don't quite belong to any people except Esmond and Decca.' About this, of course, he was wrong (as he soon found out). An invigorating tonic, the Romillys were too overpowering to be imbibed on a regular basis.

Boadilla had been published by Hamish Hamilton in the autumn, at a time when the market was flooded with accounts of the Spanish conflict. It sold poorly. Esmond began looking for a more secure way of earning his living and found a job as a copywriter at the advertising agency Graham and Gillies. One of his first assignments was to write copy for Bob Martins' animal conditioners. Landing at Rotherhithe Street in the Christmas vacation, Toynbee found Esmond enthusiastically composing and enacting his doggy dialogues, then being broadcast over Radio Luxembourg. This was Esmond at his best; humorous, vivacious, engaging. There was, however, another side to the Romilly character, a side Toynbee had almost forgotten.

I met him, one evening, outside his office in the Strand, and we made our long way back to Rotherhithe, often stopping for a glass of beer. I became querulous when he dropped the quart bottle which I'd paid for, took half-a-crown off me to buy another, and then refused to give me the change. Here was all the worst and toughest in him coming out again. Back in the house we began to tussle amicably,

173

drunkenly and without, on my part, the least concern about who won or lost. But as we wrestled on the floor and as, since I was taller and stronger than Esmond, I began to get the better of him, his methods became more and more drastic. His teeth were sunk into my arm, and he was pulling my head sideways to the ground by the short hairs. Suddenly, influenced by the beer, influenced by the physical pain, but principally in horror at Esmond's methods, I began to weep. I felt almost satisfyingly humane, but Esmond and Decca were utterly bewildered. They could not understand that such fighting as this was intolerable to me, the thin edge of a hideous wedge.

The Christmas visit was not a success, marred not only by the above incident but by the hosts' habit of ganging up on their guest. It was annoying and dispiriting always to be voted down two to one, and this was invariably the case, as Decca took her husband's part on all occasions. It may have been very flattering for Esmond to have his views reinforced by an adoring wife, but this automatic partisanship was often rather wearing on friends.

The Romilly's child, a girl, was born on 19 December 1937 and christened Julia Decca – Julia after the adored damsel of Robert Herrick's poems:

> How rich and pleasing thou, my Julia art
> In each thy dainty, and peculiar part.

Nellie Romilly offered to help with the baby, but the parents refused; they had their own ideas on bringing up their daughter: 'We planned her future,' wrote Decca, 'growing up among the rough children of Rotherhithe Street, born to freedom and May Day parades, without the irksome restraint of nanny, governess, daily walks and dull dances; or perhaps we'd take her to Paris to live, a little gamine trudging to a *lycée* with books in satchel....' The dreams apart, Decca proved to be a competent mother, and impressed friends by her 'easy maternalism'. This solicitude did not, however, prevent the baby from catching measles when an epidemic broke out in the spring.

... the health clinic nurses assured me there was nothing to fear – a breast-fed child was immune to such illnesses. Perhaps they did not know that immunization can only be conferred by a mother who has had the disease; or perhaps, in that teeming part of London, it never occurred to them that a person might reach maturity without having had all the usual childhood illnesses at some time or other. In any case, they were tragically wrong.

The baby died on 28 May 1938. A week later Esmond resigned his job with Graham and Gillies and fled with his wife to Corsica; 'shielded', wrote Jessica Mitford, 'from the sympathy of friends'. Shielded too from the self-righteous reproaches of the Establishment, whose members, as Philip Toynbee noted, while enjoying a 'season', 'spoke of the Romillys with a spitefulness which was out of all proportion to what they themselves had suffered from them'. It was as if, thought Toynbee, they regarded the Romillys as some kind of insidious enemy, or worse, sagacious deserters.

18
Corsican Summer, Munich Winter

My wishes now come homeward,
Their gallopings in vain,
Logic and lust are quiet
And again it starts to rain;
Falling asleep I listen
To the falling London rain.

LOUIS MACNEICE, 'London Rain'

The Grande Hôtel de Calvi was small, bourgeois, and by English standards, very cheap. The Romillys moved in on arrival and remained there for three months, swimming, sunbathing, eking out their savings on plain food and cheap wine.

In the thirties Corsica was a haven for the impecunious artist and the down-at-heel member of the governing classes. Esmond and Decca soon struck up a friendship with one such denizen: the island's remittance man. Every Friday the man trekked into the town to collect the family's bribe, then he went on a spree, inviting the Romillys to join him in food and drink. A life-saver on many occasions, the remittance man was far and away the island's most reliable inhabitant.

'In 1938', Jessica Mitford recalls, 'Corsica was a very revolutionary place. Many of the young men were involved, or had been involved in the Spanish Civil War. Others were enmeshed in these tremendous island vendettas. We would make friends with someone and then suddenly he would disappear and we wouldn't hear from him for weeks. Although dying to know where these people went to, we decided it was unwise to show too much interest.'

A curious place for a rest cure, Corsica nevertheless worked its own peculiar magic on its visitors, as the writer William Sansom found when, in the company of Peter Nevile, he visited the Romillys in August. Peter Nevile:

We – the Romillys, Sansom and I – made a trip along the West coast from Calvi to a little village called St Florent, spending one night along the way at the Hotel Napoleon Bonaparte at Ile Rousse. Here Bill Sansom imagined himself one of Napoleon's marshalls, drinking freely and intemperately at the battle's end. As he quaffed the shots of Tokay he tossed the glasses cavalierly into the open grate. The landlord looked on sympathetically, while making a liberal assessment of the damage.

Sansom later kneaded the incident into one of his first short stories, *Through the Quinquina Glass.*

Esmond too had gained an idea for a story, although the plot had nothing to do with romantic and picaresque Corsica. His own story – a novel – concerned a public school, and was symbolically abandoned in mid-term.

The Romillys returned to England in early September, just in time to witness the Prime Minister's frantic shuttles to Germany and their insidious culmination. On 30 September Chamberlain and Hitler signed the Munich Agreement, transferring Czechoslovakia's Sudeten-land and all the country's major fortifications to Germany. 'You shall today level no reproaches at those who have forsaken us in our hour of direst need,' the Czechoslovakian President, Eduard Beneš, told his people. 'History will pass judgement on the events of these days.' History's judgement was rapid, so rapid in fact that it is often forgotten quite how popular Chamberlain had been before he passed into popular myth as an unprepossessing comic cut. 'I believe it is peace for our time', were the old man's words as he waved his achievement above his head. His audience cheered.

There would be no war, and yet aircraft production was mushrooming, the Hyde Park trenches – symbols of Munich-week panic – remained, and those monstrous masks continued to lurk in one's home. Looking into the future, as was his wont, Esmond saw, to his horror, 'One vast OTC, with overtones of an eternal Boy Scout jamboree. You wait and see, in no time there'll be a wave of Grey-haired Motherism (barely choking back the tears you understand) and the small matter of who we go to war with, and why, will be entirely lost sight of.'

Esmond could muster no enthusiasm for the coming European embroilment, his own belligerence having declined with the Spanish Republic's fortunes. By October 1938 both had reached a very low ebb.

In July the Republic had launched its last-ditch Ebro offensive – an attack designed above all to convince France and Great Britain that, given a free arms market, it could still prosecute the war. But, whilst sending seismic waves throughout the Nationalist camp, the

177

Republic once again failed to create the necessary ripples within the Quai d'Orsay and Whitehall. Lacking adequate artillery, the Government's thrust quickly lost impetus, the Ebro offensive becoming one long dispirited retreat. By November Franco, aided by a new shipment of German arms, had not only reclaimed all the lost territory, he had also captured or destroyed the best part of the Republican army. Thereafter his victory was a foregone conclusion.

The Romillys had taken a furnished room near the Marble Arch; an expedient move, precipitated, as Jessica Mitford admitted, by her ignorance of household economics. 'No one had ever explained to me that you had to pay for electricity; and lights, electric heaters, stoves blazed away night and day at Rotherhithe Street.' When a process server arrived hot on the heels of the electricity board's final demand the Romillys made a stealthy exit.

A particularly tenacious member of his profession, the process server had, however, given chase, forcing the fugitives to adopt a number of 'the most transparent disguises' to circumvent the incriminating scrap of paper. But the subterfuge game had soon ended, the Romillys, in languorous mood, having taken to their beds to avoid the daily drudge. On occasion, Jessica Mitford recalled, they would remain in bed for up to two days – amusing respites for themselves, maybe, but 'a source of irritation' to the advertising agency Graham and Gillies, who had magnanimously re-employed Esmond after his return from Corsica.

In the circumstances Decca's 'great windfall' – a trust fund of £100 – came like manna from heaven.

The sum of a hundred pounds seemed just the right amount for the purposes of emigration. It was neither large enough to start a business or invest for income, nor small enough to spend on a few parties and good meals out. Yet a third of it would purchase two one-way steerage tickets to America, leaving a nice round sum, over $300, at the prevailing rate of exchange, to live on for a while until we found work.

Unfortunately, the American Consul didn't agree. Try again, suggested Peter Nevile, with a 'Land of Opportunity–Rugged Individualism' line. Esmond did so, with stunning effect. Jessica Mitford:

If Esmond had suddenly assumed the appearance of a cross between

Mr Oover in Zuleika Dobson and Spencer Tracy, the Consul didn't seem to notice. As Peter had predicted, the words had an enormous, almost mesmeric effect on him. With a faraway look in his eyes – which were no doubt seeing the windswept main street of some Mid-western town, swarming with rugged individualists – he uttered the words of consent: 'Well, I guess I'll take a chance on you kids.'

Turning over the possible ways of making a living in the New World Esmond alighted, characteristically, on the most spectacular: a coast to coast lecture tour. Decca could talk on 'I was an English Debutante', he himself on 'I Ran Away from An English Public School'; kindled by the new sparks his mind spat out the endless possibilities. Of course what he really needed was a lecture troupe. Tony Hyndman, back from his depressing Spanish excursion, was an obvious recruit, so too was Esmond's old Parton Street friend, Sheila Legge. Both spent their lives bobbing aimlessly and precariously on the London current; both were perennial candidates for an escape clause. Then there was Toyn-bee . . . .

Since leaving Oxford in the summer Philip Toynbee's affairs had gone from bad to worse. At his final Oxford ball he had proposed to Isabel Campbell (a pseudonym), daughter of Liberal politician Sir Roderick Campbell, and had been accepted. But the girl's parents had refused to countenance the match on the grounds that the suitor was a communist sympathizer and known to inhabit dissolute circles. They counselled a six-month separation in order for their daughter to examine her feelings more fully. Stunned into acquiescence, Toynbee went off to Birmingham to take charge of Frank Pakenham's news-paper, the *Birmingham Town Crier*; and, as if in confirmation of his worthlessness, proceeded to cut its 10,000 readership in half.

When he met up with the Romillys in November, Toynbee was more than ever before a ready target for Esmond's gleaming arrows. He could join the troupe and lecture on life at Oxford University, Esmond told him; or on his famous father: 'Arnold Toynbee – Historian, but first and foremost "Dad".' Why indeed shouldn't he persuade Isabel to come and lecture too? Toynbee scoffed at this last suggestion, but his frail defences were pierced.

. . . it is another proof of Esmond's hallucinatory powers over me that I did seriously think it possible that Isabel would come with us, even if she would not be persuaded on the lecture platform . . . [Esmond] talked about this radiant project until late at night; and as I listened to his stuttering enthusiasms, as I watched his

179

indefatigable face, I believed that he would be able to have his way even at the heart of my own ill-managed life, even with Isabel, even with her parents.

Depressed by the political scene, on the look-out for diversion, Esmond saw in Toynbee's impoverished love life the bare bones of a *cause célèbre*. Clearly his friend too readily accepted the dictates of the girl's family. Without action – precipitate action – the cause was lost. Toynbee gave his uneasy assent, and Esmond began the campaign. 'He would persuade me to let Decca telephone to the Campbell's house, pretending, if one of the parents answered the call, to be one of Isabel's most respected friends. Or he himself would ring up in the improbable rôle of her art master or dressmaker: it was a situation from which I hadn't the heart, the will or even the desire to exclude him.'

Toynbee and Isabel met, but the meetings – often spent in the company of the Romillys – were not as successful as he had anticipated. Isabel was nervous, distant even; undoubtedly the Campbells' measures were achieving the desired effect.

Esmond was all for quitting the subterfuge and openly carrying the standard to the enemy camp. He would personally confront the father with the tour idea. Hadn't Toynbee told him that Campbell's chief objection to the marriage was that his daughter needed to see more of the world? '"If her father really wants her to see more of the world," he said, "here's his chance. And if he suggests that Decca won't do as a chaperone, I shall be damned insulted."'

Horrified by the spectre of a Romilly–Campbell encounter, Toynbee rejected the plan. The relationship floundered on into further disappointment.

I had come up to London on a Sunday for one of my rare clandestine meetings with Isabel, to find that she was to spend the day with her parents, visiting her brother at Eton, and would not see me until the evening. In savage disappointment I was in the right mood for Esmond's stirring advice, and went at once to the Romillys' room. For a reckless moment I was persuaded that their methods were the only possible ones – that only violence could succeed against this entrenched and uncompromising family. Esmond gave the battle-order as soon as I had explained the situation to him.

They would follow the Campbells to Windsor and confront them there and then on the playing fields of Eton.

The Eton trip was a fiasco. They did not meet up with the Campbells and after a long tiring afternoon of pounding the school grounds took solace in entering the chapel cloakroom and stealing the boys' top hats. Esmond proposed sending a notice to *The Times* – 'Look out for your boaters! We strike at Harrow next.' Just like the 'Out of Bounds' jaunts, thought Toynbee, just like of old. But it was a paltry, self-conscious parody of those earlier escapades, and defied the heavy social argument which Toynbee was later trapped into conferring on it when confronted by Isabel's condemnation. '"How monstrous!" said Isabel. "How unpardonable!"' and the argument began, adding even more ballast to the rapidly plummeting affair. As for the hats, Esmond sold all thirty of them the following morning to a second-hand clothes dealer.

After the Eton incident the final rift came quickly. Pressured by Toynbee into revealing her feelings, Isabel admitted that she was not in love with him. Dejected, he slunk across London to the Strand offices of Graham and Gillies to present the sad tidings to his friend.

We sat in a bar, side by side on bar-stools, while Esmond summoned all his great strength for the unfamiliar task of consolation. His methods were as blunt, as brutal and very nearly as effective as his methods of hostile attack. In this very first shock, not only of loss but of indignity, I doubt whether anything could have been better for me than Esmond's tremendous simplicities. He tried to persuade me that Isabel had never been good enough for me, had always lacked the courage and the generosity which I would need in a wife. (I was able to forget that he had urged me on to conquer her only a week before.) I protested, at first, that the very opposite was true, and that it was I who had proved inadequate; but my protests grew feebler and feebler as this flattering new carpet was unrolled before me in all its richly consoling colours. I began to see myself as a generous, open-hearted man who had been betrayed by someone too small and mean for him, as a kind of rougher Swann betrayed by a less colourful Odette....

It was not a true picture, but neither, I suppose, was my own self-abusing picture any truer.... Whatever was true it was certainly true that Esmond really saw the situation just as he expounded it to me; and the vigour of the convictions gave me at least a temporary comfort. What he made me feel, without expressing it, is that unhappiness is a dirty disease which must never be encouraged, or even tolerated.

The lecture tour had fallen through, the fellow travellers dropping out one by one for lack of money, verve or the intrepid spirit. Toynbee – the last to fall – admitted his decision was dictated by his instinct for self-preservation. 'My personality, already depleted by guilt and loss, would have been obliterated in their tremendous company, and without another companion to support me against their undeliberate but crushing domination.'

And so when the ss *Aurania* pulled out of Southampton on 18 February 1939, only the Romillys were aboard to wave a bleary goodbye to the blessed plot. On the previous evening they had held a farewell binge in London, crammed with faces from the Romilly past, but Esmond's sights, Toynbee noted, were already set on future events: 'I remember that Esmond and Decca became bored before the end of the party and left their guests to shout and drink without them.'

19
New York

The Romillys had booked into the 'elegant' Shelton Hotel on Lexington Avenue.

The Shelton [wrote Jessica Mitford] turned out to exceed our wildest dreams of American mass-produced luxury. The magnificent lobby and bellboys, the immense size of the place, the thickly carpeted corridors had nothing in common with any English hotel. The dark gloom of the London Ritz with its elderly, grave staff, the genteel, organized discomfort of English middle-class hotels, seemed much more than a mere thousand miles away; we seemed to have stepped on to another planet.

Cushioned in such sumptuous surroundings, it was inevitable that the impressionable Esmond should soon drift into his own American dream: a dream centred on the rich and glamorous world of New York advertising. 'For two months', he wrote, 'I spared no effort. I wrote stacks of letters. I said "good morning" breezily to shoals of secretaries. I established hundreds of those magic things called "contacts"....' But the New York advertisers were unimpressed. His London experience was worthless, he was told. (British advertising, according to the Americans, was still howling in the pre-Pavlovian dark ages.) If however he was really interested in making a career for himself with an American company he could do no better than persuade someone to take him on from the bottom – teach him everything, 'even wrapping up parcels and emptying wastepaper baskets ... the office boy's routine ... then after twelve months or so....'

Forced out of their luxurious room in the Shelton by a nagging bank-balance the Romillys took refuge at No. 16 Christopher Street, a tiny apartment in the heart of bohemian Greenwich Village. Esmond described the new home in a letter to Dorothy Allhusen:

> We have a one-room flat (or rather an 'apartment'), in which the divan becomes two beds and the cushions become pillows at night, and the kitchen is behind a thick red curtain which looks very nice, and there's a door to the bathroom. I'll try to enclose a photograph published by Time Magazine of us which shows the scene.... The picture is completed by a small cat that we got from a home, which is black with a white waistcoat, white gloves, socks and spats. The cat has been suffering from rickets but is now making a splendid recovery, and wakes us up at seven every morning by walking over our faces, purring.

Meanwhile, Decca had become the family breadwinner. Setting her sights lower than her husband's she had probed the shop-assistant market and had landed herself a job with the fashionable Fifth Avenue dress shop, Jane Engels. She had been working there just a few days when she received a call from a very dubious-sounding character with a broad northern English accent and a line about wanting to help fellow Brits. Perplexed, Decca gave the man the Christopher Street number and asked him to get in contact with her husband.

The man – he told Esmond he was jockey Steve Donahue's brother – was a racecourse racketeer, paying journeymen jockeys $100 to throw a race so the horse he was betting on would win. In fact he was betting on a couple of certs that same day. Would his young friend like to make a small wager? Esmond wrote out a cheque for forty dollars.

He knew Donahue was a trickster, he told his wife, but he believed he was the big-time kind. He probably thought they had plenty of money, in which case he would let them win say $500 to gain their confidence, then go for the kill. But after the first few bets they would, of course, pull out. If, however, Donahue turned out to be the cheaper kind of crook he would stop the cheque first thing in the morning.

Conforming exactly to the role Esmond had outlined for him Donahue turned up later that evening with the news that the Romillys had won $70. The pay-off was the following day at Jack Dempsey's bar. He would have some more tips for him then. Donahue introduced Esmond to Jack Dempsey – a very good friend of his. Dempsey said 'Hello'. About the money? Esmond asked.

Donahue said he didn't have it – he had assumed that Esmond had wanted to bet it all on another couple of certs. He would have to bring it round to him later in the day. But Donahue did not come round, and he had not seen him since.

And did he expect to see him? asked the incredulous journalists of the New York *Daily Mirror*, to whom Esmond was relating the sorry episode. Esmond said he thought so. 'If we had such an introduction to England on our first trip over', the journalists wrote, 'we'd brew a horrible curse upon the country. But not these two. We've never seen two such healthy-minded, gloriously happy individuals.' Appropriately the greenhorns' story appeared in the tabloid's column, 'Only Human – by Candide.'

Disappointed with the response of the New York advertising world Esmond had turned his attention to freelance writing. Write something on the situation in England, a literary agent advised, and he would do his best to place it. Inspired by burgeoning dollar signs – acquaintances had told him he might make up to $1,000 for an article – Esmond dashed off a commercially gloomy 'Escape from England'

> People in England aren't excited or hysterical any more at the idea of the coming war. People are adjusting themselves to a kind of half-life – a life where it's no good making plans, no good thinking at all of the future.... People don't talk politics very much, either. What's the use? No-one can feel any more that they have the remotest control over what is happening. Their only role is to do what they are told....
> After escaping from England what shall I do if war breaks out? The answer is that I shall go back....

The view that he had left a country on the edge of despair and had entered one brimming with enthusiasm was one which Esmond returned to time and again during those first weeks: 'England is one of the saddest places in the world', he told *Time* magazine; and to the New York *Daily Mirror*: 'I'm becoming an American citizen you know. I simply couldn't stay in England.... The only place democracy exists in the world any more is in America.'

The analysis was, to say the least, highly subjective. How many Englishmen believed that 1939 represented the high-water mark of thirties despair? For most, whose views on misery were more akin to Mr Micawber's than to Esmond Romilly's, the late thirties was a period of growth and expansion. Indeed, in economic terms England presented a much healthier picture in 1939 than the United States which, after escaping the Slump's trough, had become trapped in a minor recession.

185

Politically, of course, the picture was quite different: in England the thirties had been the period of the 'Old Gang' – MacDonald, Baldwin, Chamberlain: old tired men who at best wore a face of resignation, at worst of complacency and insouciance. In the States the thirties was the decade of the New Deal and Franklin D. Roosevelt: a leader who exuded an aura of enormous energy and compassion. It is easy to overestimate the material importance of the New Deal's copious legislation, but it is impossible to underestimate the psychological impact of the President on a shell-shocked nation. 'His bold approach,' writes the historian J.A.S.Grenville, 'his faith in democracy and desire to help the ordinary people, the disadvantaged and the poor, not only brought hope where there had been despair, but significantly changed American society and attitudes.'

Nevertheless, by the end of the decade there were signs that Roosevelt and the New Deal policies were losing support. The country had escaped the mire but there was no sign of a return to prosperity; and with one foot placed unsteadily on the economic ladder Middle America had begun questioning whether such a prize was indeed within the bureaucrats' grasp. But was there an alternative government? Hadn't the *laissez-faire* policy of the Republican Party been responsible for the dire state of things in the first place?

It was in this atmosphere of uncertainty that other, irrational voices were gaining an ear.

Only five days before Esmond and Decca arrived in New York the pro-fascist German-American Bund had packed Madison Square Garden with 22,000 of its supporters, and while it is an exaggeration to suggest that the United States was teetering on the brink of fascism, the activities of the Bund and similar home-grown groups reveal a thirties cancer by no means confined to Europe.

More dangerous, however, if only because they made their appeal to the nation's well-established xenophobic tendency, were the rantings of Texas congressman Martin Dies. Dies's House Committee on Un-American Activities (HUAC) had begun its campaign in the summer of 1938, labelling 'Red' 640 organizations, 483 newspapers and 280 labour unions within the first weeks of its activities. However ludicrous these barbs, they stuck; however unprepossessing Dies's stooges, however outlandish the senator's claims, they attracted an audience – at least for a season. Why then was the Dies threat short-lived? The answer surely lies in the mood of reason which, despite the New Deal's declining fortunes, continued to pervade the country. Let a future Dies sweep across a starker, less humane landscape and the result would undoubtedly be more ominous.

'Escape from England' roamed the New York market for four months before being placed with the *Commentator* in July – by which time Esmond's luck had taken an unexpected and abrupt turn for the better.

The prospector had at last hit pay dirt. The name of the find was the Topping and Lloyd advertising agency, and it had offered a handsome $100 a week for his copywriting services. There was, of course, a catch, but he was by no means certain what it was. 'My job situation grows more and more amazing,' he told Peter Nevile (letter of 5 July):

You remember that I didn't do very much work at 'Graham and Gillies'. Well, I certainly do less than that now. But with an important difference. There's no more of this tiresome business of getting in at definite hours and working a full day on Friday and often on Saturday morning, or anything like that. Here is a typical day.

10.10 a.m.	Arrive. Seat myself in huge office towering over Madison Avenue, which I share with Vice-President.
10.15 a.m.	Open and begin study of *New York Times*.
11.10 a.m.	Cheerfully greet Vice-President. Put *New York Times* in waste-paper basket.
11.10–12.00	Do a bit of work.
12.00	Wash, pack up shirt, shorts etc., and depart to play tennis with somebody at Tudor City.
12.20–1.25	Play tennis.
1.20–2.20	Changing, lunching, drinking, relaxing.
2.40	Arrive back at office.
2.40–3.00	Read *New York Post*.
3–4	Work.
4–5	Chat with someone.
5–5.30	More general chatting.
5.30	Depart.

The Vice-President has a very pleasant habit of going away for the week-end every Friday morning at eleven thirty (meaning he just drops in to collect the mail or has a boy send it down), and gets back immediately after lunch the following Monday. Sometimes he goes away on Thursdays instead. And the last week-end – the 4th July weekend – we had a holiday from Thursday evening till the following Wednesday.

Well, you see, Nevile, in this country hard work, starting right at the bottom and working up is what counts. Seriously, I keep expecting to wake up every morning and find the whole thing's a dream . . . .

Amazingly enough, it hasn't affected our way of living much. First, we had to catch up on a lot of back rent, telephone and electric light bills, and now we're trying to save some cash to be able to motor for three or four years all over America in as romantic a manner as possible, taking in both swell hotels and migratory labour camps,* you know, the sort of thing that never works out like that but you always hope it'll be fun and it usually is.

The Romillys' original idea had been to remain in New York until Christmas, banking Esmond's pay cheque while living off Decca's weekly $25 – she was now selling tweeds in the 'Merrie England' concession of the World Fair. But, counter to expectations, Esmond's advertising agency turned out to be one thin and rapidly exhausted seam. In fact Topping and Lloyd was not an advertising agency at all but a front chosen by millionaire Andrew Topping to lose a large amount of highly taxable income. This target reached – in the middle of August – the deputy to the vice-president (Esmond's official title) was given two weeks' wages and the well-deserved push.

Thus, the nationwide tour, planned, as Decca recalls, 'to allow for any fascinating contingency', began not in December but at the end of August, with a jaunt up to New England. In a battered old Ford picked up for $40, the travellers rambled north out of the fervid city into the lush New England byways; their destination the sumptuous country estate of Mrs Murray Crane, patron of the arts, and all-round soft touch.

The Romillys had met Mrs Murray Crane – the heiress to a toilet empire – soon after they had arrived in New York. Amused, the lady invited them to her Park Avenue penthouse for cocktails. At the door they met Wystan Auden and Christopher Isherwood on their way out. '. . . as though by common consent', wrote Jessica Mitford, 'both they and we confined our greetings to a distant bow as we passed in Mrs Maine's† foyer. "Trying to muscle in on our racket! They've got a hell of a nerve," Esmond muttered. Judging by their expressions, the thought was fully reciprocated.'

Esmond and Decca arrived at the Murray Crane estate just as the summer house-party was getting under way. The hostess introduced them to their fellow guests, all crisply turned out in country casuals, and suggested that for dinner the new arrivals dress likewise. For Esmond this posed an embarrassing problem: the only half-decent

* 'There is a wonderful book which is a best seller over here called *The Grapes of Wrath*.' (Letter to Dorothy Allhusen, 29 June 1939.)
† In *Hons and Rebels* Jessica Mitford refers to Mrs Murray Crane as Mrs Curry Maine.

thing in his meagre travelling wardrobe was a second-hand dinner suit. Self-consciously he donned the stuffy, formal garment and strode out to join the cool relaxed party. It was 'one of those few occasions', his wife wrote, 'when he seemed genuinely embarrassed and ill at ease'.

From Woods Hole, Massachusetts, the Romillys crossed the sound to Martha's Vineyard. With them went the tennis player and socialite Babe Alexander (another of Mrs Crane's week-end guests); all three bound for the island retreat of Menemsha Inn and a new host, Selden Rodman.

Esmond had first met Selden Rodman in May while on the magazine trail. Rodman, co-editor of a small liberal magazine, *Common Sense*, had been curious to know why the Englishman had chosen 1939 to leave home, and had been treated to Esmond's well-aired views on the European situation. Should the US enter the coming affray? enquired the editor. Absolutely not, opined the visitor. It was a dismal, hypocritical imbroglio and they should stay out. Rodman, a confirmed isolationist, agreed.

Since then the isolationist-interventionist question had become a major political issue. Roosevelt, a pro-interventionist, favoured an immediate repeal of the US arms embargo, allowing 'friendly' nations to purchase arms. But Congress, mirroring public opinion, was less enthusiastic, voting on 11 July to postpone discussion of the repeal until the next session. Losing ground, the President resorted to hyperbole. European war was imminent. The repeal of the embargo, if enacted immediately, he avowed disingenuously, might avert the conflict. 'I've fired my last shot,' Roosevelt told the senators. 'I think I ought to have another round in my belt.' In the circumstances it was a singularly inappropriate allusion, and moved no one.

At Chilmark (Martha's Vineyard) the conversation again focused on war. Rodman had invited to lunch the political journalist (and friend and biographer of Leon Trotsky) Max Eastman, who was in knowing, cynical mood over what he saw as Stalin's latest treachery: the Soviet–German pact. Eastman turned to Esmond: did he seriously believe that there was a communist volunteer left who wasn't cynical after what he had seen of Soviet policy in Spain? He did, and he resented the accusation. There was a heated exchange, Rodman eventually interceding 'lest Max and Ilyana [Eastman's Russian wife] start throwing things'.

The weather, sunny when they arrived, suddenly turned chill. Dark clouds rolled across the horizon and it poured. Noting that the

Menemsha innkeeper was not too punctilious, the Romillys had quietly squatted in a vacant room in the same cabin complex as the Rodmans. Their days were spent in a series of furtive leaps and bounds, dodging prevailing storm and innkeeper's glance.

They were seen here and there about the grounds [wrote Rodman], sweeping the [tennis] court, scuffling through cloud-bursts with newspapers over their heads and borrowed ponchos, playing poker in one of the empty rooms, taking turns in the dining-room as one of us would sit out, or munching pieces of cheese on the porch and speculating whether the prevailing shower was the storm's death rattle. Babe [Alexander] would run madly to the useless phone and consult boat schedules (he had intended to stay 6 hours and had already been here 48).

Two strange girls appeared in one of the untenanted rooms and were immediately lured into a game. A pale youth came to another of the rooms Tuesday, left a suitcase and was not seen again. We speculated whether his body was in one of the damp locked closets or in the suitcase. We still laughed but almost hysterically now. Seven card high-low became the only game. I began to lose heavily. The tension was terrific. Babe speculated whether Christmas would see us here shovelling the court instead of mopping it. Hilda [Rodman's wife] went to bed on a permanent basis to escape the game, Decca's increasingly querulous voice and E's wearing bumptiousness.

At 4.30 Friday morning the last hand was played. It had been decided that our 3 guests were to leave on the 6.30 morning boat. I knocked off for 2 hrs sleep, the others cleaned out the carnage in the poker room so that it would still look un-tenanted in the morning.

Esmond, still wound up like a watch spring, juggled with an empty beer can, a pair of scissors and a safety razor, in front of the strange girls' dresser. Then opened one of the cans which exploded all over the double bed. At 5.30 he changed his mind for the fourth time and decided to stay in the room with the suitcase. Babe threw up his hands and I began to lose my temper. I drove Babe to the harbour.

We speculated whether Esmond was mad or childish, brilliant or foolish, funny or disagreeable. We never decided. At seven I climbed into bed. At eight E's voice, now as exasperating as a buzz saw, awoke me and announced that within an hour I must drive to Vineyard Haven again or they'd miss another potential host in Woods Hole.

I was so mad that I looked at him and said, 'If you ever get to Vineyard Haven it will be under your own steam.' And as his face reddened and he started to answer, the missing pale young man appeared from behind a doorway and announced calmly, 'Germany invaded Poland at 5.45. The war has begun.' He took his suitcase and left.

20
The Tour

The pale young man's announcement was premature. Chamberlain did not declare war on 1 September, but, to the increasing consternation of both sides of the House, fumbled towards another peace agreement. Only a cabinet revolt and the threat of a parliamentary vote of no confidence on 2 September brought home to the Prime Minister that this really was 'war'. The message was announced to the British public at 11.15 a.m. on Sunday 3 September. 'This is a sad day for all of us,' Chamberlain lamented, 'and to none is it sadder than to me. Everything that I have worked for, everything that I have hoped for, everything that I have believed in during my public life, has crashed into ruins....'

But these were meagre, egotistical sentiments and fell short across an auditorium prepared for an altogether loftier oration. It was left to the new Lord of the Admiralty, Winston Churchill, to fill the vacuum, in a speech to the Commons on 3 September:

In this solemn hour it is a consolation to recall and to dwell upon our repeated efforts for peace. All have been ill-starred, but all have been faithful and sincere. This is of the highest moral value – and not only moral value, but practical value – at the present time, because the wholehearted concurrence of scores of millions of men and women; whose co-operation is indispensable, and whose comradeship and brotherhood are indispensable, is the only foundation upon which the trial and tribulation of modern war can be endured and surmounted. This moral conviction alone affords that ever-fresh resilience which renews the strength and energy of people in long, doubtful and dark days. Outside, the storms of war may blow and lands may be lashed with the fury of its gales, but in our hearts this Sunday morning there is peace. Our hands may be active, but our consciences are at rest.... The Prime Minister said it was a sad day, and that is indeed true, but at the present time there is another note which

may be present, and that is a feeling of thankfulness that, if these
great trials were to come upon our island, there is a generation of
Britons here now ready to prove itself not unworthy of the days of
yore and not unworthy of those great men, the fathers of our land,
who laid the foundations of our laws and shaped the greatness of
our country.

Churchill would now go on to replace Chamberlain as head of the
Government, Esmond asserted. Rodman commissioned an article.
'England's Next Prime Minister' appeared in October's *Common Sense*.
Churchill, the article argued, had been in the wilderness during the
inter-war years because there was no place for a politician to the right
of the official Tory Party. Only with the recent collapse of the Government's appeasement policy had he begun to make any impact on Parliament, the unrepentant imperialist finding himself in accord with
Labour's 'Collective Security' measures, although for quite opposite
reasons. Now, in the wake of appeasement, Churchill was in a position
to unite those disaffected elements within Parliament and head a coali-
tion government; 'but', opined his nephew, 'it will be on his terms
and his terms alone'.

A specious enough argument; but Esmond had omitted one very
important consideration: to many members of his own party –
appeasers and non-appeasers alike – Churchill's name was anathema.
He was a traitor: a careerist whose personal ambition had led him
into an affair with the Liberals, and then, when the floosy had lost
her charm, led him back, head bowed, to the Tories. Compared to such
venality the incumbent prime minister's faults were considered mere
misdemeanours. As Lord Beaverbrook told a friend, the Tories may
have forgiven Winston 'for ratting to the Liberals long ago, but they
cannot forgive him for returning to the Tory fold'. Winston Churchill
would be Britain's next prime minister as the article predicted, but
in September 1939 the issue was by no means as clear-cut as Esmond
believed.

So much for predicting Churchill's future; what of his own future
now that the long-anticipated conflict had at last arrived? 'We haven't
any plans for coming over for the present at any rate,' Esmond wrote
to Peter Nevile on 25 October. 'As you say, there doesn't seem to be
any point. Another thing is that we have our first citizenship papers
here, and don't want to spoil them unless there's really a terrific reason
for doing so.'

There was no 'terrific reason' to return. Well into its second month of inactivity, the war had already been labelled 'Bore War', 'Funny War', and – Chamberlain's description – 'This strangest of wars'. The American Press, with its penchant for chic, had another name for it – 'phoney'.

It's really amazing to find [Esmond to Peter Nevile] after the first shock of the declaration, how things go on normally (I mean of course on this side of the Atlantic). It's rather like being in London during the war in Spain, no not really, it's much more distant and far away than that even. It's quite extraordinary how absolutely unanimous everyone here is about one thing – namely that America shalln't get involved.... What's more, I'm quite sure that when the Embargo is repealed (as it undoubtedly will be) America's neutrality will be more certain than ever, as everyone will then feel, well, they've done their bit, and there'll be no cause for a pro-British wave of sentiment along with the cry of 'Lift the Embargo' – which might well happen otherwise. One thing I had never realized when I was in England was the American attitude toward the last war, namely, that they were dragged in, when they oughtn't to have been. Personally, I can't quite see any truth in this, but it's what almost everyone here believes today.

I think that when Hitler marched into Poland, there was a tremendous feeling of enthusiasm behind the idea of supporting a country defending itself against a bully. But now that part of the war's over, and the West Front seems to be quiet, and people are talking about possibilities of peace, etc. all that enthusiasm seems to have gone. Not that the Gallup Poll hasn't shown that ninety percent or more people want the Allies to win. It's simply that just at the moment there's very little enthusiasm or excitement about the war....

In marked contrast to this apathy towards the Old World was Esmond's continuing interest in the New, an interest now focused upon Washington – the Romillys' latest port of call – and the New Deal. 'It's amazing how enthusiastic all the young people are in the various Administration departments,' Esmond wrote to Peter Nevile, with a *brio* lacking in his earlier war analysis. 'They rush round insisting you take stacks of literature about all the wonderful New Deal projects they're working on and attacking the "reactionaries". Imagine the same thing in a British Civil Service department!' And to Selden Rodman:

I'd no idea how terrifically keen and enthusiastic the spirit would

194

be among the New Deal people. But this gives an example: I went to the Department of Agriculture and was seized on and stacked up with piles of pamphlets, etc. without any questions as to what sort of credentials I had, and instantly everyone began writing letters for me from the United States Government saying to inspect their farm projects all over the country.... What a contrast to New York! Instead of the rather wearing kind of sophistication of endless radio-ish repartee, etc. you get a lot of people sitting round talking about a 'social program'.

Esmond's enthusiasm had not always been so complete. The first few days in the capital had been very dull, he told Rodman. Then he had met a man called Michael Straight 'and from then on we were in the centre of everything'.

As a presidential speech-writer and scion of the wealthy American heiress Dorothy Whitney, Michael Straight was well-equipped for the role of social and political guide to the capital. Naturally, Esmond took full advantage of the situation, and cultivated the acquaintanceship further. The young men became friends, a friendship cemented, unex-pectedly, by some old school ties.

Although born in the United States, Michael Straight had always regarded himself as English. England had made him; first the English progressive school, Dartington Hall (founded by his reform-minded mother and stepfather in 1926), later Trinity College, Cambridge. It was at Cambridge that Straight was introduced to the Communist Party. It was here he became friends with the formidable John Cornford, and the young, charming aesthete, Anthony Blunt. It was here, in 1937, that Blunt sounded him out on becoming a Comintern agent.

Esmond and Decca were not, of course, made privy to Straight's double life. To them he was purely and simply a New Dealer – a rather moderate New Dealer at that. Paradoxically, this impression was pro-bably nearer the truth than that gained by his communist employers, of a committed revolutionary. As Straight explains,* his involvement with the underground network had stemmed not from a dogmatic belief in the inevitably or necessity of communism, but from an equivocal attitude towards his own family's wealth and privileged position; his continuing, albeit ineffectual, association with the network the result of an almost pathological incapacity to confront an insupportable situa-tion. It appears that the organization soon gave Straight up as a bad

* Michael Straight, *After Long Silence*, Collins, London, 1983.

job, and made no demands on him, although he continued to remain in psychological detention throughout the next forty years.

In 1951 two of Straight's Cambridge contemporaries, Guy Burgess and Donald Maclean, were exposed as Russian spies (Burgess was then working at the British Embassy in Washington); both made eleventh-hour escapes to Moscow. In 1963, Kim Philby, another Cambridge man, and for many years a high-ranking official of MI5, followed suit. Then in 1978 the book *The Climate of Treason* – an investigation into the Cambridge spy phenomenon – was published, and it became clear that the network did not stop at the so-called Cambridge triangle of Philby, Burgess and Maclean. Andrew Boyle, the author of the book, mentioned no names, but the Press soon sleuthed out the facts. In November 1979 Anthony Blunt, then employed as Keeper of the Queen's Pictures, was unearthed as the fourth mole, and the race was on to bag a fifth and a sixth.

For Michael Straight the subterfuge, for what it was worth, came to an end in March 1981, when a member of that august body of Red-baiters, the *Daily Mail*, called at his home in Washington and confronted him with the fatal line: 'Mr Straight, would you mind if I asked you a few questions?'

Romilly and Straight shared the English radical youth experience, but this apart they had little in common. Excitable, even gauche, Esmond nevertheless bubbled over with self-confidence. Outwardly urbane, Straight was essentially a shy man whose inner fastidiousness recoiled from his friend's extroversion. 'He showed no restraint,' says Straight, 'no discipline. He was an adventurist. Where the action was he was there. He seemed incapable of settling down. That's all right when one's twenty-three, but what about when one's thirty? You can't drag a wife and child* around with you for ever.'

Other Washington acquaintances were less critical of the newcomer. As Michael Straight adds, 'Esmond's brand of boisterousness was generally found entertaining'. To Virginia Durr Esmond was the most entertaining person she had ever met: 'He was so vitally alive, like a shooting star, there was so much radiation coming out of him.' Mrs Durr recalled her first meeting with the Romillys, at a party given by Michael Straight:

Decca was absolutely beautiful – lovely slanting Mongolian eyes, beautiful white skin and black hair – but mute. Esmond was having

* The Romilly's second child, Constancia, was born on 22 February 1941.

this terrific discussion with Congressman Jerry Voorhis about the Spanish Civil War. He was fascinating. I invited them over to meet my husband. Cliff [then General Counsel to the Reconstruction Finance Corporation], who had much greater wisdom than me, adored him. He thought he was brilliant; a man of great principles and courage.

Another Washington acquaintance, soon to prove himself a very valuable friend, was Eugene Meyer, owner of the *Washington Post*. Esmond and Decca had first met Meyer in the summer through his nephew, and friend of Peter Nevile, John Cook. Esmond had written to Peter Nevile with details:

We've become very friendly with John Cook and like him very much ... through him, we went to stay last weekend, with his uncle, Eugene Meyer, who turned out to be a terrific Washington big-shot with an aura of cigars, badly sequenced liquors and huge-stomached business friends, in fact really fascinating. I thought at one point he was just like an American 'Washington figure' in the movies. All true too, as I expect you know his name, he was the chairman of some Reconstruction Finance corporation, now he's a big newspaper owner. Decca asked him if – as though in conclusion – he was a supporter of the capitalist system. He said he was, and we got along absolutely fine. In fact, I think I'll try and get a job from him when he comes back from Europe where he's going for a few weeks. . . .

Once in Washington Esmond made good his threat, and for his pains he and Decca were commissioned to write a series of articles on their States experiences. The series, which appeared on consecutive Sundays from 28 January to 10 March 1940, was given the syrupy but appropriate title of 'Baby Blue Bloods in Hobohemia'.
'Introducing Two Youthful Escapists Who Fled To America With a Song in Their Hearts', the first instalment began:

We were living in a furnished bed-sitting room near the Marble Arch in London when a wonderful thing happened to us. We learned one day we had suddenly acquired £100.
This was far and away the biggest sum of money we had ever possessed. . . . Suddenly we hit upon the one obvious thing to do with our money. 'Let's go to America.' That was it. The instant we said it we realized what a wonderful plan it was. . . .

As Esmond wrote to Peter Nevile, even compared to the Second World War, 'Baby Blue Bloods' was 'very small beer'.

While in Washington Esmond and Decca became regular visitors to the Meyer home. On one occasion, recorded by Decca in *Hons and Rebels*, the host engaged a group of his guests in an after-dinner conversation on the United States' moral commitment to the British:

'There are those who claim the British are trying to put one over on us,' he was saying, and added with great emphasis, 'I say the British are incapable of stealing from us!'

As though drawn by sympathy to the representative in their midst of the gallant little island, all eyes turned to Esmond, who had quietly slipped away from the circle by the fireplace and was busily and methodically stuffing his pockets with some excellent Meyer cigars.

Far from being annoyed with us, Mr Meyer treated the whole thing as a huge joke.

Looking as always for diversion and extra money, Esmond had answered one of the myriad newspaper ads for a 'Young man, must be intelligent, alert, ambitious, personable ... NO SKILLS OR EXPERIENCE NEEDED', and had returned with a cardboard briefcase (deposit $5), several matchbook-like containers – 'mending kits' – and a wad of company blurb: reinforcements to 'Realsilk', the stocking company's 'unique' sales method. There was also the company song sheet, containing such rousing ditties as 'It's a Great Gang ...' (to the tune, 'It's a Long Way to Tipperary'):

It's a great gang that's selling Realsilk
It's a great gang to know
We are all full of pep and ginger
And our watch-word is 'Let's go,'
Hey! Hey!!

'"And how are we today, Mrs Graham?"' – Eugene Meyer's daughter Katherine (now chairman of the *Washington Post*) recalls Esmond's sales parody. 'He would jam his foot menacingly in between the door and launch into this high-powered phoney sales talk, while Decca hitched her skirt provocatively to show the goods. "Now don't run away with the idea that we're selling stockings." Then they'd sing the Realsilk songs. It was a great party piece.' This show-stopping performance was unfortunately limited to private gatherings. In the Realsilk arena Esmond lasted just two weeks and made $5.52.

At the end of October the Romillys quit society drawing room and New Deal bureau and headed south, toward the sun and the winter tourist season. While in New York in the summer Esmond had taken a crash-course in bartending and was now lucidly plotting a career for himself among the palms and tropical refrains of a southern resort.

The original idea was to make for New Orleans, but a full day's driving found them on the road to Miami. Reluctant to turn round, Esmond canvassed opinion at a roadside gas-station, and was told that the Florida resort was indeed the place he was looking for. They pushed on towards America's so-called 'playground'. Jessica Mitford:

> The playground of America proved to be the most unattractive town I had ever seen, from the stunted, ratty-looking palm trees to our motel room, from behind the spanking new white walls of which cockroaches came out by the thousands every night. Here was not the cosy, settled filth of London bed-sitters, nor the warm, smelly and somehow human dirt of the Hôtel des Basques, but rather a crawling, mean sordidness.

From the counter of a downtown drug store – she was again the first to find work – Decca extended her study to include the Miami citizens: 'a humourless, suspicious, narrow-minded lot', who perfectly 'matched their surroundings'.

And Esmond's opinion? Judging by his letters to friends he agreed with his wife: Miami was mean, murky and meretricious; it was also a unique experience and as such demanded to be savoured and indulged.

Finding no work as a bartender – it appeared that the Miami bars were run on a family-trusted-friend basis – Esmond had answered an advertisement for an experienced waiter, and by confecting a glittering past (as an employee of the Savoy Grill) had got the job. It was a brave deception, even foolhardy, Esmond being renowned (in his wife's words) 'for his inability to carry a teaspoon from one room to the next without dropping it'. Letter to Selden Rodman:

> Did you realize that waiting is quite a skilled, technical job? I certainly didn't. I thought anyone could do it, and it just meant going up and being pleasant to people and finding out what they'd like to eat and going to fetch it, and then perhaps discreetly suggesting they order some wine – in fact, rather an enjoyable pastime for a

while – it sounded. Well, it'd take too long to go into all the details of just how wrong this idea was, but I daresay you can imagine.

Esmond lasted just two days as a waiter, but was retained by his Roma Inn employers, at a cut in salary, as a bus-boy-cum-cleaner; a much pleasanter occupation, he told Selden Rodman, 'as the business of pretending I knew a whole lot I didn't was steadily wearing me to a frazzle'.

It was after three weeks of scrubbing floors and running errands that Esmond approached the owner, John Marrugat, with a proposition. The restaurant had a small bar, which owing to the cost of a licence – $1,000 – had remained closed. Esmond proposed buying the licence, providing he was made barman and the bar was run on a profit-sharing basis. Marrugat agreed. On 26 December he shuttled up to Washington to talk business with Eugene Meyer. Jessica Mitford:

The interview with Mr Meyer proved extremely brief. As Esmond described it on his return, two days later, Mr Meyer had leaned back, a fairly godfatherly twinkle in his eye, and said, 'A thousand dollars? Yes, I think I can lend you a thousand dollars.' Esmond, expecting long resistance, was so completely taken aback that the only rejoinder he could think of was, 'Oh! Well, I hope it won't leave you short.' Mr Meyer was exceedingly tickled by this remark, and the discussion ended in gales of hilarity. . . .

'My father was much amused by Esmond's request,' Katherine Graham recalls. 'Esmond told him how he had resources in England and how, if necessary, he could bring money over to repay him, explaining in some detail how this was possible. My father, who had previously headed the Reconstruction Finance Corporation, eventually called a halt. "Yes, Esmond, I do know a little about international exchange."'

The resources were, of course, non-existent. Nevertheless, Esmond did pay off the loan, and in fairly regular instalments, his last payment being a £50 cheque sent from London in October 1941, six weeks before his death.

Once established behind his bar, Esmond had developed a number of Hollywood personae to test on the Roma customers – 'Damon Runyan "tough-guy"', 'courtly, old-fashioned English servitor', 'sophisticated Ernest Hemingway self-made-world-traveller-at-home-in-five-continents type'. His enthusiasm, as usual, was boundless. Letter to Selden Rodman:

I feel well qualified to write a brochure on the subject of 'The Man From Ohio's Sub-conscious When Under The Influence of Alcohol In A Miami Bar.' You know, stage one – a bit of nationalism, 'How'd you like America? Isn't it a fine country? Yes, Sir'; stage two – a bit of regionalism, 'Denton Ohio – that's where I come from'; stage three – mainly physical and concerned with the desire to shake as many hands as possible with an endless repetition of details of name and place of origin; stage four – a sudden urgent inspiration to produce evidence of identification – we got to spot this stage so well that often I could say to Decca while the hand was still fumbling in the waistcoat pocket, 'Here comes the driver's licence,' and sure enough, out it came. . . .

Esmond 'radiated warmth and life', wrote Jessica Mitford, 'developed all sorts of wild plans for the future of the bar, set to work doggedly to learn the ins and outs of liquor merchandizing, the ways and means of attracting and keeping customers. As usual, he was the centre of a whirlpool of activity of his own making, into which he drew everyone around him.' Decca's enthusiasm was more constrained, at best vicarious. She had taken a dislike to Miami on arrival and carried the impression with her like the reminder of an approaching and unwanted appointment; '. . . at times,' she wrote, 'I felt that something unpleasant would spring out at us from behind the façade of that horribly tinselly town'.

On 3 September 1939, the day Britain declared war on Germany, Decca's sister, Unity, a friend of Hitler and a staunch Nazi supporter, left her flat in Munich's Agnesstrasse, entered a city park and shot herself in the head. The suicide attempt failed (German doctors were, however, unable to extract the bullet from her skull), and after spending several months in a Munich clinic Unity was sent home to convalesce. She arrived in England on 3 January 1940, and the Press on both sides of the Atlantic swooped on the story.

'A journalistic storm of huge proportions broke over us,' Jessica Mitford wrote. 'The telephone rang continually with calls from newspapers all over the country demanding to know the "inside story": was it true that Unity had been shot by the ss? That she had had a violent quarrel with Hitler just after the outbreak of war? Where had she been for the last few months?'

For Decca it was a terrific ordeal. An unbridgeable gulf had long separated the two sisters, but for all that there was still a chord of sibling love which continued to link them. Decca grieved for her estranged and troubled sister, albeit in silence : 'I knew I couldn't expect Esmond, who had never met her, to feel anything but disgust for her, so by tacit understanding we avoided discussing her.'

For Esmond – if not for his wife – the war remained a distant issue. To Philip Toynbee he joked that he had a 'TALK NEUTRAL' sign hung over his bar; while to Peter Nevile he wrote, 'I wonder if leaders in England fully realise what a great disappointment this war is being at present to the American public, which feels definitely tricked by the whole thing ! !' This opinion (his own) was in fact not so far removed from that in England where relief – at not being invaded in September – had become irritation against War Office apathy. Why were they taking no positive steps, now that Hitler had so obviously missed the bus ?

'In another week or so', Esmond wrote to Selden Rodman, 'we're leaving to continue our tour – with immediate prospects of a job – already offered – on a cattle ranch in Arizona.' The letter, which made no mention of the war, was dated 18 March 1940. Three weeks later, on Tuesday 9 April, Hitler's phalanx struck at Norway and the Second World War began in earnest.

For two days the British Navy had trespassed into Norway's neutral waters, laying mines to prevent Germany's merchant ships from reaching the iron ore port of Narvik. It was a calculated act of provocation. Germany depended upon the iron ore shipments, and would, it was felt, retaliate by attempting to invade Norway, leading it into confrontation at sea with the superior British Navy. But the Germans had long been expecting the manoeuvre and had already shipped thousands of soldiers into Norwegian ports in merchant vessels to await the invasion signal.

Dispatched to Narvik by the *Daily Express* to report on the minelaying, Giles Romilly recalled the scene as he awoke in the early hours of 9 April to find himself in German-occupied territory.

A sound sleeper, I was surprised when I awoke to find that it was only twenty minutes to five. Through half-drawn curtains I could see the usual dense unhurrying snowstorm and a leaden half-light, neither of night nor dawn. The window banged shut loudly – strangely, because there was no wind. The irregular, friendly rattle of the trains and the hoppers was missing; the pall of silence seemed wrong. Then came two abominable, insulting bangs. Lifting the receiver of the room telephone I heard blurred sounds of distress and confusion; the voice of the hall clerk: 'Yes. Yes. It is trouble in the river.' I dressed fast and ran downstairs. On the landings, at the doors of the bedrooms, were officers of the Norwegian garrison, in flowing nightshirts, in pyjamas of thickest flannel, buttoning shirts over hairy chests, fumbling with boots, buckling belts, some standing as though rooted, picking sleep off their eyelids. The hall, a mass of dressing-gowns and tousled heads, looked like a country house party surprised by fire.

Outside, soldiers were tumbling helter-skelter, rifles clutched anyhow, down the steep, slippery slope that led towards the harbour. The slope ran out into a straggling square, bounded on the right by the railway, sunk in a bridge-spanned cutting. On the left was a covered market. In the centre, to the right of the road, stood a small, lighthouse-shaped kiosk, and near it some trucks were parked. Directly below, a few hundred yards further but invisible, lay the harbour. The heavy, whitish mist, leaving only a ragged snow-drenched clearing between sky and land, made all beyond a region of mystery, now also of menace....

A sound cracked the almost palpable silence. There emerged, statically sudden, as if the sound alone had set it on the mist-screen, an oblong panel of forms kneeling on one knee, elbows supporting the weight of aimed guns, lines from knee to ground as close, straight, and fixed as altar-rails. Minute against the endless front of the mist, this green-grey tableau suggested, in some sickening way, an appeal for forgiveness. Not more than thirty yards divided it from the Norwegians. Already all was too late. The Norwegian soldiers whispered together, and one of their number ran out of the ranks, pulling a white handkerchief from his pocket and waving it aloft. The tableau sprang to life.

At first interned with a group of British merchant seamen cut off by the raid, Giles was later isolated – it had been discovered that he was Churchill's nephew – then flown to Germany, where he was imprisoned in a Bavarian castle called the Wülzburg. Eighteen months and an escape attempt later he was transferred to the towering fortress, Colditz, beneath whose grey battlements he passed what was left of the war.

After Narvik it took Hitler's forces just two months to overtake northern Europe, defeating Holland, Belgium and France in rapid succession until, by 22 June 1940, only Britain remained outside the German net. The Foreign Secretary, Lord Halifax, urged the Government to seek peace terms. Churchill rejected the idea. As British Prime

Minister, he told the Commons on the day after his appointment, he had only one aim: 'Victory – victory at all costs, victory in spite of all terror, victory, however long and hard the road may be....'

'To Esmond' wrote Jessica Mitford 'this was the turning-point, the moment when all doubts as to whether or not the war would be fully prosecuted were at an end, and the course of English policy was once and for all clear.'

The Romillys abandoned their tour and returned to Washington.

21
Shoulders and Cradles

Isn't the machine-gun vocabulary amazing – I mean
talking of 'shoulders', 'cradles', 'housings', etc.

Letter to Selden Rodman, 21 April 1941

Selden Rodman (journal entry, 3 July 1940): 'Esmond and Decca blew
in from Washington today. Between the whirlwind of tennis, poker
and drinking that that meant I pieced together something of their story.'

They had left Miami at the end of May, after breaking even in the
bar, and had headed back to Washington where Esmond approached
the British Ambassador, Lord Lothian, with a request to join the Canadian Air Force. The Ambassador had arranged this with a letter,

describing E., whimsically, as something of a rolling stone, who
would, nevertheless, make a good airman. Esmond said they had
spent about two hours with the Ambassador and liked him. Like
Winston, whatever he is he's not a stuffed shirt, Esmond said. The
first question he asked Esmond was, bluntly, 'Are you a member
of the Communist party?' E. was about to say no, a little indignantly,
but Decca was quicker. 'Are you?' she said.

The following day an equerry phoned from the Embassy to ask
Esmond, as a nephew of the Prime Minister, to write an article for
the American Press telling why he had taken up arms for his country.
Esmond agreed, but warned he would say he was doing it out of curiosity
and love of adventure alone. 'Needless to say', wrote Rodman, 'they
did not press the point.'

Reluctant to be drawn into the British Embassy's proselytizing,
Esmond was nevertheless critical, in private, of Capitol Hill's increasingly spurious isolationism. From the midst of all the 'bally hoo' and
'hypocrisy', he told Peter Nevile, why couldn't someone step out,

and say in effect: 'We all realize America is very much concerned
about Europe for reasons of its own defence, and it's possible that,

in looking after that defence, we may get involved in war, but we must take that risk.'

If anyone said that they'd be branded as a warmonger. You remember the way the Conservatives in England used to meet demands for a stronger collective security by saying – 'Well would you go to War about it? You want War then.' It's the same here, except that the amusing thing is that both sides are manoeuvring to try to be in that position viz a viz the other, e.g. today I see in the paper that the Democratic Party is going to be even more anti-war than the Republicans! Enough of politics and don't spread all this around, as I want to come back to the US after the war.

If he was ever involved in war again, Esmond had resolved in 1936, while watching Junkers roar invincibly above the Castilian plain, he would make sure he remained above it. But why choose the Canadian Air Force? For one thing he would be away from British Blimpism – or so he believed. More important, he would be near Decca, who, provided his training programme was not too peripatetic, might even be able to join him. The problem: who was to be entrusted (persuaded) to look after her in the meantime? Virginia Durr:

A few days before Esmond was to leave for Canada he and Decca came over for a farewell dinner. I was in the kitchen preparing the food, when Esmond appeared. 'Old Virginie' – he used to call me 'Old Virginie' after the song 'Carry me back ...' – 'could you possibly take Decca for the weekend as I'm going off to Canada and she'll be all alone.' He was the most irresistible character. I said, 'Well, Esmond, I'm going to the Democratic Convention in Chicago this weekend.' (I was going to make a presentation for the resolutions committee on the poll tax.) He said that would be marvellous, it would take Decca's mind off his leaving. He absolutely got round me.

The two women set off for Chicago, Decca asking to stop at each service station along the way to go to the toilet.

I thought, my God, we're never going to get there. I went into the toilet and she was puking up. 'Are you pregnant', I asked. She said 'Yes'.

When we got to Chicago we went into the Sheraton Hotel [Roosevelt's campaign centre] where we met Lyndon Johnson and Alvin Wirtz who were trying to get Roosevelt re-elected. They asked us

to sit with them and made us honorary delegates to the Texas delegation, with big badges and sombreros. When we were seated in the
convention Decca noticed that we were a long way from an exit.
'What happens if I want to throw-up?' she said. Maury Maverick,
the mayor of San Antonio, handed her his sombrero. 'Madam,' he
said, 'use my hat!' She said she felt just like Queen Elizabeth.

'Had you been in the gallery, just above the Texas delegation', Decca
wrote to Esmond, 'you would have seen, sitting with the delegates and
wearing an alternate's badge, ME ... I've still got my badge – I've
put it in the Interesting Things File!! You must admit, it was a *terrific*
triumph!' And now 'Virginia has very kindly (and entirely due to you,
you clever old thing) asked me to stay as long as I want.' Decca agreed
to move in for a couple of weeks, and stayed two years.

From the radio, he had got the impression that the Democratic Convention was 'even more bombastic, horrible, dishonest, etc than the
Republican one – which should make it fun'. His own week-end had
been spent in New York with Selden Rodman, playing poker and watching a double-header baseball game: 'It was terribly dull, and I got
Babe [Alexander] and Selden quite annoyed by continually telling them
it was the same game played by English children under the name of
rounders.'

He was now in a hotel in Buffalo – still a long way from Ottawa
and the recruitment centre – and thinking about his wife:

I have missed you enormously the last few days – it has been similar
to a prolonged dull kind of stomach ache, and so I'll be glad to get
to Canada to get started on something. The car, driving around, having meals, club breakfasts, arriving in new places etc. have all point
removed when done without you. Well, there is one thing – not seeing
you all this time will certainly give me something terrific to look
forward to. Be sure to write me exactly what you're doing, and be
sure to have a nice and exciting time, and enjoy yourself. I shall
be doing the same.

Had Decca objected when Esmond had joined up? Philip Toynbee
asked his friend when they met again in the summer of 1941. Esmond
seemed surprised by the question, explaining that it had been something for him alone to decide. For all its anti-Establishmentism, Toynbee concluded, the Romillys' marriage was an old-fashioned affair in
which Esmond made the decisions and Decca lent the moral support.

Esmond arrived in Ottawa on a sultry July evening, signed in at the recruitment centre and awaited his induction. A week later – still waiting – he wrote to Decca: 'I'm changing my first favourable impression of Ottawa – it now appears the dullest place on earth.' His days revolved around cheap meals, bad cinema and baking hot afternoons secluded in his guest-house bedroom. Even chance acquaintances had proved disappointing, with the sole exception of an 'oldish man' whom he had met sitting on a bench by the river, and who had 'invited my opinion as to whether most harlots preferred it "the French way or the straight way ...". This man was very persistent in his speculation. He appeared convinced that I knew the answer. Finally, I said it would be necessary to conduct a Gallup Poll to find out. "No, seriously," he said, "which do you think?"'

The apogee of the week's events had been a four-hour medical, from which, after enduring a particularly rigorous ear examination, Esmond passed 'in a very high category'. The problem with his hearing concerned a mastoid, operated on when Esmond was five years old and which the doctor believed had left him deaf in one ear.

Even after I'd repeated with deadly accuracy the sweet murmurings like 'sixty-six' and 'forty-four' which he wafted tantalizingly far from my left ear he had doubts as to whether I had any ear drum there at all, and sent me to another air force doctor to find out. The latter stabbed away at it in a desultory fashion for a while, trying to dynamite a passage which would afford him a good observation post from which to view the drum:

'He's deaf in one ear' I heard an assistant mutter. 'No, no,' I protested, and a few minutes later was proved to be right, and the ear to be in excellent shape.

Esmond's first training centre, called a 'Manning Depot', was in Toronto; his first days spent 'mostly in parades, shining up brass buttons and boots, drill parades, physical training and generally learning our way round'.

In reply to a letter from Decca describing in detail a magnificent week-end spent at Eugene Meyer's country house, Esmond supplied an unofficial picture of a day in the life of an RCAF recruit:

The place of the maid answering a bell is taken (and very adequately) by a singularly strident bugle note, which I'm sure you'll have heard

208

of via the movies, etc. called Reveille. At this point I can already claim my day is better than yours, for I have a 3½ hour start and waste none of the precious hours of these long summer days – i.e. Reveille goes at 6 o'clock.... Social life at this moment projects itself into the scene in the form of the two dangling feet of the man in the bunk above. After an ample breakfast of cereal and milk, I decide that the day is too good to be wasted indoors. So I put in an appearance at the physical training squad, at which a roll call is taken to find out whether everybody else took a similar decision. After a lot of creaking and groaning of joints to get my right hand to touch my left foot and generally pivot and wheel and bend on various hips, balls (of feet) etc., we go indoors. I reach the conclusion it might be an idea to change into some regulation clothes and saunter out onto the parade ground in time for the fall-in at 9 o'clock. This, in fact, does turn out to have been a pretty good idea – as in this way I have something to do the whole morning instead of hanging idly around. Drill ends at half-past eleven, starts again at one, and at 4.15 I have to do my own planning of diversions, as the day is officially over. Seriously though....

And, send-up apart, Esmond was serious. He had recently taken a science and mechanics test and had made 'a most awful mess'. This had prompted him to buy a book on elementary mechanics, 'and this afternoon, after a couple of hours' diligent study I've mastered the principles of how a piston works, this may lead in time to something further, I feel'. He had even begun to be more fastidious over his dress, and was eating slower 'on the theory that in this way the percentage of food matter transferred to my clothing can be cut to a minimum.... Of course, all this unfortunately doesn't have much connection with flying, but some time some place that will come along.'

Esmond's first flight – a purely fortuitous occurrence, and not repeated for another six months – came after a month's training. The recruits had been transferred to Camp Borden, Ontario, for a week's guard duty before entering on their technical training programme at Regina, Saskatchewan. Standing idly by the airfield one morning watching the bombers take off, Esmond was approached by two officers who asked him if he would like to accompany them on a practice flight: 'I sat next to the pilot,' he told Decca, 'and as it was a dual control plane, he let me fly it (or drive it or steer her or whatever the expression is) for quite a bit, and at one point even climbed out of his seat to make a sketch of something for a minute or two, which, as you can imagine, was really fine.'

The rest of the time at Camp Borden was spent in 'an endless succession of polishing, sweeping up, parading, waiting around, falling in on marches, right dressing, carrying kit somewhere else, answering roll calls, being assembled in alphabetical groups, waiting to see what's next, being formed in new groups, drilling in the sun, preparing barracks for inspection, and folding sheets and blankets "Camp Borden style", as opposed to the "Manning Depot" style'.

Nor were there any radical changes at Regina. 'The actual instruction here is rather fun – maths, morse code, Air Force regulations, accounts, etc. – but so far polishing, parading and drilling have loomed largest in the prospectus.'

It had taken a two-day train journey to transfer the men to Regina: 'a nice and airy and pleasant city in the middle of miles and miles of fuck all ... I suppose the main thing now in Washington is the news from England', Esmond wrote on 15 September. 'Up here one feels terribly cut off from everything ...'. He was now 1,500 miles from Ottawa, 2,000 miles from Washington and, seemingly, light years away from the London bombing.

In September the war, which for the previous two months had been dictated by the Luftwaffe's attempts to immobilize the Royal Air Force, entered a new phase: the plan to invade Britain was shelved, and the German Juggernaut pointed towards Eastern Europe. The dynamic Battle of Britain gave way to that long, destructive and, from a strategic point of view, ineffectual pounding: the Blitz.

'It seems as though what everyone expected in the first weeks of the war is happening now, and London will soon be in ruins', wrote Esmond to Decca on 22 September. Before the war had started it had been generally held that if subjected to continuous large-scale raids the capital would be crippled within six months. With this claim in mind, the Prime Minister addressed the Commons on 8 November. 'Statisticians may amuse themselves', he told the House, 'by calculating that after making allowances for the working of the law of diminishing returns, through the same house being struck twice or three times over, it would take ten years at the present rate for half the houses of London to be demolished. After that, of course, progress would be much slower.'

Lacking her brother-in-law's versatility, Nellie Romilly's accounts of the situation rarely rose above the histrionic. Letter to Esmond, 8 July 1940:

Well Uncle W. is wonderful and never in 30 years have I known him rise to grander heights. I feel like Aunt Clemmie, glad to be alive today, glad we shall be fighting together for this blessed island – come what may. My dear boy I wish too that you were here. I feel grieved for all who aren't. Poor tepid, frightened America, her whole attitude is pitiful – 'Yes, yes – help them if it keeps the danger off our shores – will it, won't it?' The help we need is the help that doesn't count on gain – the help that the volunteer gives regardless of danger to himself. I don't feel angry with America, just so sorry for her – and God how I wish we could win the war without her.

The last few months had been a particularly stressful period for Nellie: her eldest son had been taken prisoner at Narvik in April, in May her husband had died of cancer, and now, as German bombs rained on London, she faced the prospect of evacuating her home of twenty-five years. It was unthinkable, therefore, that Esmond should write anything but a sympathetic, rallying reply; 'As you say [Esmond to Decca] the mater's last letter was a real stiff upper lipper, and I suppose I should write back to say: "While there are people like you in London Hitler cannot/must not/cannot hope to/etc. etc. ..."' This was, however, a concession to circumstance alone. As Esmond made clear to his wife, his attitude to his mother's melodramatic displays remained as intolerant as ever: 'Really, though, something will have to be done. There must be a law one could dig up to prevent people from publicly surviving a new calamity twice a year.'

On the basis of their performance at Initial Training School, Regina, the men were to be placed in one of three groups: pilots, observers, and gunners/radio operators. Letter to Decca:

How the selection is made – whether on the basis of how many are called from 'Ottawa', or our marks in examinations, further medical tests (compression tanks etc.) or a bit of each, is a matter of absolute speculation. But I am sure of one thing – that it's quite useless to have any special preference, as I've a very strong suspicion that the selection may even follow something of the pattern and be achieved by the same illogical minds that execute our movements from place to place.

The classifications would inevitably cause disappointment as almost everyone wanted to be a pilot. For his own part he was determined to see advantages in all three groups:

211

viz:

PILOT. Far more fun learning to fly a plane than learning wireless, gunnery, navigation, photography, etc. The whole job would be far more exciting and far more fun in every way.

OBSERVER. The only advantage is that this is the most responsible, most difficult, most highly paid of the three.

GUNNER. The dullest course (24 weeks are spent, I believe, in studying wireless alone!) But the actual job is very exciting. And there's another very important thing – the social side would be more interesting and far more fun, as this is the least 'aiming to become an officer'-ish branch – therefore the people would be more palatable, etc. etc. . . .

The classifications were published on 24 September. Esmond was an observer.

On the whole, I'm pretty glad about the choice, as I think I'm more suited to the dropping of bombs on defenceless women and whatnots (at least, I sincerely hope they will prove defenceless) than all this 400 mile an hour power drive, guns screaming on the tail of a Messerschmitt etc. A pleasant half hour over a cigar plotting the course, a nice plane ride watching out for scenery, instructing the pilot if I have a whim to look at the Black Forest, arrive nicely at the objective, release the switch and home again is – I think – definitely more up my street, and I'm sure you can see me much easier in this role. The only snag is, of course, that I don't think observation has so far been my main quality – in fact even recently I've lost my way on a number of occasions inside the buildings here, and of course the consequences of this sort of thing on a wide territorial scale are quite horrifying to consider.

There was a definite end-of-term atmosphere at Regina as all the men prepared to leave for the specialized training stations. Esmond thought it probable that he would be posted to an observer school near Toronto, in which case Decca might well be able to join him. Amidst the excitement and speculation, however, a note of anxiety was sounded.

Before announcing the classifications the Air Force had subjected each man to another rigorous medical examination. Once again Esmond's mastoid operation caused problems. 'I still haven't heard the final result of my last medical over the mastoid question,' he wrote to his wife on 27 September. 'Seeing the way things are, it wouldn't surprise me to find there was a regulation tucked away about it somewhere which would cancel out the last $2\frac{1}{2}$ months!'

In fact, although he made no mention of it in the letter, Esmond had already been shown a copy of Air Force Regulations in which a radical mastoid was listed as an automatic disqualification from air-crew. However, as he had shown no signs of deafness, and in all other respects was 100 per cent fit, the doctor had told him he was sure the medical board would waive the regulation. When, a week later, the classifications were announced and his name had not appeared on 'X' flight (the classification for those unfit for air-crew) Esmond had assumed that the regulation had indeed been waived.

This was the situation when he wrote to his wife on Friday 27 September. But three days later, and on the eve of his transfer to air-observer school, Esmond was called before the Squadron Leader and told that he was being placed on 'X' flight – the medical board's decision being that the regulation concerning radical mastoids was 'to be rigidly adhered to in all cases'.

Staggered by this sudden body-blow, Esmond asked for an immediate discharge (the prerogative of all those placed on 'X' flight). The Squadron Leader was sympathetic, but told him there were another fifteen men in the same position, and his release, which had to go through Ottawa, might take some time.

On Monday evening Esmond bought a bottle of Scotch, checked into the town's hotel and drowned his sorrows. Appearing, bleary-eyed, on parade on Tuesday morning he discovered he was still on the observers flight roll-call and was required to sit an examination the next day on navigation, reconnaissance, armament and morse code; 'so – to find something to do – I studied up on them on Tuesday evening, and got a certain morbid satisfaction out of writing around 95% or so correct'.

On Wednesday afternoon preparations for the air-crew draft began, Esmond watching the proceedings from a Nissen hut window. Letter to Decca:

I'd often thought that if one was compounding a little journalese on the subject, one'd probably throw in a line or two about the one or two men from 'X' flight in each room – you know, the old stuff: standing by the window, listening to the shouts of whoopee, watching the lads rush to get their flying suits on so they can get their picture taken in it, looking at the lines of bleak iron bedsteads and noting which ones have already been stripped of kitbags, blankets, etc. ...

It was his first failure in adult life, and for several days he unashamedly abandoned himself to that most terrible of virulences, self pity. 'The last week has been just about the most hellish thing I've

213

known in my life,' he wrote to Decca on 7 October. 'I only tell you this now because as I write this letter all that is over.' It wasn't over, of course, but at least the debilitating hollowness had passed. He had even begun to look at the situation with something approaching stoical levity:

> Meanwhile life in the flight is becoming quite a lark. (A large proportion of it, by the way, consists of mentally and not physically unfit.) There's a certain lack of military preciseness about the parade ground manner of this lost brigade. After roll call at 8.15 in the morning, when the other boys march off to school with all the old bright face and satchel stuff, the sergeant-major comes over and after receiving the corporal's 'All Present and Correct, Sir,' he says, 'All right, carry on your duties.' which makes quite pleasant hearing as the duties are undefined and non-existent. Occasionally, a few are caught and brooms and mops thrust in their hands, but they usually tire of playing with these after ten minutes or so and mysteriously melt away till the next roll call at 1.15.

Esmond was using much of this unofficial free time to keep up-to-date with his navigation and meteorology studies, in the hope that he might yet be reinstated to the observer course. However, if this proved forlorn, he would – with Decca's approval – return to England, and try again there. 'I'm quite sure I'll be able to get into the Royal Air Force (I even think I'll ask Mrs Romilly to use her influence if necessary with brother-in-law). That means that I'll be back in Canada for advanced training within a very few months – you can then come to wherever I am, and everything will be just fine.'

At the end of October Esmond was transferred to a 'Manning Pool' at Brandon, Manitoba, where he was once again put through 'the whole weary business' of applying for a discharge – 'What takes time is even getting them to locate your files, then considering your case, then to Ottawa, etc. ...'

After five days of drilling with the new recruits he was made a fire piquet (fire warden) which meant an automatic exemption from daily parades, drills and inspections. 'Best of all [letter to Decca, 4 November] it means one is not shoved around. So as an AC2 fire piquet "entitled to occupy public quarters and draw rations", my morale is at the state where I'm prepared to sit it out till hell freezes till that discharge comes through.'

As it turned out he had only to sit out another eighteen days. On 22 November 1940 – two weeks into Franklin D. Roosevelt's third term of office – AC2 Esmond Romilly was officially discharged from the Canadian Air Force.

Away from the military middle-men, it took Esmond just a few minutes to get himself reinstated to the air-observer course; this was achieved by phoning a Canadian MP, J.E.Matthews, who was friendly with the Air Marshal's secretary. How Esmond came to know Matthews, however, no one can recall, not even Selden Rodman, to whom he related the story four days after his release. 'Esmond dropped in from Canada tonight with amazing tales to tell', Rodman recorded in his 26 November journal entry. The 'amazing tales' were of his four months of training which had left him, according to his friend, 'disheartened, if not thoroughly disillusioned with his whole experience.... Four months at camp and still he hasn't seen the inside of a plane. Why? The most god-awful bureaucratic inefficiency. No doubt the training is as good as can be had but the force seems to be pointing at 1944, rather than 1941.'

For *Per Ardua Ad Astra* – the RAF's motto – read *Per Ardua Ad Aspera*, Esmond told Rodman. Why not *Per Ardua Ad Asperin*, Rodman suggested, 'which he allowed was best of all'.

Christmas 1940 was spent in Washington with the Durrs. Virginia Durr:

> Esmond was the most delightful person in that period. He said he'd never had a Christmas tree which he considered fully decorated, so we had a tree which was the most gorgeous thing you've ever seen in your life. And he made stockings for everybody, and when we woke up they were pinned to the bed full of gimmicks and things. So radiant, so full of life. He took Decca and me to a small French restaurant where you could get lunch for $1.25. He asked to see the Maître d. and wanted to know the best wine and what they recommended for an entrée, all in a terribly British accent. Everything he did was an event.... He was delighted with the prospect of the baby, and took Decca for two-mile walks every day.

Decca, who had been working as a tightly girdled dress-shop assistant until Christmas, had now retired to the Durrs' spacious Seminary Hill home to await the happy event, letting it be known – one suspects more out of mischief than maternal madness – that she was determined to have the baby in the family barn. 'Just going out and dropping it

215

there. How romantic! We thought we'd go crazy. In the end we persuaded her to have it at Columbia Hospital.'

The baby, a six-pound ten-ounce girl, was born on Sunday 9 February 1941 and christened Constancia. Decca:

Constancia was my choice, after the Spanish aristocrat Constancia de la Mora, who had become a Communist and had sided with the Spanish Republic. Esmond wasn't too keen on the name, he thought it would be contracted to Connie or Con: a needless worry – the Democratic Donkey having already secured the baby's familiar name: 'The Donk', which became in time 'Dinky Donk' and 'Dinky' and has ever more remained.

Esmond was a month into his air-observer course at Malton, Ontario, and flying almost every day, but feeling no closer affiliation with those momentous events taking place across the Atlantic. He confided to Selden Rodman:

One thing I notice sometimes is a coma of sublime inactivity that grips me in the air. Perhaps it is the speed of the aircraft, the sight of the pilot hurtling this imponderably technical apparatus through the air at a colossal speed tends to make me feel that all's well anyway and how could a silly futile gesture like writing out a slip of paper or change of course have any effect on such things. Much the same type of coma gripped me the other day when we went up to do a Reconnaissance of a small town. I had a sketch all ready prepared and a pencil in my hands to fill in the pertinent detail, and we whirled around the town for about ten minutes drinking in all the 'activity at rail heads', etc., but the curious part about it was that at the end of the time I discovered I hadn't made a single actual note – written or mental – of anything. In fact, it appeared, I had done nothing. Curious.

Fortunately the 'torpor' passed before the end-of-course examinations, from which Esmond emerged joint first, and graduated to No. 1 Bombing and Gunnery School, Jarvis (Ontario). Here he spent six weeks learning to bomb lakes and – with some difficulty – assemble the 197 parts of a Browning machine-gun, before entering the Air Navigation School at Rivers, Manitoba, for the final phase of his training, in astral navigation.

In June the Canadian *Standard* caught up with him at Rivers, and later ran a five-page pictorial on his training. 'Typical of the keen-eyed, romantic young "Aerial Key Men" I found at "No. 1 ANS" was Sergeant Observer E.M.D.Romilly, nephew by marriage of Winston Churchill. Briskly alert, he was classed by Squadron Leader Gillson, officer commanding the Ground Instruction School, as "a rattling good observer ...frightfully keen"'; a further encomium this, Esmond having already been voted by his fellow trainees 'man most likely to succeed'.

At the end of the month Esmond was back in the States and celebrating a pre-embarkation leave in the breezy glades of Menemsha Inn, Martha's Vineyard. Selden Rodman was once again on hand to record events. Journal entry, 23 June 1941:

The Romillys arrived on Thursday from Washington.... In a sense it was the happy nightmare of September 1st, 1939 repeating itself. But in another sense like the second act of a mystery play whose end is still unforeseeable. (In the first act war declared, now Russia's entry,)* Neither the possibilities of death nor the much less likely happy ending could rob us of the delirious present. I received my 2nd notice to appear before the draft board as Esmond was getting ready to go to England. I asked him if he had any misgivings about going on a raid and not coming back. 'None', he said, decisively, but matter-of-factly 'I have no doubt at all that I will survive this war whether shot down or not.'

'Friday was a recapitulation of childhood', wrote Rodman. He and Esmond had played tennis all morning on 'liberal' hostess Evelyn Preston-Baldwin's tennis court, before retiring, in elfish mood, to her kitchen for a drink.

We asked her if we could get a drink from the house. 'You know where the kitchen is', she said. We knew she meant the tap. Nevertheless we opened the ice box, found a big jug of lemonade and decided a couple of glasses removed from it would hardly be noticed. Our thirst was not slight. 'I think', said Esmond, with a mischievous gleam in his eye, 'that we have no recourse now but to finish this jug, wash it carefully and replace it on the shelf. Our guilt will be apparent from an empty pitcher, whereas if we finish it there are several possibilities. One, the evidence can never be more than circumstantial, second, there is a good chance the boys [the Baldwins' sons] will be whipped not for taking it but for denying that they took it. Third, the cook may be fired, a flagrant injustice that may promote a class

* Germany invaded Russia on 22 June 1941.

217

struggle. Four, can we really be sure that she didn't intend us to drink it. If we didn't take it might we not place her in the unenviable position of thinking, "Romilly left to fight and die for civilization without having taken this lemonade".' A small thing to be sure, but the thing that meant most to him at that moment. Five, couldn't we do away with the jug itself thus leaving them totally baffled. For surely they would argue that Romilly and Rodman might steal the lemonade but it would be beneath them to steal the kitchen-ware as well. All these possibilities we argued at length, finishing the lemonade with some difficulty because of laughing.

Saturday was 'another hilarious day'. They had joined forces with some other holiday-makers, played tennis twice, swum three times 'and tried at the same time to get from place to place in three cars. On one such occasion after standing in the middle of the road for 15 minutes arguing, Esmond remarked that the difficulty lay in an over-abundance of resources. Too many tennis courts, too many beaches, many too many cars, and much too much ocean.'

On Sunday morning they discussed the Russo–German war, speculating on how long it would take the *Daily Worker* and the communist anti-war organizations to 'adjust themselves back to the old line'. At 3.00 p.m. Uncle Winston addressed the world, embracing the Russian people in the common fight against fascism. Rodman thought this 'an extremely fatuous utterance and at least some attempt should have been made to dissociate democratic war aims from the plight of the new totalitarian partner'. Esmond was equally

scornful of business as usual defence in this country, and gave a classic take-off of Roosevelt's wordy fireside speech the night before. Perhaps as a result of his experiences in the IB where communists fought hardest for Spain he is still a fellow-traveller. He did not agree that in practice Nazism and communism are opposite sides of the same coin. He thinks that now the communists will fight hardest to win the war and win it for socialism.

In the evening they went to a drinks party, and then played poker until midnight. 'In the morning Esmond left for the boat. Several days of sun came to an end with a stiff north-easter and heavy rain.'

22
The Grey and the Black

After escaping from England what shall I do if war breaks out? The answer is that I shall go back ... to fight for the grey of British Imperialism allied to Polish and Rumanian Fascism against the black of German–Italian Fascism.

ESMOND ROMILLY, 'Escape from England'

'It was frightful when you left,' Della wrote from the Vineyard. 'I immediately went for a long walk to get myself together, but everything's all right now. I shall go back to Virginnie's as soon as I hear from you. I'm sure Halifax will be simply beastly....'

Not beastly, wrote Esmond, just 'as dull as ditch-water', but quite bearable had it not been for the commission business which had marred his arrival.

When I got here on Tuesday night I was told I had a commission, and learned, immediately afterwards, that George Moss did not have one (nor a single one of my friends for that matter). Next morning, when it came to filling out forms in connection with the commission I said I didn't want it. This caused a temporary check in proceedings, and later on I had an interview with the officer responsible. The gist of it all was that I already had the commission, had had it in fact since June 10th, and that the only way to get out of it would be to go about resigning it, which would mean new enlisting if able as an AC2. Knowing what this would mean – endless waiting around for interviews and documents, continual stalemates ... I let the matter go. Since then, I've had moments of bitterly regretting that I didn't more or less push the thing to the limit. The reason for these feelings is, of course, the experience of the last two days. The form here has been pamphlets on how to behave as an officer, officers segregated in a separate barracks and separate mess, exultant ordering of officers' uniforms and other fancy adornments in the Halifax

219

stores, groups of disappointed sergeants sitting together bleakly in cafés in the evenings, never a whisper about the war from a soul. Right here, right now, you might say we have the logical sublime climax of the competitive promotion seeking, mark-grabbing, on-with-your-career ideology which has been nurtured by the powers that be and is apparently the one they think best suited to the morale of a group of men who've volunteered for war service. Jack Bryant said to me yesterday, 'You know, Esmond, we were coming up on the train Sunday, and I don't think anyone gave one moment's thought to Russia coming in the war, we were so worrying about the commissions.'

As I said though, in a few days, or weeks or however long it is till we get to England I shall look back on this as just as bizarre and unreal as seemed the political fractious meetings with Lorrimer Birch at Albacete when we looked back on them a while later. Actually, as soon as it looks as though we were to move you notice a change already in the atmosphere.

The situation did not improve on board ship, but was exacerbated by assigning the officers to separate decks and bars and providing them with waiter-service while the sergeants were expected to line up for their food and wash their own dishes: petty discriminations which did nothing to bridge the official rift between men who up until two days ago had existed on terms of absolute equality. There was, however, a ray of hope: 'One of the most cheering things is that all the RCAF P/O's and quite a few of the RAF ones are worried a lot about it all – and wondering what can be arranged.'

There were, too, those young officers – RAF men according to Esmond – who seemed to be actually basking in their superiority. Larry Hagget was one.

Our flight was the 'duty' flight today; Larry Hagget (small, no sense of humour, technical, competent, boastful) was orderly in charge of the flight, and myself and three other officers were supposed to be assisting him. On the parade this morning he said 'all right, smartly on parade, you'll just make it that much easier for yourselves.' At lunch time in the airmen's mess, it seemed that some people had had their butter and sugar rations removed by some others. He said to the orderly sergeant: 'I'm going to look into this very carefully, Sergeant. I mean we can't have that sort of thing. It isn't done, especially on shipboard.'!! And when he went into the mess at supper-time, he made an announcement: 'Now, understand men, this sort of thing can't go on. If it does, we shall have to take disciplinary action.'

At breakfast the next morning, when Esmond was orderly officer, the butter problem again emerged: 'lack of, or missing, or taken, or somesuch business. Final solution was to buy a pound tin at the canteen – very weak indeed.... This leaves one very open to attack, of course. Roughton-Bermondseyish and not very serious!'

On the second day he had gone down to the sergeants' deck to celebrate the embarkation with a friend, George Moss. Moss produced a bottle of rye, and officer and sergeant were loosening-up on rye and apple-juice cocktails when Moss's cabin-mate, who had refused a drink, began to take exception to Esmond's presence. 'The other sergeant says, "We don't usually allow officers in this cabin." "Oh yes," says George, "we have a new comrade for the revolution here." "Good Party member, I hope?" "The Party's doing all right," says the other fellow. "And we're not going to let any of the officers in...."' Esmond and Moss left the cabin and continued their celebration on a secluded area of deck. Later Esmond met his antagonist ('his name's "Marx"') again, drew him out on his politics and discovered they shared many views. They parted on amicable terms.

To relieve the tension several of the officers, including Esmond, had organized a series of activities: a mixed-team tug-of-war, a sergeants versus ship's company quiz, a concert party, and a sing-along.

For community singing it was things like 'Roll Out the Barrel', 'Oh Johnny', and 'Irish Eyes'. When they came to songs like 'Wings Over the Navy' nobody knew any more than the first verse. When they sang a very popular army tune which has words like 'There'll be no promotion this side of the ocean, then bless all the sergeants and wo1's, bless all the corporals and their darling sons, bless them all,' it was sung just like that; whereas usually this goes with a terrific bang as everybody sings: 'Fuck all sergeants and wo1's, fuck all the corporals and their bastard sons, fuck them all.' Apparently the Captain, who constituted a censor on the material – in the words of the ship's doctor – 'Doesn't like anything that's a trifle blue.' ('Blue' is a new one on me.) However, the concert and the tug-of-war etc. have definitely made for a much friendlier spirit on the boat.... Even Larry Hagget had some sergeants in his cabin to give them a beer.

Before disembarking Esmond questioned his commanding officer, an RAF man, on the 'form' in England.

'You'll find they pay more attention to that over there than they do here' [the man said], meaning the commission/non-commission distinction. I asked him if there hadn't been some sort of a social revolution in England, and he said 'ah yes, that was in the civilian population and in the civilian services, you noticed a lot of it there.' Even here, it's true the English RAF people seem to have far more reverence for the badge of authority than the Canadians or Australians.

Braced to expect the worst type of Forces captiousness at his Operational Training Unit, OTU Abingdon in Oxfordshire, Esmond had been surprised and relieved to encounter instructors who, apart from a rather 'self-confident slanginess', were quite tolerable people. Later, as a member of 58 Squadron, at Linton-on-Ouse in Yorkshire, he found, to his amazement, that this situation actually improved. There were still 'dragons to be slain' of course, he told his wife, but in the main there existed a 'great feeling of friendliness among the Air Crews.... People who have done a lot of trips go out of their way to be helpful to newcomers, and, even more, to be genuinely friendly. It makes for a most agreeable atmosphere.'

'And England?' Esmond wrote three weeks after his arrival:

The amazing thing about England is that there is nothing amazing at all yet. People stood the raids, got ready for the invasion, endured the boredom, fear, regimentation of their lives with patience and courage that could hardly have been bettered – but through it all, tho' individuals' lives were broken up and habits of work and pleasure radically changed, yet the economic structure and the class divisions, the control-organization of society as a whole has not changed. The towering giant of conservatism ... stands astride England today happier and more confident than ever.

Expecting, unrealistically, to encounter a *Zeitgeist* of social revolution, Esmond had confronted instead a society which, in the bleakest period of the war, longed for nothing more idealistic than a return to the status quo.

On all fronts 1941 was proving a disastrous year. In the first half of the year German submarines had sunk over 300 merchant ships, imports had fallen to two-thirds of the pre-war figure, and the population's diet was poorer than at any other period in the War. Added to these domestic privations was the appalling news from overseas where the British forces had recorded a litany of defeats in the Balkans and North Africa, while their Russian ally was offering only scant resistance to a German Army bent on engorging Moscow before Christmas.

No less depressing were the events on the other side of the Atlantic where, at Placentia Bay, Newfoundland, Churchill and Roosevelt were drafting the Atlantic Charter. 'The greatest cordiality had prevailed,' the Prime Minister told his cabinet, 'and the Americans had missed no opportunity in identifying themselves with our cause.' But to the nation, expecting something more substantial than cordiality, the agreement was yet more unction on the downward slope to 1942.

For Esmond the most emotive news of 1941 was that being relayed from the Russian front, where an ill-prepared people was trying to fend off its powerful invader; a stand, in Esmond's eyes, as dramatic and heroic as the stand made by the Spanish Republic in the winter of 1936. 'The news [from Russia]', he wrote to his wife on 22 September, 'has the same dull torturingness that the news about the war in Spain used to have – accepting one new blow after another, resigning yourself, then finding it wasn't so bad after all, then hopes for counter-blows then suddenly another sickening thud – Malaga and Kiev – the same process all over again.' And in a letter of 16 October:

The news from Russia is really agonizing – just like the way it used to be from Spain – and though we're actually fighting in the same war with them, it is startling and rather horrifying how very detached we seem to be from that agony. Of course, in America this would be even more so the case – or perhaps not? Is there more enthusiasm now among the New Dealers and one time fellow travellers – or still the 'democrats since June 22nd' angle?

Esmond had mellowed, thought Toynbee, himself a reformed character, married and serving with the Welsh Guards at Wilton Park. Esmond had turned up at his Wilton home one Friday evening in August bristling with discursive conversation and urgent theories: 'I remember

223

that he had just read Koestler's *Darkness at Noon* – with the ecstatic, unrestrained enthusiasm of the desultory reader – and that he was resolutely on the side of the inquisitors.' But to Toynbee the claim was merely 'bravado', plangently out of tune with his friend's increased sensibility :

Before his departure for America he had already become more mellow, but his mellowing had taken the form of a more indulgent good-humour rather than a greater gentleness or pity. Now, walking under the summer sky at Wilton, he told me that his only political motive was his dismay at human unhappiness. I was surprised, almost alarmed, not so much at the sentiment itself as at Esmond's confession of it. No earlier Esmond would have allowed himself to be so emotionally forthright, and I had a sudden superstitious fear that by admitting his own goodness of heart he had made himself vulnerable ; that this, without his knowing it, might be a preparation for his own death.

Esmond had changed, but not as dramatically as the above might imply. In any event he had not lost his vivacity or sense of humour, and while this did not run counter to a philanthropic outlook it at least militated against the stuffier aspects of the belief. Toynbee :

This had been by far the longest of our many separations and my life had changed so much during the past two years that I was uncertain how our old relationship could be resumed.... But from the first moment that I saw him I felt a delighted excitement at his presence which assured me that nothing awkward had grown up between us. He was still asleep when I came home in the morning [Toynbee had been on night duty when Esmond had arrived], and the sight of his heavy, sleeping face poignantly returned me to a sad but adventurous past. But when he woke, when he at once began to chatter as if we had last seen each other only on the day before, it was no longer nostalgia that I felt, but present joy in acquiring again what I had lost.

The relationship renewed, the friends began to meet regularly, on occasion spending a free evening together in London, as at the beginning of October, when Esmond accompanied the Toynbees to a fashionable London dinner party. He wrote home excitedly with details :

The other evening Ivan Moffat (he was at Dartington Hall and I knew him in the old 'Out of Bounds' days*) and his girl friend, Natalie, gave a dinner party in their flat in Soho – a dinner's a frightfully rare thing and this was delicious with chicken and wine and a lovely room. Philip and Anne were there and Brian Howard and Dylan Thomas and his wife, and Nancy Cunard with a coloured Trinidadian airman and the odd German professor, and it was a terrifically good party. The only thing was that later in the evening Philip and Ivan and myself seemed to form into a mutual admiration clique consisting of each one doing a terrific act and never pausing without giving an opening for the next one. At the end of each act, the other two would say, 'Brilliant, brilliant, Ivan, brilliant,' and he'd reply, 'Come on, now, Philip.... All right, Philip has the floor', so one or two of the other guests thought they had rather a thin time, but most people enjoyed it enormously.

But for all his good-humoured participation on this occasion and on other occasions, Esmond's thoughts seemed elsewhere – with his wife, thought Toynbee, although even now, even in his 'more self-revealing mood', it was impossible to tell quite how much the separation was affecting him.

'I will never be able to explain how tremendously I miss you,' he wrote to Decca on 22 September; and, on 16 October: 'I am thinking of you all the time and simply longing to be able to see you again.' Yet in none of his letters had he asked her, unequivocally, to come over; indeed, at times he appeared to be advising against it. He now knew the name of his operational base, he wrote on 5 October, so she could come over if she 'really frightfully wanted to and it was possible. ... But', he warned, 'I do still think that everything I said previously about things being more fascinating and interesting and life satisfactory for you in America are true absolutely.' And again, a fortnight later: 'Well now I am pretty well settled down at an operational station, and have found out that if you were able to come over, this would be very nice to know. However, there are of course a lot of things to be considered....' So what did he want her to do? Probably, to relieve him of making the decision; although, understandably, this was not a responsibility she was eager to accept. 'GOOD POSSIBILITY SHIP

---

* Ivan Moffat, 'Dartington Hall School: An Experiment in Education', 'Out of Bounds', Vol. 1, No. 3, Winter. In 1941 Moffat was working with Dylan Thomas, writing scripts for the documentary unit, Strand Films.

TRANSPORT', she cabled on 8 November. 'HAVE MADE ROUTINE AP BUT WILL ONLY COME IF YOU ARE 100% PRO.'

'Yes,' he wrote, 'more than anything else in the world.' But it had taken a major shock and the prospect of his own death to shake the confession from him.

Sandwiched between OTU Abingdon and the operational base at Linton-on-Ouse, on the Yorkshire coast, was a week's leave. Most of this was spent in London, meeting old friends – 'Peter [Nevile] is just the same as ever, much more tolerant of everything though' – hobnobbing with a few literary figures – 'I have seen Cyril Connolly, whose magazine *Horizon* is really very good, I think, and Stephen [Spender], who has a new wife ...' – and generally chasing up acquaintances, a group of people he tended to compare unfavourably with its American counter-part, as he wrote to his wife:

> After the wonderful simple nice naïveté of the Americans it was rather fascinating to get back to the subtleties and nastiness and under-currents of a lot of the sort of English people we know, where a remark doesn't mean what it seems to but is a sort of rapier thrust of some kind. Incidentally, I haven't seen Nancy [Mitford] (whom this remark brings to mind) or any of your family....

Nor had he seen his mother, except on one occasion, a luncheon in the summer, and although he replied conscientiously and chattily to her letters he was always careful to parry any invitations to further meetings. Eight years after the 'Out of Bounds' affair, he was still determined to regard Nellie as a particularly dangerous predator, to be kept at arm's length. Letter to Decca:

> I ran into [X] who's sort of being built up as Giles' fiancee, but per-sonally I think she is so much in contact with Giles' mother, who is building another cage for Giles by remote control, that Giles will absolutely associate her with the cage: and even if when he first comes back he is so broken down by his terrible time that he lets himself wallow back in it as the easiest and laziest solution, he'll soon want to be out again.

On 9 October Esmond moved to 58 Squadron, a light-bomber detach-ment based in the East Yorkshire town of Linton-on-Ouse. He viewed the move with a certain amount of trepidation, hence the telling analogy with first days at school. Letter to Decca, 22 September:

I shall be a new boy at school again but for the last time, and the most important.... Quite obviously I am going to have no time in my mind at first for anything except the struggle to avoid committing some ghastly blunder such as losing my protractor under the seat, plugging my oxygen tube into the aircraft radio circuit, breaking the points of all twelve of the pencils I shall persuade myself it's necessary to take, taking an astro sight on an enemy searchlight, releasing a few thousand pounds of high explosive bombs accidentally on the ground while checking the bombsight before take-off, using the nautical mile scale instead of statute miles, mistaking the Atlantic for the North Sea, and other farcical items of this nature. However funny all this sounds there may be more 'drame' than 'comédie' to it at first.

Offsetting this technical nightmare there was, however, as always, the 'human drama':

... i.e. being posted to a crew which in our case will consist of the first pilot (who is the Captain), a second pilot, a wireless operator, a tail gunner, and the Navigator (oneself); the same crew stays together for quite a large number of trips, so that the relationships and personalities involved are quite fascinating ... I will be certain to write to you about all this, and it will of course require no effort, because it is the aspect which interests me most of all.

After two mission cancellations, Esmond made his first trip, a raid on Ostend, on the evening of the 16th. The aircraft took off at 18.21 hours, attacked the primary target at 20.20 and the secondary at 20.25. The results were not observed. One 250 lb bomb had been held up and had to be jettisoned into the sea before the aircraft returned to base, at 23.15. These were the statistics, entered into the Operations Book by the captain, Pilot Officer F.G.Mounsey. In a letter to his wife Esmond presented the 'human drama' of the occasion:

When I got into the plane at first I simply couldn't get the navigator's table up, and had to struggle for ten minutes with the aid of some of the ground crew before it would stay up. (I think you can imagine the type of scene of frustrated fury – like trying to get out of the cupboard that time in Corsica.) A short while after we got going, the Captain began saying something to me which sounded at first like 'chum' – it turned out to be 'chewing gum' – after a lot of frenzied searching around in awkward places I finally found some among

227

the rations, and with a sigh of somewhat indignant relief, plonked it into his lap. This was the signal, however, for further crackling and fuming in my ears through the inter-com. After an exchange of continual malentendus, I gathered the gum was to be chewed up and stuck over some light inside that was too bright. This incident closed, I thought I could apply myself to the navigation, but not before a particularly bitter struggle with some window curtains, the manner of fastening of which was amazingly simple to everyone except myself. And this was not the end. The wireless operator rapped peremptorily on my desk and thrust into my hand a grubby sheet of paper. This, on inspection, contained nothing but a series of gibberish, so I gave him an understanding nod of acknowledgement – a sort of quick 'thumbs up' signal to indicate that the matter was completely under control, stuffed the paper in my pocket and prepared to regard the incident as closed. You can imagine my feeling of annoyance when I heard the captain's voice say – 'What was in the message, no. 3?', followed by the reply, 'I don't know, Sir. I passed it to the navigator to be decoded.' 'Good Lord', I broke in, 'does this mean I've got to decode the thing now?' It did. When we were over the target area, I chanced to pass the observation that there seemed to be a great number of bomb bursts and flashes going on everywhere – and indicated a few particularly vivid flashes in one quarter. 'Those aren't bomb flashes', our captain tersely informed me. 'That's their Ack-Ack firing at us.'

And there were more anxious moments to come. After releasing the bombs over the target area – the observer's job – Esmond had returned to a scene of 'horrid desolation'.

Everything – pencils, dividers, rulers, protractors, notes, log sheet, star tables, almanacs – were on the floor, somewhere – but by no means in the same place.... But it's amazing how adaptable one is – eventually, somehow, things got straightened up, and I began to get the return trip under control. Half-way to England there was one wild moment of gnawing uncertainty occasioned by the cheery remark from the tail gunner, 'Hullo, number 2, we seem to be running along parallel with the enemy coast still. Is that right?' 'Hello, no. 6', I said in as stern a tone as I could muster, 'no, that is not right. That (rather quieter) is not possible.' Nor was it (thank Heavens). ... Actually, though, I learned an enormous lot of useful practical things (like not leaving all your instruments so that they will fall off the table when the twists and ducks begin), got along very well

228

with the captain, and was left with an amount of confidence for the future.

The worst part of the raids, he wrote to Decca on 28 October, before what was to have been his fourth trip, was the take-off:

... getting in, bumping one's head on something, struggling to get the heavy bag of navigational equipment and the sextant and the parachute etc. in place, and then the bitter struggle to get the table up, and make the legs fit in the holes on the floor – and get the speaking tubes and oxygen plugs stuck in their right places and then sort out the maps and charts and get the main ones stuck to the desk with drawing pins, and have all the rest of the pencils and dividers and protractors and rulers and calculators and star almanacs deployed in such a manner that one can grab onto them when the plane jolts across the ground at the take-off. Tonight is cold and wet outside which will add to the general bleakness also of piling onto the lorry, dressed up like a stuffed animal, for the ride across the hangar to the plane, treading on someone's hand and upsetting their equipment as you get in. Once 'airborne' the outlook becomes very much better....

And the account continued with a description of the target area:

... soon there's a blaze of activity everywhere. Lights of every sort and colour flash and blink and twinkle ... long thin spidery yellow searchlights whirling around, rising and falling, seeking to form a spider's web in the sky ... vivid red flashes which illuminate the ground for a few seconds which I used to mistake for bomb flashes, but apparently are the flashes from their heavy anti-aircraft guns. The exploding shells make dark brown-grey puffs of smoke which hang in the air sometimes right in front of you to the right and to the left. In the distance, perhaps, you see a beautiful arc of red streaks curving upward across the sky – the path of incendiary bullets fired from hundreds of machine guns. All the while the plane is ducking and weaving and diving and twisting to avoid the shells and the searchlights. Then there's another item to the November 5th display – huge red flares strewn across the sky, floating gradually earthwards – the ground beneath is lit up as though by a dazzling electric light. Still twisting and weaving, the plane edges round toward the target, straightens out for a second, the last intricate settings are made, the last words of guidance given to the pilot, a gentle pressure of the thumb, the plane gives a convulsive leap in the air

229

and the pilot hears the welcome phrase – 'Bombs gone'. The night's work is over – except of course for the business of getting through searchlight belts and shells and night-fighter patrols to the coast, and on across the sea to the English coast and home – but the rest is mainly cold and worry and hard work and complicated problems of navigation, and hence any sort of description would be out of place in such a highly romanticized account as this.

'As for last night's trip,' he wrote, picking up the letter the next day, 'we never went. It was "scrubbed" at the last moment. This is very indicative of the non-Hemingwayishness of everything.... You can't even sit down and write a letter with the tough drama of "This is written just before take-off ..." etc. etc. with all the old understatement racket, because the probable thing is it'll be cancelled at the last moment!'

For Esmond one of the few consolations in being posted to the other end of the country was the presence of Philip Toynbee, based during October and November just twenty miles away from Linton, at the resort town of Bridlington-on-Sea. Given a twenty-four-hour leave at the end of the month, he paid his friend a visit.

'It was a time', wrote Toynbee, 'when the infantry often regarded the airforce with gnawing and unconfessed hostility. Home-based infantry officers had done no fighting at all, at least since Dunkirk, and they were secretly jealous of the glamour and publicity which had been won by air-crew and fighter pilots.' Esmond, he noted, had read the situation immediately and when introduced to a group of young officers in the officers' mess played down the role of the bombing crews while praising the unsung heroism of the Army. 'He laid this on very thick, grinning at me when I caught his eye – but he was right in thinking that none of it would seem preposterous to his grateful audience.'

Later that evening Esmond again demonstrated his great social ease, this time among a group of privates in a Bridlington pub. For the past month Toynbee had been going into the pub's bar (bars were officially out of bounds to officers) and had succeeded gradually in establishing a casual and friendly relationship with the other drinkers. 'But Esmond needed no such long preparation. He was at ease with them at once and had made them easy.... His supreme social gift', wrote his friend, 'was the real interest which he felt in the lives and opinions of others.'

Esmond's second and final visit to Bridlington, on 10 November, was a more serious occasion. He spoke about the probability of death while disguising, ineffectually, his own fears with a purported conviction of his indestructibility. He had improbably survived at Boadilla, he told Toynbee, therefore, he would, improbable though it might seem, survive the present conflict.

But sober reality returned the next morning when he arrived at Linton to discover that two aircraft from the previous night's mission were 'missing'. One of these, containing four people whom he had come to regard as his best friends at the base, had come down in the North Sea. A search was organized, in which Esmond acted as a look-out, but nothing was sighted.

With two of the men, Esmond told his wife, the friendship had been based on sharing the same experience combined with a general 'agreeableness of manner'.

One of them was one of the Canadians I had been right through the course with – when I wrote you a few months ago describing the people who were with me at OTU he was the broad thick all things to all men cheerful 'good sort' one. The other in this category was an Englishman I had made all but one of my trips with – and as a result we had both developed quite an affection for the other on a fairly humorous basis of joint boastings and 'line-shootings' about our trips. The other two – one Canadian and one English – were really close friends. They were the people I used to discuss things with all the time, they both had more or less the same views on most things as me, and so we formed quite a circle. For the last week or two we used to spend most of our evenings in my room discussing books and politics and life in general and the changes that we hoped would be made after the war, etc. ... there is no sort of attitude or line you can take to a thing like that happening, the truth is one is very untough, and this sort of thing makes you cower down for a second like a cruel blow from something against which it is utterly impossible to strike back, it is so huge and powerful and at the same time so vague and shadowy there is no place on which you can grip at it. ...

It was, he now realized, wrong of him to have discouraged her for so long against coming over.

It's awfully hard to go into long explanations as to why all this happened, and of course now I wish tremendously that I'd taken a different line right away. But of course I didn't know just how things were going to work out. Now it isn't only that I can see you

231

will really be happy over here in spite of all the factors I mentioned and irrespective of myself, it is also that I am being utterly selfish over the whole thing and want to be with you again more than anything else in the world.

In the following week Esmond made two more flights, shook a nagging toothache which had been plaguing him since his return to base and 'generally got out of the slough'. He wrote again on 23 November, a letter devoted entirely to Decca's coming to England. Was she bringing 'The Donk'? Surely it would be better both in terms of the child's safety and Decca's 'usefulness' if she were to leave her in Washington: 'I know that when you come here you will terrifically want to be taking part in the war and the general life of everybody and all the changes, etc., and looking after a child would definitely cut out an enormous part of it.' And, in a passage that might have stood as his personal philosophy:

If one is in it, there is the barrackdom and grumbling and the overwork and exhaustion and meeting new types of people and general fascinatingness, but if one is out of it, then the whole thing is utterly bleak and pointless. I wonder if you see what I am getting at.... Nevertheless, I do absolutely see the arguments in favour of bringing the donk, and of course all the above difficulties are not insuperable.

How were the arrangements coming along anyway? Was the Embassy being obstructive?

Not at all, she wrote. In fact, it all seemed very straightforward – at least in theory. The arrangements were exactly the same as in peace-time, except there were fewer vessels, therefore a much longer waiting list. She was told she would definitely get a passage but it might take as long as three months. 'Of course one can't really tell whether it is quite as easy and normal as they made out, but it certainly was awfully encouraging.'

In the event the arrangements took just three weeks. Elated, Decca cabled the news on 1 December: 'LEAVING FRIDAY SO TERRIFICALLY EXCITED DARLING STOP DECIDED TO BRING DONK DO WIRE THAT YOU AGREE HOW SHALL I CONTACT YOU JOURNEY WILL BE VERY COMFORTABLE GREATEST LOVE – ROMILLY.' The reply came the next day, from Ottawa. 'REGRET TO INFORM YOU THAT ADVICE RECEIVED FROM ROYAL CANADIAN AIR FORCE CASUALTIES OFFICER OVERSEAS YOUR HUSBAND PILOT OFFICER ESMOND MARK DAVID ROMILLY CAN J FIVE SIX SEVEN SEVEN MISSING

ON ACTIVE SERVICE NOVEMBER THIRTIETH STOP LETTER
FOLLOWS.'

Esmond's aircraft had set off, as part of a nine-plane raid on Hamburg,
at 4.30 p.m. on Sunday 30 November. At 8.16 it signalled that it was
abandoning the mission due to low oil pressure in the port engine.
At 8.30 it radioed in again, asking for its bearings from the base, and
finally at 8.42 with an SOS. At this point direction-finding radio indicated its position to be over the North Sea, approximately 105 miles
east of the base.

Heavy fog prevented a search being organized until late in the morning of 1 December, when three Air-Sea Rescue aircraft went out and
searched until early evening. There was no trace of either the aircraft
or its dinghy, the only observation a large patch of oil about thirty
miles south-west of the point from which it had last radioed in. Wide-
spread fog on 2 and 3 December prevented a further search, and on
the evening of the 3rd the operation was abandoned. The Air Ministry
could offer no hope for Esmond's survival.

Notes

Chapter 1

2   'This is a sad old place': (Clementine Churchill to Winston Churchill, 21 April 1924), Mary Soames, *Clementine Churchill*, Cassell, 1979, p. 213.

2   'I went with Nellie to the Casino': ibid.

2   'Both my grandmother and Aunt Nellie': Lady Soames, interview.

3   'We often made the trek': Jessica Mitford, interview.

3   'The bud herself': (H.H.Asquith to Venetia Stanley, 1 February 1915), *Clementine Churchill*, p. 90.

3   'all cheap emotion': (Clementine Churchill to Winston Churchill, 14 August 1914), ibid.

3   'The men of the tattered battalion': John Masefield, 'A Consecration'.

4   'What nonsense it all was': Anna Gerstein (Nellie Romilly), *Misdeal*, Cassell, 1932, p. 22.

5   'My head is burning': *A Memoir of Sir Samuel Romilly*, p. 30.

6   'In everything he was as persistent as a hound': Philip Toynbee, *Friends Apart*, MacGibbon & Kee, 1954, and Sidgwick & Jackson, 1980,p. 164.

6   'I don't think she loves him at all': (Clementine Churchill to Winston Churchill, 12 November 1915), *Clementine Churchill*, p. 134.

6   'What's this?': Anthony Robinson, interview.

7   This information is taken from *Misdeal*.

Chapter 2

For an excellent and amusing account of the British community in Dieppe between the wars see Simona Pakenham, *Pigtails and Pernod*, Macmillan, 1961.

9 'My summer holidays at Dieppe': Esmond Romilly, *Out of Bounds*: *The Education of Giles Romilly and Esmond Romilly*, Hamish Hamilton, 1935, p. 164.

10 'He was one of the most unconventional players': Alister Cameron, interview.

11 'where one had to knock off the heads': *Out of Bounds*, p. 166.

12 'Our parents particularly deplored': Simona Pakenham, letter to the author.

12 'One morning I called at St Antoine': ibid.

13 'Over the bedwetting': Mary Marshall, interview.

13 'Half our summer holidays': *Out of Bounds*, p. 166.

13 'He was always scruffy': Lucinda Romilly, interview.

14 'Esmond was tough': Lady Wakeman, interview.

15 'year after year the same party gathered': *Clementine Churchill*, p. 233.

15 Esmond, *Out of Bounds,* p. 211: 'Giles and I used to be called "The Lambs", an appellation which we strongly resented. But before we were considered old enough to come down to dinner, my mother would leave the table "to see how the lambs were". My uncle thought this a great joke.'

15 'The Christmas tree caught fire': Esmond kept a diary from Christmas 1932 to June 1933. Most of the entries were later torn out.

16 'I think we both had chicken pox': Lady Soames, interview.

17 'The rumour that Esmond was Churchill's son': Jessica Mitford, interview.

17 'Nancy had a wonderfully active imagination': the Winston Churchills did go on honeymoon with the Jack Churchills in 1908; perhaps Nancy Mitford's story was based on this trip.

18 'Esmond's father, Bertram Romilly': Lady Soames, letter to the author.

18 'Nellie indulged both boys': Lady Soames, interview.

18 'One of the things we always thought': Simona Pakenham, letter to the author.

19 'Both Giles and Esmond had complexes': Sir Stephen Spender, interview.

19 'Giles as a schoolboy': T.C.Worsley, *Flannelled Fool*, Alan Ross, 1966, p. 99.

Chapter 3

The material for this chapter is taken from *Out of Bounds*, Part I, chapters 1 and 2, and Part II, chapter 1.

22   'Giles could be very amusing': Sir Stephen Spender, interview.

Chapter 4

32   'The story of Esmond's first term': *Out of Bounds*, p. 135.
32   'I can remember little': ibid, p. 53.
32   'Esmond was not unhappy': ibid, p. 135.
33   'I used to hate the meals': ibid, p. 187.
33   'Almost as soon': ibid, p. 70.
35   'philistine to a degree': *Flannelled Fool*, p. 63.
35   'The masters were just as restricted': Rupert Horsley, interview.
35   'I have had an opportunity': (Lord Derby to F.B.Malim), David Newsome, *A History of Wellington College, 1859–1959*, John Murray, 1959, p. 335.
35   'the complexity of': (F.B.Malim to Lord Derby), ibid, p. 335.
36   'Needless to say': *Flannelled Fool*, p. 102.
36   'He looks at every boy': ibid, p. 101.
36   'There always seemed to be': Rupert Horsley, interview.
36   'It was palpable': *Flannelled Fool*, p. 101.
37   For the cap incident see *Flannelled Fool*, pp. 91–4.
38   'Kindly understand, Worsley': despite Malim's speech, the school dormitory remained unliberated. Writing in 1959 in *A History of Wellington College*, David Newsome pointed out that a major criticism still levelled against Wellington was 'that the dormitory spirit is so powerful that individual dormitories can be described as possessing characteristics which have a greater formative influence on a boy than anything derived from the school as a whole'.
39   'Looking through the Murray lists': Rupert Horsley, interview.

Chapter 5

The Esmond Romilly quotations in this chapter are taken from *Out of Bounds*, Part II, chapter 2.

42   'I "became" a Communist': *Out of Bounds*, p. 141.
44   'It was astonishing': Henry Swanzy, letter to the author.

Chapter 6

The Esmond Romilly quotations are from *Out of Bounds*, Part II, chapters 3 and 4. For an account of the Parton Street bookshop see Rosalind Wade, 'The Parton Street Poets', in *The Poetry Review*, Winter 1963/4.

50	Parton Street, a small alley linking Red Lion Square to Theobald Road, was demolished in 1947.
51	'Archer's affairs were always': Sir Stephen Spender, interview.
54	'If there had been': Rupert Horsley, interview.
55	'The portrait Esmond drew': Cecil de Sausmarez, letter to the author.
56	Amusing though they no doubt are, the Scotland Yard and Foreign Office files on Romilly are not available for public perusal.
56	'I remember Malim': Rupert Horsley, interview.
58	'He was a lone wolf': *Flannelled Fool*, p. 98.

Chapter 7

The Esmond Romilly quotations are from *Out of Bounds*, Part II, chapters 5 and 6.

59	'We all acted at Christmas': (Clementine Churchill to Margaret Street, 14 January 1934), *Clementine Churchill*, p. 234.
61	How did the FSS discover Esmond? Possibly from the *Student Vanguard* subscription list or from one of the Reading University comrades whom he secretly visited from time to time.
66	'I do hope that you will make': (letter, Nellie Romilly to Esmond), *Out of Bounds*, p. 252.
67	'I hope you will think twice': ibid, p. 257.
69	'I remember going over': Rupert Horsley, interview.
70	'Malim was exceptionally good': Trevor Russell-Cobb, interview.
70	'Although the battle': Rupert Horsley, interview.

Chapter 8

72	'Nancy sent the little boy': *Misdeal*, p. 120.
73	Lady Soames: 'I remember, as a child, my mother making references to "Your Aunt Nellie's Mr Cox", although I have

no idea who this man was. I doubt very much whether
Cox was his real name.'

73   What did Colonel Romilly think of his wife's sensational
literary excursion? The answer, if there is one, is
contained within the Romilly trust.

73   The letters of 12 June and 26 June 1932 are taken from
the Esmond Romilly papers in the Romilly trust.

Chapter 9

My main source for this chapter is an unpublished account of the *Out
of Bounds* episode written by John Peet in 1964.

75   'Has anybody who cares': John Stevenson and Chris Cooke,
The Slump, Jonathan Cape, 1977, p. 182.

76   'Dear Comrade': taken from John Peet's 1964 account.

78   The *Daily Mail*, 5 April 1934.

79–81   John Peet, letter to the author.

83   'perhaps I should be expressing it': *Out of Bounds*, pp. 284–5.

84   '*June 7th* 1934': *Friends Apart*, p. 17.

Chapter 10

87   'This is a boy': from an unpublished essay on 'Out of Bounds'
written by Esmond in 1939.

87   For Esmond's views on Bedales see 'Out of Bounds' No. 3,
'Modern Schools'; and *Out of Bounds*, chapter 8, 'Co-
Education'. See also 'Pioneers' by E.L.Grant Watson in *The
Old School*, ed. Graham Greene, Jonathan Cape, 1934.

88   'It was a school': Alexander Lourie, interview.

88   'Well, haven't you ever seen': *Out of Bounds*, p. 306.

89   'After three months of fast life': from Esmond's unpublished
essay.

89   'There were plenty of "affairs"': *Out of Bounds*, p. 305.

90   'Calmly and convincingly': from Esmond's unpublished
essay.

90   'It is perhaps no exaggeration': H.W.Stubbs, letter to the
author.

90   'I challenge anyone': *Out of Bounds*, p. 299.

91   'I wrote the poem': Gavin Ewart, interview.

91   'The second issue': *Out of Bounds*, p. 283.

92   'She completely captivated': John Peet, letter to the author.

93	'It occurred while I was at Bedales': *Out of Bounds*, p. 278.
94	'He was like a wild animal': Alexander Lourie, interview.
94	'scruffier and wilder': Philip Toynbee, interview.
95	The H.W.Stubbs account of Esmond's Charterhouse visit is taken from a letter to the author.
97	For Toynbee's account of the drinking episode see *Friends Apart*, pp. 31–3.

Chapter 11

99	Esmond's account of his period in the Remand Home is among his papers in the Nellie Romilly trust. The account was, it appears, originally intended for *Out of Bounds*. Esmond probably omitted it because he was still on probation.
100	The 1944 Inquiry was called after Fleet Street had published the case of a seven-year-old girl who, having been abandoned by her parents, was placed in the girls' Remand Home at Marlford Lodge. The other residents, it was discovered, were all adolescents; most had criminal records; several were young prostitutes suffering from venereal disease.
103	'I remember arriving': Peter Nevile, interview.
103	'The sea was getting rougher': ibid.
104	The delivery man episode was told to the author by Jessica Mitford – 'This was one of Esmond's favourite stories.'
104	'The blind gave excellent credit': Peter Nevile, interview.
104	'He was not an attractive personality': *Flannelled Fool*, p. 98.
104	'When I was seventeen': Gavin Ewart, interview.
104	'Since I've been in London': quoted from Paul Ferris, *Dylan Thomas*, Hodder and Stoughton, 1977, p. 124.
105	'Of Esmond I soon despaired': *Friends Apart*, p. 64.
106	'We stayed in': Peter Nevile, interview.
106	The *Daily Mail*, 3 June 1935.
106	The *New Statesman*, 8 June 1935.
108	'Our idea': from Esmond's unpublished essay.
108	David Gascoyne, 'An Elegy – R.R. 1916–41', *Collected Poems*, Oxford University Press in association with André Deutsch, 1965.
109	The Reading School incident was told to the author by John Boulting and J.N.Hall.

Chapter 12

111   The Toynbee account of Esmond as a commercial traveller is taken from *Friends Apart*, pp. 57–9.

112   'I was bullshitting': Philip Toynbee, interview.

112   'Esmond represents rotten meat': *Friends Apart*, p. 32.

112   'A good man': Esmond Romilly, *Boadilla*, p. 21. *Boadilla* was published by Hamish Hamilton in 1935, and by Macdonald (with an Introduction by Hugh Thomas) in 1970.

113   'He was trying to present': Harry Watt, interview.

113   'We thought in our madness': Basil Wright, interview.

114   'The head of the Unit': *Boadilla*, p. 23.

115   'His determination': Forsythe Hardy, *John Grierson: A Documentary Biography*, Faber, 1979, p. 254.

115   'My worst moment': *Boadilla*, p. 25.

115   'These offices of his': *Friends Apart*, p. 84.

116   'he had a considerable measure': Maurice Carstairs, letter to the author.

116   'I was in the office': Basil Wright, interview.

117   'I guess we would refer': Sir Stephen Spender, interview.

117   It is possible that Esmond had made an abortive attempt to get to Spain in the summer. In *Boadilla* he says he had contemplated going to Spain during his summer vacation but had refrained for fear of being of no use. Yet in *Friends Apart* Toynbee writes of a postcard received from Esmond in August and postmarked Luxembourg, in which he wrote that he was on his way to Spain.

117   David Gascoyne, *Journal 1936–7*, Enitharmon Press, 1980, pp. 36–7.

Chapters 13 and 14

The material for these chapters, unless otherwise stated, is taken from *Boadilla*. For an account of the Spanish Civil War and an explication of its complex origins see Hugh Thomas, *The Spanish Civil War*, Hamish Hamilton, 1977, and Penguin, 1980.

126   Arthur Ovenden, interview.

127   In *Boadilla* Romilly called Vaciamadrid Melilla, probably because he had forgotten its real name.

130–1   Sefton Delmer, *Trail Sinister*, Secker & Warburg, 1961, pp. 304–5.

132   'This is Madrid': quoted from *The Spanish Civil War*, p. 325.

134   'in strict accordance': ibid, p. 327. '

136   *Trail Sinister*, p. 311.
136   The *Daily Express*, 23 November 1936.
136   The *Star*, 23 November 1936.
138   'This is a pretty good argument for Huxley pacifism':
        Esmond took an odd selection of books to war. One was
        Aldous Huxley's *Eyeless in Gaza*; another was Norman
        Douglas' *South Wind*.
144   'Romilly was almost crying': Arthur Ovenden, interview.
144   Esmond and Babs had met up with Aussie ... left putting
        on his boots. Arthur Ovenden: 'There was a joke about
        Aussie always putting his boots on. Almost every time he
        sat down he took his boots off. I imagine his feet were
        bad from tramping so long. He should never have been
        fighting really. He was totally demoralized.'

Chapter 15

147   The *Star*, 6 January 1937.
147   'I had the insane hope': Jessica Mitford, interview.
147   'When my mother was first married': ibid.
148   'Of course I had been in love': Jessica Mitford, *Hons and
        Rebels*, Gollancz, 1960, p. 100.
150   'which made me worried': Jessica Mitford, interview.
150   'but I'm sure': Jessica Mitford to Lady Redesdale.
152   'Esmond was worried': *Hons and Rebels*, p. 119.
152   'Of course I would never confide': Jessica Mitford, interview.
152   'we could only hope': *Hons and Rebels*, p. 120.
155   'FIND JESSICA MITFORD': ibid, p. 123.
156   'Stephenson told me': letter, Esmond to Peter Nevile,
        20 March 1937.
157   'I am with': The *Daily Express*, 15 March 1937.
159   'to say she will not': letter, Esmond to Peter Nevile, 13 April
        1937.

Chapter 16

161   My account of the Bilbao blockade is taken from *The
        Spanish Civil War*, pp. 409–10.
161   'fit to be tied': Jessica Mitford, interview.

Chapter 17

165   'working steadily': letter to Peter Nevile, 2 April 1937.
165   'I used to watch': *Hons and Rebels*, pp. 133–4.

165 'I might have gone back': *Boadilla*, p. 196.

166 The abandonment of non-intervention, i.e. a free market situation, could only have been to the advantage of the Republican camp, which was still in possession of the country's gold reserves.

167 'When he spoke of boule': *Hons and Rebels*, p. 137.

168 'A whole cross-section': Bernard Gutteridge, letter to the author.

168 'Bring a bottle': Arthur Calder-Marshall, letter to the author.

169 For an account of the Hyndman affair see Stephen Spender, *World Within World*, Hamish Hamilton, 1951, and Faber, 1977, pp. 221–4.

169 'I'm not so worried': Arthur Ovenden, interview.

169 'in quite the opposite direction': *Friends Apart*, p. 93.

170 'The high marks': *Out of Bounds*, pp. 103–4.

171 'Esmond was much more mature': John Peet, letter to the author.

171–4 See *Friends Apart*, chapter 9.

174 'We planned her future': *Hons and Rebels*, p. 148.

174 'the health clinic': ibid.

175 'spoke of the Romillys': *Friends Apart*, p. 116.

Chapter 18

The Jessica Mitford quotations are taken from *Hons and Rebels*, chapters 21 and 22.

176 'In 1938 Corsica': Jessica Mitford, interview.

176 'We – the Romillys': Peter Nevile, interview.

177 'One vast O T C': *Hons and Rebels*, p.153.

179 For the 'Isabel' affair see *Friends Apart*, chapter 12.

Chapter 19

I have quoted Jessica Mitford from *Hons and Rebels*, chapters 23 to 27.

183 'For two months': article in the *Washington Post*, 11 February 1940.

184 'We have a one-room flat': letter to Dorothy Allhusen, 29 June 1939.

185 'England is one': *Time* magazine, 3 April 1939.

186 'His bold approach': J.A.S.Grenville, *A World History of The Twentieth Century*, Vol. 1, Fontana, 1980, pp. 322–3.

190   'sweeping the court': Selden Rodman, journal entry,
1 September 1939.

Chapter 20

The Jessica Mitford quotations are taken from *Hons and Rebels*,
chapters 30 and 31.

193   'for ratting to the Liberals': A.J.P.Taylor, *Beaverbrook*,
Hamish Hamilton, 1972, p. 336.

194   The embargo was lifted in November, allowing belligerent
countries to purchase arms providing they shipped them
themselves. This favoured the shipping nations, Britain and
France.

194   'I'd no idea': letter, Esmond to Selden Rodman, 6 November
1939.

196   'He showed no restraint': Michael Straight, interview.

196   'He was so vitally alive': Virginia Durr, interview.

197   'We've become very friendly': letter, Esmond to Peter
Nevile, 5 July 1939.

198   'And how are we': Katherine Graham, interview.

199   'Did you realize': letter, Esmond to Selden Rodman,
29 November 1939.

200   'My father was': Katherine Graham, interview.

201   'I feel well qualified': letter, Esmond to Selden Rodman,
18 March 1940.

202   'TALK NEUTRAL': *Friends Apart*, p. 159.

202   'I wonder if': letter, Esmond to Peter Nevile, 24 December
1939.

202   'In another week': letter, Esmond to Selden Rodman,
18 March 1940.

202   'A sound sleeper': Giles Romilly and Michael Alexander,
The Privileged Nightmare, Weidenfeld and Nicolson, 1954,
pp. 5–6.

Chapter 21

205   'and say in effect': letter, Esmond to Peter Nevile, 15 July
1940.

206   'A few days before': Virginia Durr, interview.

207   'Had you been in the gallery': letter, Decca to Esmond,
undated (July 1940).

207   'It was terribly dull': letter, Esmond to Decca, 15 July 1940.

Chapter 22

names even when they were back on the station. This
was to be checked at once. Growling with contempt,
Esmond and his fellow-Canadians had walked out of the
lecture.' Esmond did not include this incident in his
letters to Decca, probably out of deference to the censor's
pen.

222 'great feeling of': letter, Esmond to Decca, 3 November
1941.

222 'The amazing thing': letter, Esmond to Decca, 23 August
1941.

224 'Before his departure': *Friends Apart*, p. 162.

224 'This had been by far': ibid, p. 160.

225 'The other evening': letter, Esmond to Decca, 5 October
1941.

226 'After the wonderful': ibid.

226 'I ran into': ibid.

230 'It was a time': *Friends Apart*, p. 165.

231 'One of them': letter, Esmond to Decca, 11 November
1941.

Index

Note: pseudonyms are not included in the index. Illustrations are indicated by *illus*. ER in the index stands for Esmond Romilly; GR for Giles Romilly.